Diffusion and Adoption of Information Technology

IFIP – The International Federation for Information Processing

IFIP was founded in 1960 under the auspices of UNESCO, following the First World Computer Congress held in Paris the previous year. An umbrella organization for societies working in information processing, IFIP's aim is two-fold: to support information processing within its member countries and to encourage technology transfer to developing nations. As its mission statement clearly states,

> IFIP's mission is to be the leading, truly international, apolitical organization which encourages and assists in the development, exploitation and application of information technology for the benefit of all people.

IFIP is a non-profitmaking organization, run almost solely by 2500 volunteers. It operates through a number of technical committees, which organize events and publications. IFIP's events range from an international congress to local seminars, but the most important are:

- the IFIP World Computer Congress, held every second year;
- open conferences;
- working conferences.

The flagship event is the IFIP World Computer Congress, at which both invited and contributed papers are presented. Contributed papers are rigorously refereed and the rejection rate is high.

As with the Congress, participation in the open conferences is open to all and papers may be invited or submitted. Again, submitted papers are stringently refereed.

The working conferences are structured differently. They are usually run by a working group and attendance is small and by invitation only. Their purpose is to create an atmosphere conducive to innovation and development. Refereeing is less rigorous and papers are subjected to extensive group discussion.

Publications arising from IFIP events vary. The papers presented at the IFIP World Computer Congress and at open conferences are published as conference proceedings, while the results of the working conferences are often published as collections of selected and edited papers.

Any national society whose primary activity is in information may apply to become a full member of IFIP, although full membership is restricted to one society per country. Full members are entitled to vote at the annual General Assembly, National societies preferring a less committed involvement may apply for associate or corresponding membership. Associate members enjoy the same benefits as full members, but without voting rights. Corresponding members are not represented in IFIP bodies. Affiliated membership is open to non-national societies, and individual and honorary membership schemes are also offered.

Diffusion and Adoption of Information Technology

Proceedings of the first IFIP WG 8.6 working conference on the diffusion and adoption of information technology, Oslo, Norway, October 1995

Edited by

Karlheinz Kautz
Norwegian Computing Center
Oslo
Norway

and

Jan Pries-Heje
Copenhagen Business School
Frederiksberg
Denmark

SPRINGER-SCIENCE+BUSINESS MEDIA, B.V.

First edition 1996

Originally published by Chapman & Hall in 1996
MyCopy version of the original edition 1996

DOI 10.1007/978-0-387-34982-4

A catalogue record for this book is available from the British Library

∞ Printed on permanent acid-free text paper, manufactured in accordance with ANSI/NISO Z39.48-1992 and ANSI/NISO Z39.48-1984 (Permanence of Paper).
www.springer.com/mycopy

CONTENTS

PART ONE

Introductory Papers

1

Research Directions on Diffusion and Adoption of Information Technology

Karlheinz Kautz
Norwegian Computing Center
P.O. Box 114 Blindern, N-0314 Oslo, Norway,
Email: Karl.Kautz@nr.no

Jan Pries-Heje
Institute of Informatics and Management Accounting,
Copenhagen Business School
Howitzvej 60, DK-2000 Frederiksberg, Denmark,Email:dsjph@cbs.dk

The IFIP WG 8.6 on diffusion, transfer, and implementation of information technology has held its first Working Conference on the theme of Adoption and Diffusion of IT at Leangkollen, Oslo in October 1995. In the working group the term information technology is used in its broadest sense spanning from traditional information systems, over modern communication technology to best practice routines in system development and software engineering.

Information technology is playing an increasingly important role in many organisations, sectors and countries. The adoption and diffusion process takes place between one country and another, between research and development organisations, between commercial organisations and the open marked in general, as well as between different departments in one and the same organisation. However, there are still many problems in the practical adoption of the technology, and not often are the results expected by the use of IT achieved. This may be, among other reasons, due to inappropriate attention to the adoption process and associated change processes in communities aiming at the utilization of the technology.

This volume contains twelve contributions which reflect different aspects of diffusion and adoption of information technology. As such, they give an initial overview over the diversity of work done in a subject area which implicitly has been a part of IT research for 20 years, but which only recently has gained attention as a field of interest on its own.

When reviewing the contributions one major distinction immediately arises. Most of the work considers adoption and diffusion within or into organisations, either companies or public organisations and only few papers take another viewpoint, namely that of looking at adoption and diffusion either in sectors or between nations.

In total we have identified five lines of work. The first aims at identifying or specifying overall frameworks and models for the whole diffusion and adoption process. The second group deals with adoption and diffusion within organisations in a rather normative way. Although having sound theoretical and analytical basis, the main message is normative; recommendations are given to planners, change agents, managers etc. on how to make diffusion and adoption happen in an organisation.

Representatives of the third direction are not focusing on the whole process, but on certain selected adoption and diffusion issues. They take a mainly theoretical and analytical perspective, but the research methods used are quite different. One part of this work uses qualitative methods, such as case-studies, to make in-depth explorations and identification of important diffusion and adoption issues. The other part which we see as an group uses quantitative methods focusing on measuring and modelling the adoption and diffusion process.

In the following a brief summary of all contributions will be provided.

Frameworks and models

General models and frameworks are used to predict the course of a diffusion and adoption process. The changes of success for such an endeavour are one important part of research within the field of technology transfer.

Jaakkola discusses a collection of quantitative mathematical diffusion models which are used to describe the diffusion of a product by forecasting the number of potential adopters and users, and (if quantifiable) the benefits that the adopter community might gain from the technology. A major problem with mathematical models is that they do not cover the variables which describe the context of the diffusion. Another problem is that most of them assume a stable environment. Using the case of diffusion of mobile telephones *Jaakkola* shows one general predicament of the mathematical approach, namely that it often leads to a too optimistic prediction in the short term run and a too pessimistic one in a long term. However, it is argued that mathematical models are informative in a less precise way and that they can be a valuable supplement for other diffusion prediction approaches.

Leon proposes such a approach. However, his framework aims not at forecasting the success of a technology in general, but is directed towards the diffusion of formal software development methods in software organisations. He suggests the use of so-called adoption profiles to analyse an organisation's conditions for adopting a technology. A profile consists of contextual aspects like pressures which influence the transfer process, the formality of transfer processes, the adopters' attitudes and interdependency between providers and receptors; and technological aspects, like the adaptability, the maturity, the impact on work procedures, and the differences from technology already in use. Adoption profiles are then used to plan and choose actions to minimise the risk of failure when introducing technology. The value of the approach is demonstrated with two case studies.

Normative recommendations

From a sound theoretical basis two contributions present a very strong normative bias that offers advice and recommendations to change agents, managers and others who are engaged in technology transfer.

A proposal which results in technical support for transfer activities is based on the idea that technology introduction has to be based on a systematic process. The problem for tool support lies in identifying the replicable parts. *Comparetta, Fowler, Juristo and Levine* present the prototype of a software tool and the base model that evolved during the tool' s development process. The base model distinguishes three phases of technology transfer. These are planning and purchase, implementation and sustaining use. Eight key activities are supported by the tool: establish team, define desired process, establish current state, identify gap, develop solutions, pilot use of technology and evaluate result, roll out and ongoing use, wrap up and shut down transfer team.The prototype helps gather information about the starting conditions of a transfer project and supports the generation of an adoption plan by taking into account the tasks and sub-tasks of a transfer endeavour.

A different implementation planning model is proposed by *McMaster and Vidgen*. Again, also these authors stress the need for a planned project. However, they see implementation as a vital part of development. In contrast to *Lien* this means that implementation has to be taken into account from the very beginning of development work. The methods they use to plan the activities to handle the elusive, and partly unpredictable factors of human, not technical concern, are borrowed from the marketing research discipline. The key activity in their model is to take into account the needs of all involved stake holder groups. This means that, first of all, stakeholder groups have to be identified, then their interests have to be analysed, and the assumptions made by the analysts have to be compared in a gap analysis to the stakeholders' attitudes. As said before, interview techniques from marketing are proposed to perform these tasks. On this background the other crucial element of their model is developed: That is a communication strategy which will aid in explaining the introduction process to all involved. The benefits of such a strategy are demonstrated by a particular case, the introduction of a computer-based access control system for a car park.

Organisational Issues

Three contributions focus on one or more specific issues of the adoption and diffusion process. These specific issues which are viewed as being of major significance are very diverse, they span from learning to culture and politics.

Thoresen claims that organisational adoption of IT systems requires distribution, sharing and pooling of knowledge. To say it another way, successful adoption requires "Learning at work". *Thoresen* looks at how learning takes place in organisations, what resources are used, and what are the elements that can facilitate or hinder learning and thereby adoption of IT? Based on a qualitative interview-study and grounded theory analysis, she identifies several resources for learning. E.g. overlapping skills, expert users, meeting places, and continually overlapping groups. She also identifies several hindrances for successful learning/adoption such as division of work enforced by organisational boundaries, peripheral participation brought about by work pressure, IT-complexity, and the varying degree of IT-usefulness for different groups.

Kautz also looks at organisational adoption of IT. However, *Kautz* uses an interpretive framework to understand what can influence the adoption and diffusion process. The framework focuses on three issues: (1) The content of the IT being introduced. (2) The context in which the introduction takes place, and (3) the cultural and political processes taking place as part of the introduction of IT in an organisation. *Kautz* uses the framework in a case-study on the introduction of email in a public sector organisation. Based on interviews and studies of documents he concludes that the use of the interpretive framework broadens the analysis that is needed before the introduction of IT. That has some value in itself because it may help minimize the risk of adoption-failure.

Hughes, Kristoffersen, O'Brien and Rouncefield take up the issue of organisational politics that were also in *Kautz's* framework. Using two case-studies of the introduction of video-based communication systems *Hughes, Kristoffersen, O'Brien and Rouncefield* find that organisational politics on the one hand can drive and encourage the exploration of new IT, but on the other hand (and at the same time) foster ways of organizing and managing work that conflicts with the adoption and implementation of the new IT.

Modelling and Measuring

Whereas a strong qualitative tendency characterised the papers presented so far, three other articles are grounded in a quantitative research tradition as they use quantitative modelling and measuring to explain adoption and diffusion processes.

Watad and Ospina uses data from 140 public organisations to focus on the link between context and change enabled by new IT. They conclude that neither IT nor strategic choice alone control the change process. Instead, they say, change is moderated by factors linked to the organisational setting. Factors like structure, tasks and goals. *Watad and Ospina* also claim that their findings support the so-called emergent perspective of organisational change. Based on their findings *Watad and Ospina* recommend that managers responsible for adoption and diffusion changes have to take into account the relation between human and technical aspects and focus simultaneously on external demands and the internal meeting of those demands.

Closely related to the *Watad and Ospina* paper is the paper by *Thong and Yap*. They present a factor-based study of the relation between IT adoption and contextual factors. Contextual factors taken into account are CEO innovativeness, information intensity, adoption attitudes, IT knowledge, and competition. *Thong and Yap* sent out a questionnaire to 1200 small Singapore businesses, where "small" mean businesses with fixed assets less than 7.2 M US$, less than 100 employees, and annual sales less than 9 M US$. *Thong and Yap* got 172 (16%) completed questionnaires back. The analysis revealed that the extent of IT adoption is mainly determined by the level of IT knowledge. Furthermore it was shown that small businesses are more likely to adopt new IT when they have an innovative CEO and a positive adoption attitude. However, these two factors do not affect the extent of subsequent IT adoption.

Moore and Benbasat do not focus on the organisational level but on individual level. They ask the question: What are the factors influencing individual decisions to use IT? To answer that question, *Moore and Benbasat* distributed 810 questionnaires to users and non-users of personal work stations in 7 organisations, and got a 67% response rate. The questionnaire tested a research model with four components (usage, attitude towards adopting, subjective norm, and voluntariness), each with 1-8 dimensions. E.g. the component Usage had two dimensions: (1) Diversity of use. (2) Intensity. The research model was developed on the basis of Reasoned Action and Diffusion of Innovations theory. *Moore and Benbasat* conclude, based on statistical analysis, that the research model can be used for understanding the utilization of IT. Furthermore, in consistency with results from diffusion research, they also find that the most significant perceptions that had an effect on degree of use were: (1) ease of use, (2) relative advantage, and (3) compatibility.

Diffusion and adoption within sectors and nations

The adoption and diffusion on a regional, national, or sectorial level builds the focus of the fifth identified group of contributions.

Robertson, Swan, and Newell focus on decision making processes regarding the introduction of information technology. They are concerned with the diffusion of computer aided production management technology in a particular industry sector, the automotive sector in the United Kingdom. Attention is given to the influence of interorganisational networks on the decision making process. The article includes a disapproving critique of Roger's fundamental diffusion model because he describes diffusion as a simple, linear, sequential process, driven by the needs of potential adopters. This does not adequately address the dynamics of the relationship between suppliers and adopters and the active participation of the potential adopters in the process. The authors have analysed three cases and explain how awareness has been developed and which social networks informed the decisions. A typical network for information collection consist of free seminars organized by professional associations and performed by vendors and consultants, university courses on the subject, and support by commercial consultants. Especially important is the role of consultants as boundary spanners between the networks. Another result is that diffusion is often driven by fashion, rather than by an efficient choice perspective. The drive leads to a situation where inappropriate technology is adopted as the result of the knowledge selectively accessed by the decision makers.

The comparison of models used for strategic information technology decision making in two different regions, the Chinese and the Western world is the subject of *Elliot's* submission. He has selected one business sector, the banking business to investigate the decision making processes employed when considering the introduction of computer technology. On the basis of four cases *Elliot* concludes that there are common factors in these decisions. The business needs and requirements are especially important but the Commissioners of Banking's requirement also influences the decision to utilise or not to utilise information technology by Chinese banks. The same is true for the core processes in decision making. These comprise requirements' determination, capacity monitoring, proposal, and consideration and approval by CEOs. The final outcome of the study is that the differences between Western and Chinese decision making are not that big, at least not in the banking sector. The elucidated factors and processes in China are substantially similar to those used in Western organisations.

Together the contributions serve as an entry to the subject of diffusion and adoption of information technology, a subject in which further research results with the emergence of new technologies can frequently be expected

2

The challenge of information technology transfer and diffusion[1]

Priscilla Fowler
Software Engineering Institute, Carnegie Mellon University, Pittsburgh, PA, 15213 US, Tel. (412) 268-7748, Fax (412) 268-5758, pjf@sei.cmu.edu

An important area within information technology (IT)–*technology transfer and diffusion*–has emerged. It includes diffusion (Rogers 1983, Redwine 1984, McKenney 1995) and adoption and implementation in organizations (Kwon and Zmud 1987, Leonard-Barton 1987, Fichman 1992) of software and IT innovations. This new area has attracted the interest of both the research and the practice communities. For example, four IEEE Computer Society workshops on software engineering technology transfer have been held (Morton 1983, Przybylinski and Fowler 1987[2]). A growing community of software process improvement network (SPIN) groups has emerged (Peterson 1995[3]). Major consortia and government institutions such as the Software Engineering Institute and the ESPRIT program have been established to address software and IT issues, emphasizing technology transfer and diffusion. And a growing body of research and practice on the introduction of software and IT in organizations is being published (for example, Nord and Tucker 1987, Eason 1988, Pressman 1988, Bouldin 1989, Fowler 1990, Strauss and Ebenau 1994).

There is much to learn from research on and experience with the transfer of technologies in general (Downs and Mohr 1976, Rogers 1983, Von Hippel 1988, Tornatzky and Fleischer 1990, Roberts 1991). Nonetheless, the process-intensive nature of software and IT requires that we understand what is unique about transfer in these cases. Which models and approaches to technology transfer and diffusion are specific to IT, including information systems and methods for developing and evolving them? What does the manager, engineer, or information systems analyst need to know about technology transfer, and what is best practice? What can the research community contribute? To answer these questions, we need to understand the nature of IT transfer and diffusion.

Reflecting the increased interest in IT transfer and diffusion in a number of domains, definitions and terms vary. IT can be sold, licensed, spun out, disseminated, infused, transplanted, modified, appropriated, unbundled, absorbed, adopted, implemented, and inserted (Zmud and Apple 1992, Lien 1992). Context for the application of new technology varies widely (Fowler and Levine 1992), and can include: work groups of various sizes within an organization, entire organizations (small or large), communities, regions, countries, or the international market. Technology maturity can vary as well: transfer and diffusion out of R&D is quite different than

---

1. This work is sponsored by the United States Department of Defense.
2. These are the first and third conferences; the second and fourth had no proceedings published.
3. In a July 1995 presentation at the Software Engineering Institute, Bill Peterson, director of the SEI's Process Program, reported that in 1989, 46 people attended the first Software Engineering Process Group (SEPG) National Meeting; in 1995, 1,248 attended the (renamed) SEPG Conference. He also reported that there are now 54 SPIN groups, each representing a regional or national group of SEPGs.

that required for new product development (Moore 1991). Internal capability to "pull" technology into a context also varies; for example, small firms often do not have the "slack" resources (Rogers 1983) to track, evaluate, and integrate new products and technologies. But while there is a groundswell of interest in this emerging area, understanding of it is fragmented (Kwon and Zmud 1987); work is hampered by lack of a common perspective. IFIP Technical Committee (TC) 8's WG8.6 was established in March of 1994 to provide a forum and a focus for, and to expedite progress in, both research and practice in IT transfer and diffusion.

Based on the research and practice that has been documented, and the findings of this recent conference, there is no question that the IT transfer and diffusion is a crucial area to address. Many key technologies–avionics and high-speed ground transport, medical equipment and telecommunications networks, automobiles and entertainment systems–are now information- or software-intensive. IT and software are changing the shape of our enterprises and are demanding the evolution of new organizational paradigms. It is in this exciting context that the first official working conference of IFIP WG8.6 was convened. The program reflected a lively mix of case studies (on a wide range of technologies and adoption and implementation situations), practical methods and tools, and models. Three keynote speakers, John Leslie King, David Talbot, and Kalle Lyytinen, presented theoretical and practical issues for us to address. Participants, from a wide range of backgrounds, contributed questions, insights, and dialogue. The program co-chairs and the organizing committee prepared an excellent environment that facilitated constant and enjoyable interchange. It is clear that a community with energy and dedication has emerged, and that, with this conference, WG8.6 is off to an excellent beginning!

Priscilla Fowler

Chair, IFIP Working Group 8.6 on Diffusion, Transfer and Implementation of IT

REFERENCES

Bouldin, B. (1989). *Agents of change: Managing the introduction of automated tools*. Yourdon Press, Englewood Cliffs, NJ.

Eason, K. (1988). *Information technology and organizational change*. Taylor and Francis, London.

Downs, G.W., and Mohr, L.B. (1976). Conceptual issues in the study of innovation. *Administrative Science Quarterly 21*, 700-714.

Fichman, R.G. Information technology diffusion: A review of empirical research. In *Proceedings of the 13th International Conference on Information Systems*, Dec 13-16, 1992.

Fowler, P. and Rifkin, S. (1990). *The Software Engineering Process Group Guide*. Technical Report CMU/SEI-90-TR-24; ADA235784. The Software Engineering Institute, Pittsburgh, PA.

Fowler, P. and Levine, L. (1992). Toward a problem solving approach to software technology transition. In J. Van Leeuwen (Ed.), *Proceedings of the IFIP 12th World Computer Congress, vol. 1*, 57-64. Madrid, Spain. North Holland, Elsevier Science Publishers, The Netherlands.

Fowler, P. and Levine, L. (1994). From theory to practice: Technology transition at the Software Engineering Institute. In *Proceedings of the Hawaii International Conference on System Sciences*, Maui, HI. IEEE Computer Society Press.

Kwon, T.H. and Zmud, R.W. (1987). Unifying the fragmented models of information systems implementation. In Boland, R.J. Jr., and Hirschheim, R.A. (Eds). *Critical issues in information systems research*. John Wiley and Sons, Chichester.

Leonard-Barton, D. (1987). Implementing structured software methodologies: A case of innovation in process technology. *Interfaces* 17, 3 (May-June 1987), 6-17.

Levine, L., (Ed.). (1994). *Proceedings of the First International Federation for Information Processing (IFIP) Technical Committee 8 Working Conference on Diffusion, Transfer and Implementation of Information Technology*, Champion, PA. North Holland, Elsevier Science Publishers, The Netherlands.

Lien, L. (1992) Pricing and packaging technology for international transfer. In McGovern, J. et al. (eds.), *Internationalizing Technology Transfer: Proceedings of the Technology Transfer Society 17th Annual Meeting and International Symposium*, June 24-26, 1992, Atlanta, Georgia.

McKenney, J. (1995) *Waves of change: business evolution through information technology*. Harvard Business School Press, Boston, MA.

Moore, G. (1991) *Crossing the chasm: Marketing and selling technology products to mainstream customers*. Harper Business.

Morton, R. (Ed.), (1983). *Proceedings of the IEEE Computer Society Workshop on Software Engineering Technology Transfer*. Miami Beach, FL. IEEE Computer Society Press.

Nord, W.R. and Tucker, S. (1987). *Implementing routine and radical innovations*. D.C. Heath, Lexington, MA.

Pressman, R. (1988). *Making software engineering happen: A guide for instituting the technology*. Prentice-Hall, Englewood Cliffs, NJ.

Przybylinski, S. and Fowler, P. (Eds.). (1987) *Transferring Software Engineering Tool Technology,* Santa Barbara, CA. The IEEE Computer Society Press.

Redwine, S. T. et al. (1984). *DoD related software technology requirements, practices, and prospects for the future.* (Technical Report IDA Paper P-1788). Institute for Defense Analysis, Alexandria, VA.

Roberts, E. (1991). *Entrepreneurs in high technology: Lessons from MIT and beyond.* Oxford University Press, New York.

Rogers, E. M. (1983). *Diffusion of innovations.* Free Press, New York.

Strauss, S. and Ebenau, R.G. (1994). *Software Inspections Process.* McGraw-Hill, Inc., New York

Von Hippel, E. (1988).*The sources of innovation.* Oxford University Press, New York.

Tornatzky, L. G. and Fleischer, M. (1990). *The processes of technological innovation.* Lexington Books, Lexington, MA.

Zmud, R.W. and Apple, L.E. (1992). Measuring technology incorporation/infusion. *Journal of Product Innovation Management 9,* 148-155.

PART TWO

Research Papers

3

Adoption and Implementation of IT: An Evaluation of the Applicability of Western Strategic Models to Chinese Firms

S.R. Elliot
School of Information Systems
University of NSW, Sydney 2052, Australia
Telephone *[+612] 385 4736,* *Fax* *[+612] 661 4062*
Internet *s.elliot@unsw.edu.au*

Abstract

Much IS research has focused on the experiences of Western organisations, particularly those in the UK and USA. Unfortunately, little emphasis has been given to the international applicability of the models and frameworks ensuing from this research. There appears to be little necessity for firms in other countries to 're-invent the wheel' when considering the adoption and implementation of IT if they can learn from the experiences of Western firms. There is some uncertainty, however, as to how applicable Western strategic models would be in non-Western environments.

Case study research has been conducted to consider the strategic IT adoption decision-making practices of Chinese firms. Chinese organisations were selected for investigation due to their importance in global markets and to their widespread influence in many countries and regions. The research outcomes have been compared with Western models of decision-making for IT adoption and implementation. The organisations investigated displayed strong alignment of both factors and processes in their strategic decision-making, Further, there are strong indications of alignment between the strategic IT decision-making practices of Chinese and Western firms. Marked differences to Western firms have also been identified: there appears to be less diversity of practices both within and between the firms than would be expected from Western research. Implications of both alignments and differences are discussed.

Keywords

IS strategic planning, IS technology transfer, cultural differences, Chinese firms

1 INTRODUCTION

IS research has traditionally focused its attention predominantly on USA and UK organisations without concern for how applicable the models and frameworks developed from this research would be in an international context. Firms in other countries can learn from the experiences, and mistakes, of Western firms in the adoption and implementation of IT. There is, however, uncertainty as to the level of applicability of Western strategic models in non-Western environments. The numbers and commercial significance of Chinese firms, (not only in China, Taiwan, Hong Kong and Singapore but in many other countries in the Asia Pacific region), identify them as being of particular interest for research into the applicability of strategic Western models of IT adoption and diffusion.

In this paper, Strategic Information Systems Planning (SISP) models are those concerned with the processes of determining a portfolio of applications which can assist an organisation to realise its business goals as well as the search for such applications with the potential to create advantage over its competitors. (Lederer and Sethi, 1988). Strategic level decision-making differs from that at operational and tactical levels as its primary focus is on IT solutions to problems confronting the business as a whole. This paper reviews the range of strategic models of IT adoption and implementation; identifies differences between Chinese and Western management practices; describes the research design, case studies and outcomes; and assesses implications arising from the research.

2 A REVIEW OF WESTERN STRATEGIC MODELS

Only a limited number of models and frameworks are available to provide assistance to organisations seeking to plan strategically for the adoption and implementation of IT, see Table 1. Most strategic information systems planning models, rightly, focus on the alignment of business objectives and IT planning and the management of an applications portfolio. These models, however, provide little assistance to firms taking the next logical step: adoption of strategic IT solutions. The significant processes in adoption decision-making have received scant attention: only one model focussing on decision-making factors.

Bacon (1992) surveyed the major factors on which IT decision-making practices were based in 80 large companies in USA, UK, Australia and New Zealand. The author reviews previous work in the area and finds that,

> "little empirical work has been done on the financial and other criteria actually used in practice in deciding on project selection and capital investments in Information Systems / Technology."

Bacon categorises decision criteria (or factors) into primary - the decision to or not to invest, and secondary - the decision to purchase a specific product. The results of this survey of primary decision criteria can be seen in Table 2.

Table 1 Factor and Process Models for Strategic Adoption of IT

Author(s)	*Name of Model*	*Focus*	*Objectives*		
			Integrate Corporate Planning, SISP and IS Development	*Identify, categorise and prioritise strategic applications of IS/IT*	*IT Adoption*
Bacon, 1992	Decision Criteria	Factors			X
Huff and Munro, 1985	IT Assessment and Adoption Process Models	Processes	X	X	X
Rockart and Crescenzi, 1984	Top Management Engagement Model	Processes	X	X	X
Parker, Trainor with Benson, 1989	Information Economics	Processes	X	X	X

Bacon (1992) finds common decision-making factors, by size of organisation, across several industry sectors. Nine out of ten companies surveyed in the USA, UK, Australia and New Zealand use the top ranking criterion - support of explicit business objectives. 75% of companies use a form of Discounted Cash Flow (DCF), 67% apply budgetary constraints, and 61% respond to competitive systems.

There are several models in the area of strategic IT decision-making processes. Rockart and Crescenzi (1984) provide an overview of the critical processes in decisions to adopt and implement a Management Support System. They identify three main areas of processes: the link between IS and the management needs of the business; prioritisation; and prototyping / trialing.

Table 2 Value ranking of IS/IT Investment / Project Selection criteria (Adapted from Bacon, 1992)

Category	*Criteria*	*Ranking*
Management	Support explicit business objectives	1
Financial	Discounted Cash Flow - Internal Rate of Retu	2
Management	Support implicit business objectives	3
Financial	DCF - Net Present Value	4
Financial	Payback method	5
Management	Response to competitive systems	6
Management	Support management decision-making	7
Financial	Budgetary constraint	8
Management	Probability of achieving results	9
Financial	Average / Accounting Rate of Return	10
Development	Probability of project completion	11
Development	Technical / system requirements	12
Management	Legal / governmental requirements	13
Financial	DCF - Profitability Index Method	14
Development	Introduce / learn new technology	15

Following field studies in 10 very large Canadian corporations, Huff and Munro (1985) developed four separate models of the IT assessment and adoption process. The models were dependent on the relative emphasis given by firms to technology and to business issues. Technology emphasis is in essence a bottom-up process which is driven by the identification of an interesting technology. Conversely, issues emphasis is a top-down process where the issues have been determined by top management on the basis of business need through a formal planning process. Table 3 shows the different models.

The normative ideal model represents the approach that fully rational firms with few resource restrictions should follow, ie., it is the ideal. Processes in this model are:

- assessment of current IS environment;
- assessment of future goals of organisation;
- assessment of current and future IS applications;
- forecasts of the availability of new technology;
- mapping of technology assessments to organisational needs.

Table 3 Huff and Munro's (1985) Models of the processes in IT assessment and adoption

		Issues emphasis	
		High	*Low*
Technology emphasis	*High*	Normative Ideal	Technology Driven
	Low	Issue Driven	Opportunistic

In their Information Economics model, Parker et al (1989) suggest the starting point for decision-making and planning processes to be a common business and technology vision. The authors explain that most of the literature in this area focuses either on the vision->ideas or the planning->execution phases, but not on the processes as a whole. They expect that the specific processes will vary from company to company, but will all cover the vision->ideas->planning->execution phases. The particular processes may be formal (eg., establishment of a special planning group with a fixed agenda) or informal (eg., interaction over time between the concerned management). The diversity in decision-making processes in Western firms is confirmed by empirical studies of US and UK firms. (Galliers 1987, Wilson 1989, Premkumar and King 1991, Farbey et al 1992, Earl 1993). Earl's study (1993) of very large UK firms shows a wide variety of mainly formal SISP practices.

The number of empirical studies in this area (shown above) provides some indication of the potential significance of strategic decision-making factors and processes to both practitioners and researchers. This significance is apparent regardless of whether the IT to be adopted has been specified in advance as a complete solution (the view of the majority of studies)or, as proposed by Ciborra, the specification has arisen as a result of repeated cycles of decision-making (i.e., 'tinkering' - Ciborra, 1994). These adoption decision-making practices must be considered within an organisational context which clearly differs between Eastern and Western firms. But how significant are the differences?

3 DIFFERENCES BETWEEN CHINESE AND WESTERN MANAGEMENT PRACTICES.

Management style in Chinese organisations has been described as 'paternalistic'. This style of management is strongly hierarchical with centralised decision-making where managers are responsible for protection of the employees and employees are loyal to management. (Redding, 1990). Lu and Farrell (1990) provide an insight into differences between developed and developing countries which may have an important influence in IS use. One of the areas of major difference is management practice. In developing countries the management practices of firms typically have:

- short to medium planning horizons ;
- informal ad hoc policies and plans;
- little use of specialised staff;
- unclear definitions of authority eg., no formal organisation chart;
- high degree of centralisation;
- leadership style autocratic or paternalistic. (Lu and Farrell, 1990).

These characteristics of management practice have been found to be applicable to Chinese organisations in Hong Kong (Elliot, 1994). There is little understanding of decision-making in Chinese organisations:

> "For all we know, Chinese and Western leaders may use precisely the same data, emphases and weightings in deciding how to proceed with a given situation." (Bond, 1991).

While Chinese decision-making practices have not been formally recorded, Bond (1991) cites recent exploratory research on decision-making in Taiwan which suggests that there are basic steps (i.e., identify objectives, collect information, consider alternatives, find out disadvantages of alternatives etc.,) which are an integral part of decision-making in Western and Eastern cultures.

The literature has yielded little research into strategic IT decision-making in Chinese firms. A single study into strategic IT decision-making practices of Hong Kong Chinese manufacturing firms indicates strong alignment between Chinese and Western firms. (Elliot, 1993). However, since those manufacturers primarily market, produce and distribute internationally the degree of international influence on their IT adoption practices is uncertain.

4 RESEARCH DESIGN

The overall objectives of this research are to:

- identify critical factors and processes used in strategic decision-making for the adoption and implementation of IT by Chinese firms, and
- compare these decision-making characteristics with strategic level Western models for the adoption and implementation of IT.

The purpose of this paper is to consider the applicability of Western models of IT adoption to Chinese business organisations, with a particular focus on firms operating solely in a domestic market.

4.1 Research Questions

Questions considered by this research are:

1. How do Chinese firms decide to use IT?
2. How do Chinese firms decide not to use IT?
3. What factors are most important in these decisions?
4. What processes are most important in these decisions?
5. How do these factors compare with those used by organisations in Western countries in their decisions to invest in IT?
6. How do these processes compare with those used by organisations in Western countries in their decisions to invest in IT?

4.2 Research Propositions

Notwithstanding the exploratory nature of the research questions, and the lack of available research in this multi-disciplinary area, predictive propositions have been identified.

Proposition 1. There are common factors in the decisions of Chinese firms to utilise and not to utilise IT.

Proposition 1 addresses research questions 1, 2 and 3, ie what are the relevant factors in decision-making by Chinese firms to use or not to use IT. This proposition is based on Bacon's (1992) finding that there is commonality of decision-making factors between large firms in USA, UK, Australia and New Zealand and seeks to identify if commonality exists in the decision-making of Chinese firms. This proposition is exploratory, seeking to confirm research based on Chinese manufacturing firms (Elliot, 1993). No other studies have been identified which document IT decision-making factors of firms in Eastern countries.

Proposition 2. There are common processes in the decision-making of Chinese firms to utilise or not to utilise Information Technology.

Proposition 2 addresses research questions 1, 2 and 4, ie what are the relevant processes in decision-making by Chinese firms to use or nor to use IT. This proposition is based partly on work in Western firms by Rockart and Crescenzi (1984), Huff and Munro (1985) and Parker et al (1989) and partly on research into Chinese organisations (Elliot, 1993). Western firms show diversity in decision-making processes, however, the paternalistic / centralistic / autocratic nature of Chinese firms (Redding, 1990) as well as research identified by Bond (1991) indicates the possibility of common processes in Chinese firms.

Proposition 3. The factors and processes are substantially similar to those used in Western organisations, as shown in contemporary models.

Proposition 3 addresses research questions 5 and 6, ie a comparison of Chinese and Western decision-making practices. This proposition also seeks to confirm research based on Chinese manufacturing firms (Elliot, 1993). Details of factors and processes are provided above.

The research questions and propositions identified above meet the requirements specified by Lee (1989) research to be considered scientific, in that they are:

- falsifiable (i.e., propositions contain the potential to be shown to be false).
- are logically consistent (research questions and propositions are not mutually contradictory).
- at least as explanatory, or predictive, as any competing theory.
- potentially able to survive attempts made at their falsification. While being falsifiable, the research questions and propositions should be able to survive the research.

4.3 Research Methodology

To maximise the potential richness of the elements in this exploratory research, and to support exploration of differences between Western theory and Eastern practice, a case study research approach was selected.

There has been some contention, now largely historical, that case study research is not capable of supporting sufficiently rigorous, or scientific, research. These arguments have been laid to rest by improvements in the principles for application of case studies. Benbasat et al (1987), Lee (1989), and Yin (1989) have shown how this strategy can be conducted in a suitable manner. The strength of case studies is the ability to capture a greater number of variables than is possible with any of the other strategies. Further, it is possible through this strategy to follow up areas of interest which emerge in the course of the research which have significance to the research propositions. Historical weaknesses of this research approach included the problems associated with making generalisations from limited cases.

In order to support generalisations from case studies, the research was conducted with adherence to the formal processes for rigorous case study research proposed by Yin (1989). As the research questions are directed at a organisational level, a single organisation is the unit of analysis. Primary research findings were based on triangulation of interviews from multiple sources (including both IS and corporate management) and on documentation. A chain of evidence was established to enable an external observer to follow the derivation of any data or evidence from initial research questions and propositions to ultimate conclusions of the case study. All respondents reviewed and confirmed details and interpretations after interviews. Data collection practices were consistent with those nominated by Yin (1989) and Benbasat et al (1987): construct validity was established by triangulation, chain of evidence and formal review by the interviewees; and a case study protocol and case study data base were utilised to support the objective of reliability, ie stability of the qualitative research process. All interviews were conducted by the same researcher to minimise investigator bias. The application of rigorous site selection criteria (to identify banks which had local Chinese ownership and control) supports analytic generalisations from the research. Prior to commencing data collection the research question areas were previewed with a pilot site. Pilot testing was utilised to aid in the prediction and resolution of scaling and administration problems. Pilot testing also assisted in the establishment of reliability and construct validity. Validity has been used in the sense of the capability of the qualitative process to return plausible results based on anticipated responses and results from similar or related research. (Easterby-Smith et al, 1991). Pretesting was also used to ensure the areas of questions were easily understood and correctly interpreted without cultural difficulties. The exploratory nature of this research precluded the use of previously validated instruments, and the research instruments were grounded through the research questions, the research propositions and comparison with the selected Western models.

Case studies were conducted on four firms of different size in the banking industry. Banking is recognised as having high information intensity of the value chain and high information content of the product. (Porter and Millar, 1985). High information intensity and content in an industry indicates strategic use of IS. The banking industry was selected as being a 'best case' or most likely industry to utilise IT strategically and, therefore, one most likely to undertake strategic level decision-making for the adoption and implementation of IT. Empirical research into an industry unlikely to utilise IT strategically is not seen as being able to address the research objectives. The case study research was longitudinally oriented in order to maximise the knowledge and understanding of IT adoption practices over time.

Hong Kong is seen to be a suitable setting to research the management practices of Chinese firms since its Chinese firms have a strong, independent and internationally competitive presence and decision-making by these firms is comparatively free of political or governmental influence. The latter point is important to establish that the decision-making factors and processes are based on the organisation's needs rather than the priorities and agendas of external bodies.

5 HONG KONG'S BANKING SCENE

Hong Kong's excellent communications facilities, the absence of restrictions on capital flows in and out of the Territory and low corporate tax rates have contributed to the Territory's potential as a regional banking centre. In recognition of these benefits, and with minimal barriers to entry, about 80 of the top 100 banks in the world have operations in Hong Kong. While much of their activity focuses on off-shore banking, these banks maintain a considerable presence in retail banking. The retail banking market for Hong Kong's population of six million is characterised by over capacity and resulting intense competition. Competition for the local banks comes not only from international banks but also from local quasi-banks, i.e., restricted licence banks and deposit-taking companies, as can be seen in Table 4.

Hong Kong's three largest banks: Hongkong Bank (previously Hongkong and Shanghai Banking Corporation); Standard Chartered Bank; and the Bank of China; control the market. Since the relocation of the Hongkong Bank holding company to the UK in 1993, these banks are all foreign owned. Locally incorporated licenced banks currently represent less than 15% of the local market. Notwithstanding this dominance by international competition the local banks have managed to survive and to prosper.

Table 4 Competition in HK banking market (KPMG, 1994)

Type of banking institution	*Number*
Locally incorporated licenced banks	31
Locally incorporated restricted licence banks	32
Locally incorporated deposit taking companies	139
Overseas incorporated licenced banks	140

IT has a key strategic role in the survival of local Chinese banks. Alice Lam, General Manager of Hang Seng Bank, part of the Hongkong Bank group, stated in 1991 that due to the high costs of property and labour, it was not cost effective for banks to compete in the domestic market by adding more branches. She added that,

> "To survive in today's competitive environment, banks are making heavy investments in new technology in order to improve services without having to increase staff." (Lam, 1991).

Ms Lam considered that retail banking in the 1990s was increasingly dominated by new technologies and products since individual attention was no longer the main appeal in reaching new retail customers. The public demanded efficiency and convenience, which could only be provided cost-effectively by IT based innovative services.

The Hongkong Bank, the massively dominant force in the market, has certainly pursued IT with vigour. Attributed particularly due to technology and systems, between 1988 and 1992 the bank's real costs per transaction were reported to have declined by nearly 15%. The bank's operating costs were claimed to be 25% lower than those of a comparable Western bank. (Martinsons, 1992). No comparison of operating costs between the Hongkong Bank and local banks is available. The implications for the local banks of this aggressive use of IT to gain cost advantage on a large scale transaction base, however, must be apparent.

6 CASES

In 1993 there were 31 licenced banks, 32 restricted license banks, and 139 deposit-taking companies incorporated in Hong Kong. (KPMG, 1994) Of these 215 locally incorporated institutions, four (4) were selected for interview. Restricted license banks and deposit-taking companies, while being numerically the largest groups of institutions, were not considered as these categories are particular to Hong Kong and of questionable relevance to other countries. The use of special categories of banking institutions which are not present in other countries would reduce the utility of the research outcomes. The 31 licenced banks were reduced to 14 locally-incorporated locally-owned licenced banks, as the research was directed at Chinese companies. Several of the remaining 14 are owned by other banks, which would prevent a clear picture of their decision-making factors and processes.

The final four banks selected were identified as being local Chinese owned and operated in a range of sizes from assets of $US 9.2 billion ($HK 71.5 billion) and staff of 2,500 to assets of $US 2.0 billion ($HK 16 billion) and staff of 850. The selected banks represent medium to larger sized locally incorporated banks. (Elliot, 1994).

Interviews were sought with the manager of a strategic business unit (SBU) as well as the manager responsible for EDP. In two of the banks the SBU manager was an executive director of the bank. In the other sites, one manager was responsible for retail banking operations, and the other was the bank's corporate secretary. Consequently, both EDP and strategic management perspectives were obtained.

All of the banks were running large and very sophisticated computer systems, as can be seen from the profile of current computer usage in banking sites, Table 5. The banks have all had a great deal of experience with computer systems since they installed their first systems in the 1960s and 1970s. In the tables following, banking sites are identified as follows:

BEA	Bank of East Asia, Limited
BX	BankX requested confidentiality
LCHB	Liu Chong Hing Bank Limited
WLB	Wing Lung Bank, Limited

Table 5 Profile of current computer usage in banking sites (Elliot, 1994)

IT equipment	*BEA*	*BX*	*LCHB*	*WLB*
Mainframes	2 x IBM ES9000	2 large mainframes	NCR 9863 (6 parallel CPUs)	2 x IBM 4381
Terminals	400	>100	80*	200
Mini-computers	IBM AS/400	-	-	-
PCs	>400	>60	>70	>100
EDP staff	>90	>40	>40	>60

* using a proprietary system which supports two tellers using each PC.
\> more than

Each bank was asked to compare its level of use of IT with that of its competitors. It is important to note that the Chinese banks do not see their competition as being the major international banks. They consider themselves to be in friendly competition with other Chinese banks. Two of the banks considered they were more advanced users that their competitors, the other two thought they were about the same as other Chinese banks.

7 RESEARCH OUTCOMES

Longitudinally oriented case study research was conducted of the strategic decision-making practices for the adoption and diffusion of IT by indigenous banks. This research has produced the following outcomes:

Proposition 1. There are common factors in the decisions of Chinese firms to utilise or not to utilise IT.

Interviews identified the factors on which banking sites would base investment decisions for IT if making decisions today. These factors include those on which previous decisions have been made, as adjusted in light of their subsequent experience. The factors were unprompted, i.e. they were not selected from a list of alternatives. Priorities were assigned after consideration of all factors. Table 6 refers.

The business requirements specified included the necessity to provide competitive products or to support strategic positioning of the bank (many responses), and improvements in the speed and accuracy of processing data. The Commissioner of Banking, from time to time, establishes requirements which must be met by all banks. An example of these requirements is likely to be the establishment of a backup computer site for banking operations. Banks varied in their view of the importance of these requirements from imperative (major factor) to able to be incorporated into the bank's medium and long term plans, and therefore a minor factor. Doubtless the degree of importance given reflects the situation of each individual bank.

Table 6 Major factors (Elliot, 1994)

Major factors	*BEA*	*BX*	*LCHB*	*WLB*
Business needs and requirements	1*	1*	1*	2*
Requirements of Commissioner of Banking			2	1
Financial return	2			
Management Information				3
Operational factors				4

* Includes computing capacity planning to support current systems with high anticipated rates of growth, as well as to support additional business requirements in the future. Also includes recognition of the operational life span of a computer and the necessity for upgrades / replacements in order to meet business needs and requirements.

Financial return includes cost as a factor as well as cost benefit and returns on investment. The lower emphasis on financial return was unexpected in banking institutions. More detailed responses indicated that financial return was particularly important for non-strategic investments of IT by the banks. Given the extreme exposure to international competition and the effective absence of barriers to entry, it is not unreasonable to find that strategic investments in IT are made in support of business imperatives. Operational factors reflected a policy of the bank to more closely integrate the operation of existing systems.

Medium level factors were also considered. Three of the four EDP departments have approved corporate policies to use the latest proven technologies. Reasons given for this policy included competitive threat (potential release of competitor's products which require support of latest technology); service levels to clients which require latest technology (e.g. automatic passbook printing); service levels between banks (e.g. Clearing House and JETCO use cartridges rather than tapes); and lack of vendor support for out of date technology. This policy was reported as being not sufficient justification by itself to upgrade IT, but was taken into account for business driven upgrades.

Computer systems were not seen by the banks as providing a solution for every banking problem. All of the banks had performed evaluations on IT at various times and had decided not to proceed with its use. In each case the decision was based on the factors and processes previously identified. Reasons given for these decisions were:

> "The optical signature storage & verification system was evaluated and declined as the signatures were not sufficiently clear for Chinese characters."
> "After evaluation, we decided it was not suitable. i.e. the cost was too high and the technology was not mature"
> "The technology was no longer the latest technology."

"The total cost became prohibitive."

The reasons given are consistent with the factors specified above, however, cost figures more highly than would be expected from the table of factors. An explanation for this situation may be that the examples provided are at a minor rather than a strategic level of investment. In these minor decisions, cost and financial returns become more significant. Examples of major investments are the mainframe platform and mainframe backup machines which each cost in the region of $US 5 million. Minor investments would include optical signature storage and verification systems, automated passbook printers and microfilm storage for internal reporting. Consequently, cost is seen as having a greater influence in minor investment decision making for IS/IT in contrast to the ranking of factors in strategic decision-making shown above.

Notwithstanding the differing emphasis in minor and major IT investment decisions, there is striking commonality between the banks' major decision-making factors to adopt IT. Strategic level decisions not to adopt IT have been seen to be based on the same factors. Consequently, this proposition is considered supported.

Proposition 2. There are common processes in the decision-making of Chinese firms to utilise or not to utilise IT.

The processes identified are those which sites would adopt in investment decisions for IT if making decisions today. These processes include those from previous decisions, as adjusted in light of their subsequent experience. As with the propositions above, the processes were unprompted. Priorities were assigned after consideration of all processes. Table 7 refers.

The uniformity of these unprompted processes across all banks reflects their importance. Perhaps they may be considered to be representative of prudent practice in the planning for and utilisation of IT. All processes were considered major. The processes adopted will vary according to the situation. The full range of processes identified will be utilised for major investments. For an upgrade or a minor equipment purchase, the processes will not be as detailed nor will all be used. The core processes, however, will be applied in all cases. These core processes are requirements determination, capacity monitoring, proposal, consideration by CEO, and approval by CEO (subject to delegations).

As with proposition 1 above, all of the banks had performed evaluations on IT at various times and had decided not to proceed with its use. The processes adopted which resulted in rejection of IT investments varied only according to the relative importance of the investment. Evaluations of major IT investments completed the full set of processes. Minor investments completed a sub-set. In each case the decision was based on processes previously identified in decision-making to adopt IT. Consequently, this proposition is considered supported.

Table 7 Major processes in IT investment decisions (Elliot, 1994)

Major processes	*BEA*	*BX*	*LCHB*	*WLB*
EDP Dept advised of bank's future plans	X	X	X	X
Capacity forecasts prepared based on current requirements and future plans	X	X	X	X
Requirements determined*	X	X	X	X
Discussions with vendor on IT (ability to meet requirements)	X	X	X	X
Other vendors considered for major upgrades and replacements	X	X	X	X
Computer purchases by competitors reviewed		X	X	X
User divisions consulted as required	X			X
Development of technology plan				X
RFP** candidates determined	X	X	X	X
RFP or RF Quotes	X	X	X	X
Evaluate RFP (include trials and reference sites checking)	X	X	X	X
Prepare proposal	X	X	X	X
Reviews with senior management	X	X	X	X
Approval by CEO / Board	X	X	X	X
On-going capacity monitoring	X	X	X	X
Monitoring of IT development ongoing by senior EDP staff	X	X	X	X

* includes business requirements & functional requirements

** Request for proposals (RFP) from vendors for IT solutions

Proposition 3. The factors and processes are substantially similar to those used in Western organisations, as shown in contemporary models of SISP.

The first and second most important decision factors by the banks were business requirements and financial returns. These findings are entirely consistent with the Western model of Bacon (1992) who finds that the most important factors in decisions to invest in IT are to support business objectives and to meet financial criteria, *in that order*. The major processes identified are completely consistent with Western models of processes for IT assessment and adoption. Elements of each of Huff and Munro's (1985) four process models: issue driven, technology driven, opportunistic and normative were included. Due to the strong alignment of research findings with Western models this proposition is considered supported.

8 DISCUSSION

The outcomes of this exploratory research should be considered in light of its limitations. The Hong Kong Chinese banks focus on the domestic market and may be less subject to international influence in management practice than internationally focused manufacturers. However, the banking industry is an extreme case. Banks are strategic users of IT due to their high information intensity (Porter and Millar, 1985). They could be expected to have well established strategic level IT decision-making practices and considerable experience in this field. The generalisability of experiences from Hong Kong Chinese banks and manufacturers to Chinese firms in other industries needs to be further tested. Additionally, the experiences of Chinese firms have been considered in only one economy.

Notwithstanding these points, this research has contributed insights into the applicability of strategic Western models for the adoption and implementation of IT to Chinese firms. Where there has been uncertainty regarding decision-making practices in Chinese firms, clarification has been made. The banks displayed strong alignment of both factors and processes in their strategic IT decision-making. The banks' practices, in turn, strongly aligned with previous findings in Chinese manufacturing firms' factors and processes. Together, the studies of Chinese banks and manufacturers display alignment between the strategic IT decision-making practices of Chinese and Western firms.

These findings reinforce suggestions of some universality of basic organisational functions such as decision-making. The implications of these findings are significant both as a potential source of assistance in management practice to Chinese firms and as a rich source of future research. Chinese firms have a major influence in business world-wide. Consequently, research into the practices and experiences of these firms could be of considerable significance especially since they appear to have similarities with as well as marked differences to Western firms. There appears to be less diversity of practices both within and between Chinese firms, perhaps due to the strong cultural model of centralised authority and paternalism. Further research is required to explore these similarities, as well as differences, particularly as they relate to the adoption, implementation and management of IT.

9 REFERENCES

Bacon, C.J. (1992) The use of Decision Criteria in Selecting Information Systems / Technology Investments. *MIS Quarterly*, September, 335-353.

Benbasat I., Goldstein, D.K. and Mead M.(1987) The Case Research Strategy in Studies of Information Systems. *MIS Quarterly*, September, 369-386.

Bond, M.H. (1991) Beyond the Chinese Face: Insights from Psychology. Oxford University Press, New York.

Ciborra, C.U. (1994) The Grassroots of IT and Strategy, in *Strategic Information Systems: A European Perspective* (eds. C.U Ciborra and T. Jelassi) John Wiley, Chichester..

Earl, M.J. (1993) Experiences in Strategic Information Systems Planning. *MIS Quarterly*, March, 1-24.

Easterby-Smith M., Thorpe R., and Lowe A., (1991). Management research: An introduction. Sage Publications Inc. Newbury Park, Calif. USA.

Elliot, S.R. (1993) Strategies for the Management and Use of IT in Hong Kong's Manufacturing Industries: Is IT just in time or just for show? in proceedings of South East Asia Regional Computing Conference (SEARCC '93). Hong Kong Computer Society. Volume 2, pp 88-101.

Elliot, S.R. (1994) Strategic Information Systems Planning for Competitive and Co-operative Advantage in a Developing Country, unpublished PhD thesis, University of Warwick, UK.

Farbey B., Land F. and Targett D. (1992) Evaluating investments in IT. *Journal of Information Technology*. **7**. 109-122.

Galliers R.D.(1987) Information Technology for Competitive Advantage: Serendipity or Strategic Vision?. Keynote address of the AUSCAM National Conference. Perth W.A. October.

Huff, S.L. & Munro, M.C.(1985) Information Technology Assessment and Adoption: A Field Study. *MIS Quarterly*. December, 327-340.

KPMG Peat Marwick, (1994) *Banking Survey Report 1993 - 94.*
KPMG Peat Marwick, Hong Kong.

Lam, A. K.Y. (1991) Retail Banking: Marketing in the 90's. *Hong Kong Manager* . Nov/Dec **27**, 5.

Lederer, A. L. and Sethi, V. (1988) The Implementation of Strategic Information Systems Planning Methodologies. *MIS Quarterly*. September 445-461.

Lee, A. S. (1989) A Scientific Methodology for MIS Case Studies. *MIS Quarterly*. March, 32-50.

Lu, M-T. and Farrell, C. (1990) Information Systems Development in Developing Countries: An Evaluation and Recommendations". *International Journal of Information Management.* **10**, 288-296.

Martinsons, M.G. (1992) Global success with electronic banking: the Hongkong Bank and HEXAGON. A Case Study, *Journal of Strategic Information Systems* **Vol 1 No 5**, 290-296.

Parker, M.M., Trainor, H.E. with Benson R.J.(1989) *Information Strategy and Economics: Linking Information Systems Strategy to Business Performance.* Prentice-Hall International Inc., Englewood.

Porter, M.E. and Millar, V.E. (1985) How Information gives you Competitive Advantage. *Harvard Business Review.* July-August, 149-160.

Premkumar, G. and King, W.R. (1991) Assessing Strategic Information Systems Planning. *Long Range Planning.* **24, 5**, 41-58.

Redding S.G.R.(1990) *The Spirit of Chinese Capitalism.* de Gruyter, Berlin.

Rockart, J.F. and Crescenzi, A.D. (1984) Engaging Top Management in Information Technology. *Sloan Management Review.* Summer, 3-16.

Wilson ,T.D. (1989) The Implementation of Information Systems Strategies in UK Companies: aims and barriers to success. *International Journal of Information Management.* **9(4)**, 245-258.

Yin, R.K. (1989) *Case Study Research: Design and Methods.* Revised edition. Sage Publications Inc. Newbury Park, Calif. USA.

BIOGRAPHY

Since commencing in the computer industry in 1972 Steve Elliot has worked in Australia, Europe and Asia in business, government, education and with the United Nations. He is currently Director of the Information Technology Research Centre at the University of New South Wales in Sydney. Prior to this appointment he spent four years in Hong Kong. Steve has degrees in Economics and Information Systems from University of Sydney and University of Technology, Sydney and a PhD in strategic IS planning from University of Warwick, UK. His major research interest lies in the strategic use and management of IT.

4

A Prototype Knowledge-Based Tool for Software Engineering Adoption and Implementation

P. Fowler
Software Engineering Institute,[1] *Carnegie Mellon University*
Pittsburgh, PA, 15213 US, Tel. (412) 268-7748, Fax (412) 268-5758, pjf@sei.cmu.edu

I. García-Martín
Universidad Politecnica de Madrid
Facultad de Informatica, Campus de Montegancedo
28660 Boadilla del Monte, Madrid, Spain, Tel. +34-1-336-6923, Fax +34-1-336-7412, igarcia@fi.upm.es

N. Juristo
Universidad Politecnica de Madrid
Facultad de Informatica, Campus de Montegancedo
28660 Boadilla del Monte, Madrid, Spain, Tel. +34-1-336-7454, Fax +34-1-336-7412, natalia@fi.upm.es

L. Levine
Software Engineering Institute, Carnegie Mellon University
Pittsburgh, PA, 15213 US, Tel. (412) 268-3893, Fax (412) 268-5758, ll@sei.cmu.edu

1. The Software Engineering Institute (SEI) portion of this work was sponsored by the U.S. Department of Defense.

Abstract

This paper describes work that explores how tools can help change agents in software organizations incorporate new software engineering tools and methods more effectively. A prototype expert system was built to assist change agents in gathering information and planning tasks in a software engineering adoption and implementation effort. The knowledge engineering process for this system helped to integrate and translate research and practice from software engineering technology adoption and implementation within the field of technology transfer and diffusion of innovation for software change agents.

Keywords

Software engineering, adoption, implementation, technology transfer, knowledge-based tool, expert system, knowledge elicitation

1 INTRODUCTION

Recent interest in software process improvement (Humphrey 1989, Paulk et al. 1993) has increased awareness of the need to properly manage software engineering adoption and implementation–that is, the deployment and integration of new technologies and products within software development organizations. Increasingly, groups of people within technology receptor organizations such as advanced technology groups, tools groups and software engineering process groups (SEPGs) (Fowler and Rifkin 1990) introduce change as part of their regular responsibilities. Yet the process for adopting and implementing new software engineering technologies has been ad hoc: without automated support, slow, and unpredictable. Thus, few benefits are derived from many technologies,[1] for example, CASE tools and object-oriented design. Moreover, the difficulties encountered during integration into the organization delay use, add to budget and impede return on investment. (While software process improvement can itself be treated as a technology–albeit a large, complex one–the focus in this paper is primarily on single, component technologies such as a software configuration management tool.)

Knowledge and expertise exist which could be used by organizations to deploy software engineering technologies more systematically (Fowler 1994). This paper presents a study of the feasibility of building an expert tool to organize this know-how, and also to help individuals acting as change agents, who must guide adoption and implementation. Preliminary results are presented and the nature of the problem is discussed. The expert system prototype and its development are described, including initial feasibility analysis, knowledge acquisition, system tasks, and system design. Finally, the issues that were identified are discussed, and conclusions are given.

2 THE PROBLEM

Organizations typically track new technology, formally or informally, on an ongoing basis. When a need is identified, various technologies that may meet that need are examined more

1. We use the term "technology" broadly, per (Schon 1967): "...any tool or technique, any physical equipment or method of doing or making, by which human capability is extended." Thus products such as CASE tools are included in this definition, and also design and testing methods, peer review methods, etc.

closely. Eventually a decision is made to adopt (i.e., purchase, install, and use) a particular technology (Bouldin 1989), and a technical team (or individual) is assigned or voluntarily assumes the change agent role, which is to manage the adoption and implementation process. Most commonly, change agents work on a temporary or part-time basis while they continue their regular software development work.

Adoption and implementation of software engineering technology (Ackerman 1984; Leonard-Barton 1988a, Willis 1983) is a complex process that moves an organization, or unit thereof, from its current state to one that incorporates a new technology into routine work operations. This process involves adaptation (Leonard-Barton 1988b) of both technology and organization. A simplified view of adaptation is presented in Figure 1, which shows how most mass-market or "off-the-shelf" technologies are built to a general set of requirements.

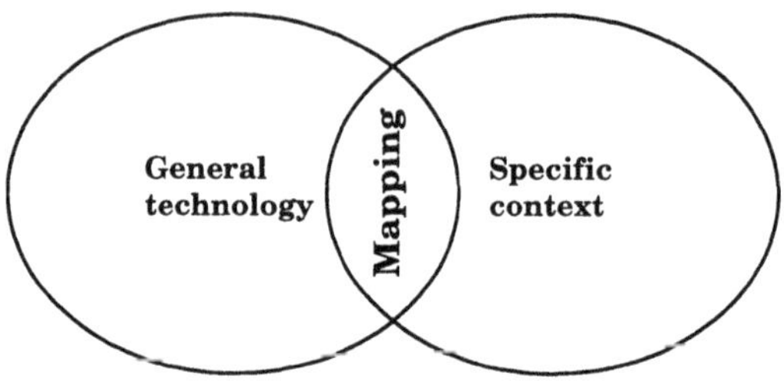

Figure 1 A simplified view of mutual adaptation.

This is increasingly the case for software engineering tools as well, for example, Cadre's Teamwork. Yet every situation in which a technology is applied is specific, and so the introduction of a technology into an organization requires a mapping of the general to the specific. This mapping process is the change agent's job. (This observation is based on interactions with change agents in context, and on their own reports at SEPG Conferences from 1988-1995.)

Individuals acting as change agents have problem solving and project management skills, but these are specific to their own product area or technical domain. They are often unaware that technology transfer, and adoption and implementation models and methods exist, or they have very limited experience. Thus they apply their skills awkwardly and with an incomplete understanding of tasks to be done.

A body of practice and literature (Fowler 1994) on software engineering technology transfer, including adoption and implementation, has emerged. From this and the more general literature of diffusion of innovations (Rogers 1983) and the related field of information systems implementation (Kwon and Zmud 1987, Eason 1988) much can be drawn that is helpful to change agents. For example, it may be obvious that during adoption and implementation, the technical environment, including software and hardware, may be modified, along with standards, guidelines, procedures, and practices. It is less apparent how the activities of managers, technical personnel, and administrative support staff may change, or that training and related materials such as job aids and guidebooks may need to be created or revised. Sometimes additional training may be required to provide background and skills in the new technology, or schedules for projects may need revision. Waivers for standards or other organizational procedures (e.g., purchasing) may need to be negotiated. Intangibles, including resistance to technology, must also be addressed. Value and reward systems may be affected and the organizational structure may need to change (Adler and Shenhar 1990, Morgan 1986). Most software engineering change agents attend to a few of these factors, but seldom consider all of them.

3 A TECHNOLOGY TRANSFER EXPERT SYSTEM (T^2ES)

For predictable adoption and implementation, each factor in the transition situation (Fowler and Levine 1992) must be considered, in an appropriate sequence. Ideally, each change agent should not recreate a method of adoption and implementation (although this is often the case). The composite expertise of experienced change agents, organized into such a method, and embedded in a tool, could guide consideration of all the factors in a software engineering technology transfer situation. It could also aid in preparing a plan for the tasks in the technology introduction process and would leverage existing research.

A prototype for such a tool was developed—the Technology Transfer Expert System (T^2ES). T^2ES work was considered exploratory: this to all accounts is the first expert system developed for this domain. The near term goals were to explore the first of these two questions: could such a system be built to organize information or "knowledge" usefully for change agents? The longer term goal was to use this as a starting point from which the expertise of other change agents could be gathered, integrated, and consolidated, and bootstrap this into a resource for the software engineering community.

Note this is called the *technology transfer* expert system, rather than the "adoption and implementation" expert system. The version of T^2ES that was built focuses on adoption and implementation–that is, introduction–of software engineering technologies within software organizations. Early in the work on this system, it was envisioned that the tool would apply to the transfer of technologies across the entire life cycle of technology maturation; however, a decision was made to narrow the focus to adoption and implementation for the first version of T^2ES because the greatest experience and knowledge was in these areas.

This work began when one of the authors, Juristo, was a Resident Affiliate at the Software Engineering Institute, and continued after her return to the Universidad Politecnica de Madrid. Knowledge elicitation and prototype system building continued via fax, email and telephone. The following sections describe the system development work: the feasibility analysis and determination of type of expert system to build; including the knowledge acquisition process; the knowledge architecture which emerged; the system architecture; and what the user sees. T^2ES development was based on the IDEAL methodology (Pazos 1988, Juristo 1995) combined with a spiral approach (Boehm 1986) and consistent with the software process model proposed by Blum (1992).

3.1 Determination of feasibility and type of expert system for adoption and implementation

In the feasibility analysis, the related issues of scope, of expert system type, and of the maturity of the domain were addressed. Even within the initial scoping to adoption and implemention it was necessary to consider what subset of the domain to include. The domain knowledge was (and still is) immature, in the sense that adoption and implementation *practice* was not consistently documented in manuals or in published articles or books. For example, books such as Grady and Caswell (1987); Bouldin (1989); Eason (1988); and Strauss and Ebenau (1994) reflect a wealth of experience, but no consistency in theory or strategy. Research on implementation has not addressed adoption and implementation at the level of detail needed by change agents. Information on practice was not readily available from more than one expert. We decided that the boundaries of T^2ES would have to emerge from the knowledge elicitation process.

This was a serious risk, so the potential for building an expert system was confirmed formally by completing an evaluation developed by Slagle and Wick (1988). This method considers 24 essential characteristics to consider when constructing an expert system. Characteristics of the expert are considered, along with the nature of the task and the potential users. The evaluation indicated that this application was highly suited for development by means of knowledge engineering[1] (Appendix 1). In addition, resources for system development existed. An expert and an experienced knowledge engineer were available, and a novice knowledge engineer was available for training as a back up.

The type of behavior to be exhibited by the system needed to be determined –i.e., which of the many tasks that can be performed by an expert system would fit adoption and implementation work (Gervater 1987). Because T^2ES must behave like an expert change agent, it must be capable of performing two main tasks: assistance and planning.

As an *intelligent assistant*, T^2ES must provide an inexperienced change agent with help in ascertaining which information needs to be gathered in each situation. It must also assist in identifying which tasks are to be performed to complete the software adoption and implementation plan. Finally, it should help and advise the novice change agent as he or she proceeds through tasks–clarifying issues, explaining essential concepts, etc. The goal is that the novice change agent will behave as if he/she is being advised by an expert, thus greatly improving the likelihood of success.

T^2ES must also act as a *planner*, and so must carry out both information gathering and plan design. Information is gathered on the characteristics of the technology to be adopted and implemented; the individual people involved; and the organization where the new technology is deployed (Fowler and Levine 1994). T^2ES must then guide the development of a plan for the particular situation, to aid in transition from the current status of the organization to the desired one, in which the new technology is fully incorporated and is routinely used. Assistance in re-planning should also be provided, because all information may not have been gathered initially; or when another organizational unit begins adopting. Also, as the novice change agent gains in experience, and as the organization proceeds with adoption and implementation of additional technologies, plans may evolve rapidly. Finally, re-planning may be needed because this is a new domain, and it cannot be assumed that T^2ES can fully anticipate all adoption situations.

These two tasks simulate the work carried out by an expert when supplying software technology adoption and implementation planning consultancy. With the help of T^2ES, the novice change agent should be able to gather appropriate information and prepare a plan to expedite software engineering technology adoption.

3.2 Knowledge acquisition

In order to build T^2ES, the knowledge had to be acquired from the person acting as the initial expert change agent. Knowledge acquisition (Juristo 1995) is the process of gathering information from any source, human or otherwise. This process is carried out in parallel with all the expert system building stages (identification, conceptualization, formalization, validation,

---

1. For details see Isabel García-Martín, Natalia Juristo, Priscilla Fowler and Linda Levine, "Developing An Expert System for Technology Transfer," unpublished manuscript.

evaluation and maintenance) (Pazos 1988, Juristo 1995). The problem for acquisition is to determine what information is needed at any time, at what level of detail and where to find it, and which technique is to be used to acquire it, etc.

The usual techniques of observing the expert and of analyzing the protocol used were tried out for this purpose, but the type of work performed by the expert was not easily observed. In a typical scenario, the expert consulted by telephone with the change agent, and then visited the change agent's organization to get a better understanding of the problem concerned. The expert's work lasted weeks, which meant that a non-standard knowledge elicitation technique was used–asking the expert directly–and then having the expert review and analyze the previous behavior during problem solving. There was some risk of uncertainty with this technique, as it was not possible to check the knowledge acquired using indirect elicitation techniques to confirm the real behavior of the expert.

The expert was asked to decompose the problem–that is, to look for a set of simpler tasks that would enable her to set the expert system objectives. The expert responded by building a diagram, divided into three phases:

- Phase 1: Software technology purchase and adoption and implementation planning.
- Phase 2: Technology deployment (implementation).
- Phase 3: Technology consolidation and support for sustained use.

As a consequence of this decomposition, each T^2ES phase was divided into a set of activities ordered by time, and each activity was defined by a brief description of the task to be performed to complete the plan (see Figure 2). The knowledge engineer, in working to derive the static domain knowledge model, decided to split the domain into three major focuses or viewpoints: users, organization and technology (the knowledge architecture). This led to a preliminary system decomposition into three main modules: one for gathering the information needed to draw up the plan, one to generate the customized user plan, and one to refine the plan through repeated interaction with the user. (This is the system architecture.)

After having acquired enough knowledge, the system scope document was drawn up, specifying that only Phase 2 of the expert diagram and the information gathering and plan generation modules would be implemented in the first concept demonstration prototype. Phase 1 was to be built into the next prototype, leaving implementation of all three phases and all three modules for the final system. The concept demonstration prototype was built and Phases 1 and 2 have now been implemented in T^2ES. Phase 3 of the diagram and the plan refinement module remain to be constructed.

3.3 Structuring the knowledge

The expert system development process consists, as pointed out formally by Blum (1992), of a transition from the identification of the task in the application domain to a software product that operates in the implementation domain. This transition is carried out through a two-level modeling process. The first is the conceptual level, which is a descriptive model of how the expert system responds to a need in the application sphere, and the second is the formal level on which the implementation is based. During the conceptualization stage, knowledge engineers are working at the conceptual level. Therefore, they should be able to get a descriptive model of the system, using a process of analysis and transformation of the knowledge acquired in the preceding stage. This transformation is carried out as a series of stages: obtaining of the concept dictionary, study of strategic, tactical and factual knowledge, creation of a

Figure 2 Phase 2 of the T^2ES Prototype

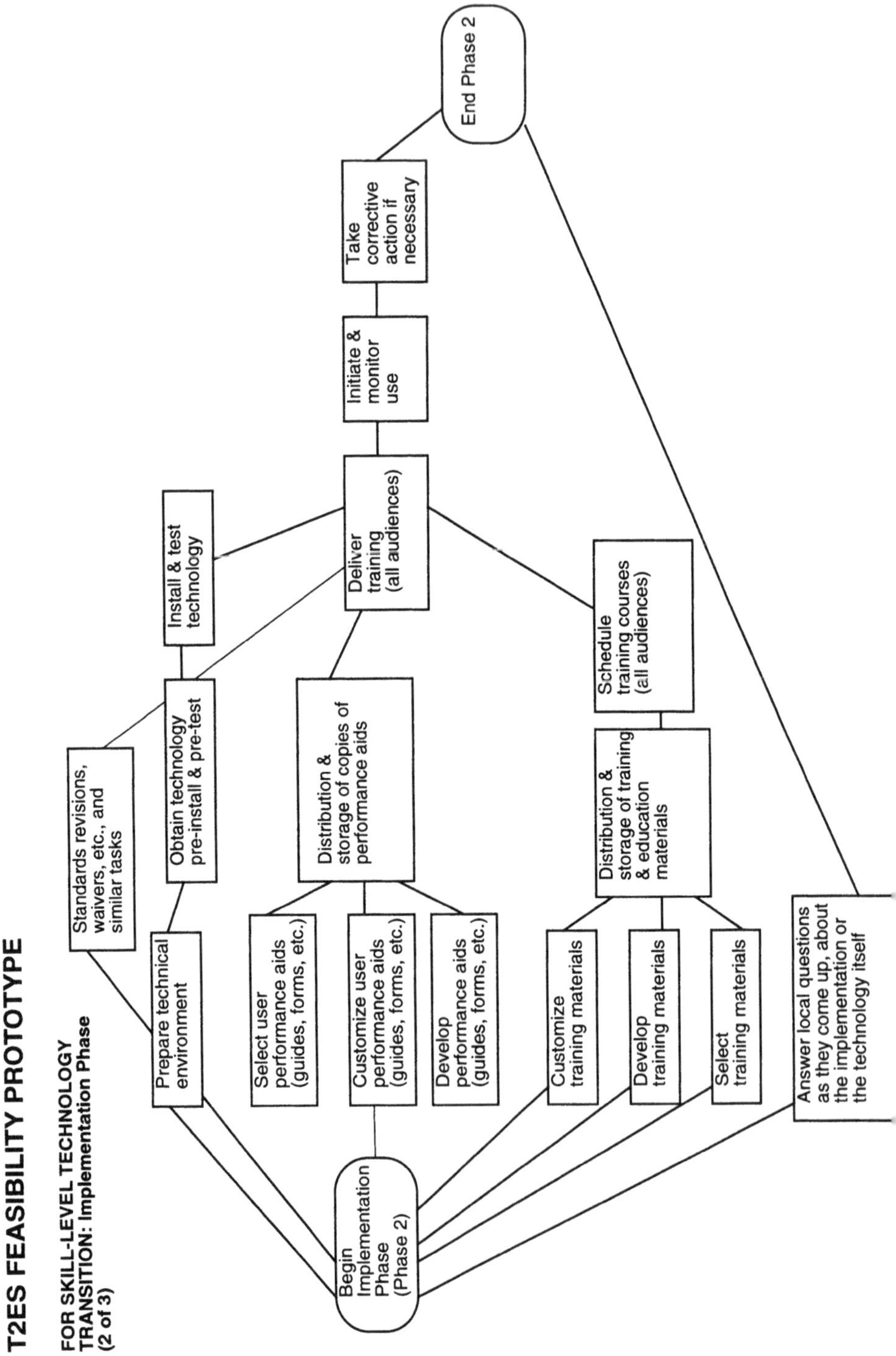

tasks model, creation of a processes model, and obtaining of the knowledge map. However, when domains are too immature and are devoid of structure, as is the case of technology adoption and implementation, a pre-conceptualization or more profound analysis of the acquired knowledge is necessary. The "amorphous mass" of knowledge extracted is structured during pre-conceptualization. In the case at hand, this in-depth analysis of knowledge acquired directly from the expert generated a structure similar to the activity models but, this time, with a forward approach (from inputs to outputs) similar to system operation. This new activity model is an improvement on the original acquired knowledge, because it provides:

- clear and final definition of the output in plan format;
- clear and final definition of the inputs as user questions, separating inputs from user questioning and inputs taken from the knowledge deduced in other tasks;
- the knowledge to perform this task is only and exclusively found in the knowledge block, and this knowledge is organized similarly to reasoning represented by pseudo rules.

The outcome of pre-conceptualization for the Training Activity is shown in Appendix 2.

3.4 Typical tasks

Some typical adoption and implementation tasks and sub-tasks elicited in the process of filling in the details for T^2ES are shown in Tables 1 and 2. Table 1 illustrates technology deployment (implementation) tasks; Table 2 shows a decision table for a sub-task that determines whether to tailor purchased training or develop training within the organization. These were identified using the diagram supplied by the expert in which she sought to reflect the steps taken in her technology transfer work. Others were taken from subsequent acquisition stages, because the expert had internalized them and was unable to bring them to light herself. For an example of how the knowledge was structured during elicitation, see Appendix 2.

Table 1 Phase 2 - Technology Deployment Tasks and Sub-tasks in T^2ES.

Tasks	*Sub-tasks*
User Selection	- Enter users depending on technology use - Type of users
Documentation	- Study and assignment of documentation production - Customize and develop technology documentation - Document costs - Distribute appropriate documentation to users
Training Organization	- Study and assign training execution - Customize and develop training documentation - Training costs - Training site - General training plan, control and follow-up
Technology Deployment	- Environment preparation - Pre-installation and acceptance tests - Installation plan and final test
Technology Use Monitoring	- Start technology use and supervision - Take corrective steps where necessary

Table 2 Decision Table for the Sub-task *Training Organization: Customization and development of training documentation.*

	The course is necessary and is not available through vendor	*The course is necessary, is available and needs changes*	*The course is necessary, is available and does not need changes*
The course is to be taught no more than three times	"Quick & dirty" development	Vendor's course without changes	Vendor's course without changes
The course is to be taught a few (4 to 7) times	"Quick & dirty" development	"Quick & dirty" customization	Vendor's course without changes
The course is to be taught many (more than 7) times	Professional course development and configuration management of course materials	Professional course development and configuration management of course materials	Vendor's course and configuration management of course materials

3.5 Implementation: what the user sees

The structure of the prototype T^2ES seeks to reflect the behavior of the expert when faced with the technology adoption and implementation problem; therefore, each of the phases implemented[1] to date (Phases 1 and 2) was divided into a set of tasks, and each task was implemented with two types of modules:

1. The *information gathering module* which was responsible for interacting with the user and extracting the information needed on the task. This module was composed of the following items:

– a set of questions about the task;

– help for answering the questions properly.

2. The *plan generation module* that draws up the customized adoption and implementation plan. This module was composed of the following items:

– reasoning underlying the task;

– output form that is part of the final plan.

The working procedure within a generic task is as follows: once the user (the change agent) has entered the task to be performed, one or more forms with task-related questions appear. The user must answer each question in order. T^2ES offers several help messages at different levels to ensure that this is done properly, depending on user expertise. It is up to the user to decide what type of help is needed to answer each question. The user may act like an expert user for some questions, but may behave as a novice in other cases; this varies according to the level of personal expertise. Depending on the user responses, T^2ES identifies the level of complexity of the current adoption and implementation process, and new or other questions will be answered according to the level. When all the questions have been presented, T^2ES starts to reason with all the knowledge supplied to that point: user responses for the current task and

1. T^2ES was implemented in a general-purpose expert system tool, Intellicorp's Kappa, a tool that enabled rapid prototyping and was PC-based.

knowledge deduced from other tasks. T^2ES then produces three types of information: the set of steps to be taken as part of the customized plan, user environment-related data, and particular recommendations for the user on when to act. All this information appears in an output form which may be displayed on screen or printed out on paper.

The different tasks are executed in an order pre-established by the expert, and the partial results of each task go to make up the complete (but not final and refined–this happens in a different session) adoption and implementation plan. In sum, T^2ES performs the complex job of adapting the general software adoption and implementation plan to a particular situation. This is possible because T^2ES takes into account these variables: the organization in which the technology is to be deployed (implemented) (Morgan 1986), the users who are to work with the technology (Adler and Shenhar 1990, Constantine 1993, Fiman 1989), and the technology itself (Rogers 1983, Leonard-Barton 1988a) (see Figure 3). T^2ES behaves like an expert consultant as it ascertains the complexity of the case and customizes the general adoption and implementation plan for the user.

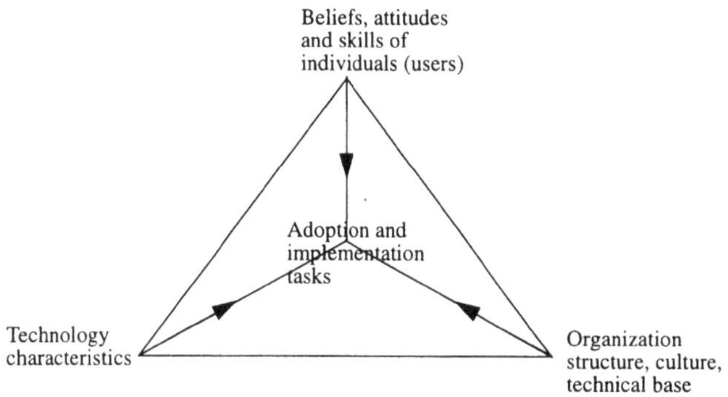

Figure 3 Relationship of users, organization and technology to adoption and implementation tasks in T^2ES.

4 T^2ES PROTOTYPE EVALUATION

A major goal of building T^2ES was to determine if knowledge about adoption and implementation could be organized for use in an expert system. The prototype system clearly demonstrated this. While the domain is immature, there is enough documentation of research and practice to provide useful guidance. And with the number of change agents growing rapidly,[1] there is clear demand for this type of assistance.

It was also a goal to determine if an expert system would be useful to software engineering change agents. This question has not been answered directly and T^2ES has not yet been evaluated by end users; this work remains to be done. However, the greatest benefit in the near term

1. In a recent presentation at the SEI, Bill Peterson, director of the SEI's Process Program, reported that in 1989, 46 people attended the first SEPG National Meeting; in 1995, 1,248 attended the (renamed) SEPG Conference. He also reported that there are now 54 Software Process Improvement Network (SPIN) groups, representing a regional or national group of SEPGs. (As noted earlier, SEPGs are an instance of software engineering change agent teams.)

is for the researchers: the knowledge elicitation work for the implementation of the T^2ES prototype provided a way to organize the expert's knowledge of software engineering technology adoption and implementation--that is, to make tacit expertise explicit enough to be used by others. This organization then provided the basis for a framework for gathering expertise from other sources, and for findings from the literature on adoption and implementation. The phase charts for T^2ES were used in consulting work to support the introduction of Fagan-style software inspections (Fagan, 1976) at a division of a large multi-national corporation. Later these charts served as the basis for the development of a more elaborate process model for software technology adoption and implementation for that same firm. (The latter model was developed using an ETVX-based software process model (Radice and Phillips 1988) on Apple's Hypercard, which allowed for rapid development by the expert, and reduced the need for support, but did not free the end user from dependence on direct expert help.) The discipline of data gathering by a knowledge engineer and the related conceptualization work were invaluable in clarifying not just system requirements but a scenario for supporting clients directly.

In using the alternative procedural tool during this past year, the role of tools in supporting the introduction of new software technologies has continued to be explored. Time and other resource constraints forced the use of a desk-top tool to meet the customer's needs; the T^2ES prototype was not complete enough to use in this situation. Despite considerable motivation (this customer was a co-developer of the process model), the change agents still needed consulting support to properly customize the model, done by creating new versions of the model. A more mature version of T^2ES can potentially perform this customization as well as produce a plan. Plans for future work in this area include further evaluation and field-testing of T^2ES.

5 CONCLUSIONS

One of the main blocks to effective software technology transfer is that many people still view the adoption of a new software technology by an organization as simply replacing equipment, installing new software and supplying user manuals, or training a few people. This may be due to the predominantly technical background of the typical change agent or wishful thinking on the part of management. The main difficulty in managing software engineering technology adoption and implementation, however, lies in the host of non-technical–that is, human and organizational–factors that come into play in the process, including: return on investment, culture of the receiver organization, resistance to change, appropriateness of technology, etc.

The complexity of dealing with non-quantitative factors with intrinsic dependencies means that the domain of adoption and implementation of software engineering technology is a good expert system candidate. Failure to perform a key task at the right point in time–for example, obtaining a management sponsor or arranging to work with a subject matter consultant–can jeopardize the entire effort, or at the least, delay it significantly. Within software organizations, incorporation of new technology is ongoing, and failure to manage the process can negatively impact schedules and budgets. Failure to manage this learning-intensive process provides one reasonable explanation why software project estimates are rarely correct: the learning curve involved in adopting and implementing new tools, methods and techniques is not yet predictable. Tool support that codifies the best know-how and practice can help to solve this problem.

6 REFERENCES

Ackerman, A.F., Fowler, P. and Ebenau, R. (1984) Software inspections and the industrial production of software, in *Proceedings of the Symposium on Software Validation* (ed. Hans-Ludwig Hausen), Darmstadt, September 1983. Amsterdam, North-Holland.

Adler, P. and Shenhar, A. (1990) Adapting your technological base: the organizational challenge. *Sloan Management Review*, 32 (1), 25-37.

Blum, B. (1992) *Software engineering, a holistic view.* Oxford University Press, Oxford.

Boehm, B. W. (1986) A spiral model of software development and enhancement. *ACM Software Engineering Notes*, 11(4), 22-42.

Bouldin, B. (1989). *Agents of change: Managing the introduction of automated tools.* Yourdon Press, Englewood Cliffs, NJ.

Constantine, L. (1993) Work organization: paradigms for project management and organization. *Communications of the ACM* (36)10, 35-43.

Eason, K. (1988). *Information technology and organizational change.* Taylor & Francis, London.

Fagan, M.E. (1976) Design and code inspections to reduce errors in program development. *IBM Systems Journal*, 15(3), 182-211.

Fiman, B. (1989) *Implementing change.* Training course licensed by Implementation Management Associates, Inc. IMA, Golden, CO.

Fowler, P. (1994).The challenge of transferring software and information technology. In *Business Process Re-engineering: Information Systems Opportunities and Challenges, Proceedings of the IFIP TC8 Open Conference* (ed. B.C. Glasson et al.), May 1994, Queensland Gold Coast, Australia, 79-88. North Holland, Amsterdam.

Fowler, P., Juristo, N. and Levine, L. (1993)*T^2ES concept and project initiation document.* CMU/SEI-92-SR 6.

Fowler, P. and Levine, L. (1992) Toward a problem solving approach to software technology transition, in *Proceedings of the IFIP 12th World Computer Congress* (ed. J. Van Leeuwen), Madrid, Spain, vol. 1, 57-64. Elsevier Science Publishers, B.V., The Netherlands.

Fowler, P., Rifkin, S. (1990) *Software engineering process group guide.* Technical Report CMU/SEI-90-TR-94.

Gervater, W. B. (1987) The nature and evaluation of commercial expert system building tools. *Computer*, 20: 29-30.

Grady, R.B. & Caswell, D.L. (1987). *Software metrics: Establishing a company-wide program.* Prentice-Hall, Inc., Englewood Cliffs, NJ.

Juristo, N., Gómez, A., and Pazos, J. (1995) *Ingenier del conocimiento: Construccion de sistemas expertos.* Ed. CEURA. Forthcoming.

Humphrey, W. (1989) *Managing the software process.* Addison-Wesley, Reading, MA.

Kwon, T.H. & Zmud, R.W. (1987). Unifying the fragmented models of information systems implementation. In Boland, R.J. Jr., & Hirschheim, R.A. (Eds). *Critical issues in information systems research.* John Wiley & Sons, Chichester.

Leonard-Barton, D. (1988a) Implementation characteristics of organizational innovations. *Communication Research* 15, 603-631.

Leonard-Barton, D. (1988b) Implementation as mutual adaptation of technology and organization. *Research Policy* 17, 5 (Oct. 1988), 102-110.

Morgan, G. (1986) *Images of organization.* Sage Publications, Beverly Hills, CA.

Paulk, M., Weber, C.V., Garcia, S.M., Chrissis, M.B. and Bush, M. (1993) *Key practices of the capability maturity model Version 1.1.* CMU/SEI-93-TR-25.

Pazos, J. and Mate, J. L. (1988) *Ingeniería del Conocimiento: Diseño y Construcción de Sistemas Expertos.* Córdoba, Argentina: Ed. SEPA, S.A.

Radice, R. and Phillips, R.W. (1988) *Software engineering: an industrial approach.* Simon and Schuster.

Rogers, E.(1983) *Diffusion of Innovations.* The Free Press, New York.

Schon, D. (1967) *Technology and Change: The New Heraclitus.*

Slagle J. and Wick M. (1988) A method for evaluating candidate expert system applications. *AI Magazine*, Winter, 44-53.

Strauss, S. & Ebenau, R.G. (1994). *Software Inspections Process.* McGraw-Hill, Inc., New York.

Willis, R. (1983). *Technology transfer takes 6 +/- 2 years,* in *Proceedings of IEEE Computer Society Workshop on Software Engineering Technology Transfer,* IEEE Computer Society Press, Silver Spring, MD.

APPENDIX 1: Slagle and Wick Feasibility Tables

Table 1 Essential Features

	Score		*Weight*		*Value*	*Feature*
1	70	=	10	x	7	Recipients agree on high payoff (Market for T2ES not yet directly assessed)
2	70	=	10	x	7	Customers have realistic expectations (Market for T2ES not yet directly assessed)
3	80	=	10	x	8	Project has management commitment
4	100	=	10	x	10	Task is not natural language intensive
5	49	=	7	x	7	Task is knowledge intensive (Yes, but very open ended because of newness of field as a practice)
6	80	=	8	x	10	Task is heuristic in nature (Yes, highly so)
7	40	=	10	x	4	Test cases are available (Yes, but not readily accessible)
8	70	=	7	x	10	Incremental growth is possible
9	100	=	10	x	10	Task requires no common sense (Sub-tasks do, and it is not an unreasonable assumption that users of the systems will have common sense in these areas)
10	80	=	8	x	10	Task does not require optimal solution
11	100	=	10	x	10	Task will be performed in future
12	70	=	7	x	10	Task not essential to deadline
13	48	=	8	x	6	Task easy but not too easy (Easy in the piece parts but not complex overall and unpredictable due to its dependencies on human systems)
14	80	=	10	x	8	An expert exists (Yes, but . . . no one expert has planned a complete transfer activity from scratch and then executed it; we are drawing a composite picture)
15	90	=	10	x	9	Expert is a genuine expert (The expert preparing the composite gained her expertise largely from experience)
16	100	=	10	x	10	Expert is committed to entire project
17	100	=	10	x	10	Expert is cooperative
18	80	=	8	x	10	Expert is articulate
19	72	=	8	x	9	Expert has successful history
20	64	=	8	x	8	Expert uses symbolic reasoning
21	70	=	7	x	10	Hard to transfer expertise (Not "hard" intellectually, but "hard" because time--consuming would require long apprenticeship)
22	100	=	10	x	10	Expert does not use physical skills
23	80	=	10	x	8	Experts agree on good solutions
24	90	=	10	x	9	Expert does not need creativity
	TOTAL	:				2003 out of possible 2400

APPENDIX 1: Slagle and Wick Feasibility Tables (continued)

Table 2 Desired Features

	Score		*Weight*		*Value*	*Feature*
1	64	=	8	x	8	Management customer (SEI) committed to follow on
2	20	=	4	x	5	Insertion into workplace smooth (We have not done market/user analysis; this would be part of the use of the first demo)
3	40	=	4	x	10	The system interacts with the user (This is essential)
4	32	=	4	x	8	System can explain reasoning (Unclear how well this will work, given differences in context and vocabulary)
5	40	=	4	x	10	System can intelligently question user
6	40	=	4	x	10	Task identified as problem area
7	36	=	4	x	9	Solutions are explainable (Yes, but . . may be long winded, and, as with item 4, depend on correct assumptions about context and vocabulary)
8	50	=	5	x	10	Task does not require real-time response
9	40	=	8	x	5	Similar expert systems built before
10	50	=	5	x	10	Task performed in many locations
11	0	=	3	x	0	Task performed in a hostile environment
12	40	=	4	x	10	Task involves subjective factors
13	0	=	3	x	0	Expert unavailable in future
14	40	=	4	x	10	Expert intellectually attached to project
15	50	=	5	x	10	Expert does not feel threatened
16	20	=	2	x	10	Expertise loosely organized
	TOTAL	:				562 out of possible 1600

APPENDIX 2: Knowledge Acquisition Example

As an example of the knowledge acquired at this stage, Appendix 1 shows the Schedule Training and Education activity model. In this case, there is an additional item called *Help to Input*. This item was created with the idea of filling it with any helpful material that the future user might need. More static domain knowledge was gathered from descriptions of adoption and implementation plan activities carried out by the expert using the activity model, thus completing the list of entities and relations. But most importantly, we began to identify the implicit reasoning used by the expert to perform each activity. This reasoning was generally extracted from the knowledge block of our model, although it appeared in a diluted form in inputs and outputs on other occasions, as is the case shown here, and even in the *Help* item. Note that the task model was built by the expert in the absence of the knowledge engineer, because of the problems of distance mentioned later.

BOX 2.4. SCHEDULE TRAINING AND EDUCATION

OUTPUT

[These items are those produced by processing the inputs using the knowledge.]

1. What individuals go to what courses;
2. Sequence for training target audience;
3. Selection of instructors (group-paced only;)
4. Availability of classrooms (group-paced only);
5. How to register students (group-paced only);
6. Conditions surrounding self-paced training;
7. Rough schedule where items 1-7 above are input (to schedule).

KNOWLEDGE

1. Match list of courses with list of individuals (who have been classified according to managers, technical support, etc.).

2. Individuals in departments or divisions who must use the technology first must be trained first. Of this set of individuals, managers and technical support must be trained before expert and casual users. If your target audience is very large and will require multiple offerings, you will need to prioritize which sets of individuals are trained first, second, etc.

3. Be sure that instructors are available and that they have the right experience for teaching the class. They need to know the material and have experience using the technology. Don't assign an instructor simply because he or she has time: be sure the instructor will be credible in the classroom. If there will be many offerings of the training and education, then the investment to train instructors formally will be worthwhile. Initially, an instructor might do the following, in the following order:

a. Attend the class as a student.
b. Attend the class as an observer.
c. Teach a part of the class and receive critique from the supervisory instructor.
d. Teach the class him or herself.

If there will be only a few offerings, the instructor should attend the class at least twice.

4. Depending upon the training and education that you are offering, you may need a particular kind of classroom.

There are several common types of classrooms:

- A regular classroom has chairs and desks (or tables).
- A computer-equipped classroom allows you to try the technology in the classroom. This type of classroom may have computers that are networked.
- An AV/Media classroom allows you to show videos to tape and replay interactive exercises, etc.
- Break out seminar rooms allow you to divide the class and work in small groups.

4A. Match the types of courses you are offering with the type of classroom that you need.

5. You will need a mechanism for registering students and for tracking attendance to ensure that everyone gets trained.

If you have a training function (or group) in your organization, use the process they have in place for registration and attendance tracking.

Because it's impossible to get 100% attendance, you will need to make provision to train those who missed classes.

6A. Self-paced instruction is designed to move at the pace of the individual student. For example, foreign language instruction frequently uses audio tapes where the student controls how much information is covered and how quickly. Computer language and tool instruction may be offered via self-paced interactive computer-based lessons.

6B.This type of instruction is effective under the following conditions:

- when students enter the training and education at different levels of expertise;
- when there aren't enough people to make a group-paced class because of work schedules or geography;
- when the technology is such that it's not essential to learn as part of a group;
- as a supplement to group-paced instruction.

6C. Self-paced instruction requires these facilities:

- adequate lighting, ventilation and seating;
- audio tape and video players, computers and other equipment as appropriate;
- private study carrels if necessary;
- in addition, students taking self-paced instruction may need tutors.

INPUT

1A. List of courses

- selected
- developed
- customized

1B. List of all individuals in target audience, classified according to following:

- managers
- technical support
- casual users
- expert users

2. Answer to the question:

What units in your organization, e.g., departments or divisions need to be trained? In what order?

3. Answer to questions:

Who are the most credible instructors for teaching the courses to be offered.

(direct)

4A.What type of a classroom do you need for each course

- Reg.

Table 3 Instructors

	Name of course	*Position*	*Back up*
1			
2			
3			

- Comp equip.
- AV
- Break out

4B.

- Course #1
- Course #2
- Course #3

(direct)

5. Answer to the question:

Do you have a mechanism for registering students and for tracking attendance? (direct)

6B. Do you have students entering the training and education at different levels of expertise? (direct)

Do you have individuals in your organization who would not be able to attend group paced instruction because of work schedules or geography? (direct)

Is it essential to learn about this technology and how to use it as part of a group? (direct)

Will you need to supplement group paced instruction? (direct)

HELP TO INPUT

1. COURSES

You may have a course serving each category: a different course for managers, technical support, casual users and expert users.

You may have a course that serves multiple categories: for example, an introductory course may be appropriate for managers and casual users.

You may have multiple courses for the same category: for example, experts may need in depth courses for several topics.

TARGET AUDIENCES (Definition)

All people who are going to use this technology or support its use in some way are the target audience. A target audience can cross organizational boundaries.

For example, for a spreadsheet technology, the target audience may include all administrative assistants (both casual and expert users) across departments and divisions. The target audience also includes their managers and those who provide technical support.

For a CASE tool, the target audience may include all department software engineers (both casual and expert users) working on a particular project. The target audience also includes their managers and those who provide technical support.

2. Change agents need to be trained before anyone. It may be possible to train change agents (either by the vendor or in-house) during the pilot or during the training for other parts of the organization.

3. The competence of the instructors who are selected to teach the courses reflect the priority that management places on the technology.

If courses will be taught many times, it is useful to create a set of instructor notes for each course. These notes might include: comments on what to emphasize in a particular section or lecture and comments on pacing and exercises.

The same instructor may teach more than one course; sometimes a course may be team taught.

4A. Make sure that the lighting and ventilation in each classroom is adequate. Try to ensure reasonable comfort in the chairs and tables/desks.

4B. Determine that classrooms will be available for the number of days and dates that you will need.

5. You must have or create a mechanism for registering students and tracking attendance.

One way to train those who missed the classroom offering is with self-paced instruction. It is unlikely you would develop self-paced instruction for this purpose alone.

6C. Do you have the appropriate facilities?

- adequate lighting, ventilation etc. (see knowledge 6C)

If you do not have the appropriate facilities, your plan will need to include time and money for acquisition of these.

7 BIOGRAPHIES

Priscilla Fowler works on the translation of research and practice in technology adoption and implementation into methods and tools for software change agents in software engineering organizations. She is co-proposer, with Linda Levine, and founding Chair of the International Federation for Information Processing (IFIP) WG 8.6 on Diffusion, Transfer & Implementation of Information Technology. She initiated and directed the AT&T Bell Labs Software Engineering Technology Transfer Program. Prior to beginning her technology transfer work in 1980, Ms. Fowler was a project manager, consultant, and software engineer at AT&T Bell Labs, IBM, and Knight-Ridder. She holds a B.A. degree from Drew University and is a member of the ACM.

Isabella García-Martín works on the development of new applications for expert systems. She completed her Master's Degree in Knowledge Engineering in 1993 and is now a Ph.D. candidate in the area of software process.

Natalia Juristo works on the relationship between knowledge engineering and software engineering. More specifically, she is working on the use of knowledge acquisition techniques for the development of traditional software systems, and the use of software engineering metrics for knowledge-based systems evaluation. Since 1993, she has served on the Program Committee of the International Conference on Software Engineering and Knowledge Engineering. Professor Juristo completed her Ph.D. in 1991 at the Facultad de Informatica, Universidad Politecnica de Madrid. She is now Academic Director of the Master Courses on Software Engineering and Knowledge Engineering and Coordinator of the Software Engineering Group at the same institution.

Linda Levine works on the diffusion and transfer of software technologies, and also conducts research in the areas of technology suppression, reasoning and argumentation, and design disciplines. Dr. Levine holds a Ph.D. from Carnegie Mellon University in Rhetoric and Communication. Recently, she has been exploring barriers to the adoption of process automation technology and investigating legal issues in technology transfer, including access to and development of technology, unfair competitive practices, and antitrust regulation. In 1992, she was co-proposer, with Priscilla Fowler, to the International Federation for Information Processing (IFIP)for the present 8.6 Working Group.

5

The organisational politics of meetings and their technology — two case studies of video supported communication

John Hughes, Steinar Kristoffersen, Jon O'Brien, and Mark Rouncefield
CSCW Research Centre, Lancaster University, U. K,
phone: +44 1524 594 186; fax: +44 1524 594 256; email: steinar@comp.lancs.ac.uk

Abstract

This paper reflects on the introduction of video based communication systems, using empirical studies of two large commercial organisations: a national high street bank and a technical research centre in a multinational manufacturing company. The study suggests that although corporate philosophy and politics can create a drive towards exploring a set of technologies, they can simultaneously encourage a way of organising and managing work that conflicts with that particular implementation. The need to resolve conflicting political and social contingencies throughout the implementation, introduction and evaluation of new technology must be recognised. Precise requirements and design implications are hard to formulate, and our proposal has important implications in that it points beyond the traditional requirements engineering and work study approaches to systems design and introduction.

Keywords

Introduction, adoption, video conferences, computer supported cooperative work, requirements engineering, work studies, politics and principles

1 INTRODUCTION

As multimedia technology becomes less expensive and easier to use, video communication will become a salient feature of many applications for Computer Supported Cooperative Work (CSCW). Video can support non-verbal communication and peripheral awareness (Pagani & Mackay 1993), informal communication (Root 1988), and contributes to the rapport within groups of geographically-dispersed individuals (Abel 1990). Users like video (Tang & Isaacs 1993), although work exists to suggest that the value added by real-time, visual communication is negligible (cited in Tang & Isaacs 1993), and that the success of teleconferencing has fallen short of commercial expectations (Egido 1988). However, few such systems have moved beyond the laboratory and, consequently, there have been few opportunities to consider and evaluate the use of cooperative multimedia within natural work settings.

While research continues to suggest the *potential* of CSCW solutions to the coordination of distributed working (Malone et al. 1987), it is still the case that organisational implementation is frequently less than straightforward, involving not merely technological issues but also important organisational factors (Orlikowski 1992). Similar experiences have been made throughout the history of IS development (Keen 1981; Kling & Iacono 84). Controlled experiments in laboratory-like environments often show increased technological efficiency and effectiveness, however, and in contrast, the move into the 'real world' of organisational use often proves disappointing (Dennis et al. 1990; Grudin 1994; Greenberg 1991; Egido 1988).

While there are technological challenges in developing effective video systems, this paper emphasises the importance of looking at the technology as enmeshed in the 'politics' of organisational life and asserts that this needs to be taken into account when assessing the implications of video technology.

The two case studies considered here allow us to offer some evaluation of video communication systems in use, albeit systems which are used for different purposes: selling a product, as in the bank, and holding a meeting, as in the technology centre. Whilst small in scale, these two examples are intended to illuminate the wider context which bears upon the effectiveness of video based systems.

2 THE ORGANISATIONS STUDIED

The first empirical study on which this paper is based concerns the introduction of a video based communication system in a large UK bank. Radical reorganisation had centralised some of the more specialised functions of the bank's services so that high street branches had to deal mainly with counter customers, calling on the centres for more specialised services. The role of the Telehelp team in the bank's national insurance centre, is to give customers advice about home insurance and related matters. A commercial, ISDN-based, desktop video conference system, with task-dedicated workflow software developed in-house, has been implemented to support the communication with customers and staff in selected branches. The video link was installed in the Telehelp team for a 6 month trial period, staffed by specially trained personnel. The study is based on 12 days' ethnographic observation, taking place over a period of several months in 1994/95.

The second study is from an investigation of a laboratory in a technology centre, belonging to a multinational company. The technology centre employs a dedicated facility video conference system to facilitate meetings with stakeholders throughout the company. Observations lasted approximately four weeks over a period of two to three months in 1994.

3 RESEARCH METHOD

The research method adopted in these studies is broadly that of ethnography. The distinguishing characteristic of this approach is the researcher's involvement in the milieu of study, and whose role is to provide 'thick descriptions' (Geertz 1983) of the circumstances, practices, conversations and activity that comprise the 'real world' character of everyday work settings. The general advantage claimed for ethnographic approaches *in design* lies in the 'sensitising' it promotes to the real world character and context of work. Such research begins by seeing the social world from the point of view of the participants, and by examining the ways in which the work activities actually get done. This emphasis provides an important analytic tool for the examination of work as lived experience, and important clues as to both the 'how' and 'why' of everyday working practices. Although the use of technology is but one aspect of these studies, *in the design context* ethnographic approaches focus on the various ways in which technologies, including video systems, are enmeshed in the everyday flow of work as experienced by those in the setting.

4 PLACING VIDEO IN ITS ORGANISATIONAL CONTEXT

Traditionally, problems associated with the introduction of systems have predominantly been defined from a development perspective (Andersen et al. 1986) in which insufficient analysis, careless design or incomplete testing and narrow communication lines on the managerial level are seen as paramount problems. Previous work also takes the stance that lack of success stems from an organisation reluctant to change, even for the 'obvious' benefit of the enterprise. Thus, the job of the system designer includes the necessary effort to persuade managers and workers into changing the organisation of work, the work procedures, or even the people and their skills, to accommodate the technology being introduced.

To facilitate the adoption of multimedia technologies to support cooperation, Francik et al. (1991) suggest that several issues should be carefully considered: i) Identifying the suitable application domain in which to introduce the system; ii) Assisting the members of the organisation to envisage future use; iii) Selecting the right group for a pilot test situation; iv) Being careful not to ignore the actual distribution of work; v) Assessing existing support for communication; vi) Assigning equipment to group members according to the nature of the work they perform rather than the traditional roles of manual office routines; and vii) Acknowledge the importance of training.

As the following empirical studies suggest, adhering to such principles is no guarantee of success: in the example from the bank a thorough 'adoption exercise' like the one outlined above *was* carried out and yet the system has failed to meet expectations. 'Video links', like many other technologies past, present and, no doubt, future, are introduced and developed in accord with a range of organisational, managerial and local priorities and policies; priorities and policies that are themselves subject to change and may even, in some instances, be in conflict (see, for example, Yates 1989).

In the bank, the desktop video conference system became the central component of the RATE (Remote Access To Expertise) project. Internally known only as the *Video Link*, it had been installed in the 'Telehelp' section of the Insurance division. One aim of this 6 month part of the project was to obtain customer and staff feedback. The bank's research department also wanted to consider other possible applications, such as in Home loans and in the Foreign and Commercial sectors, as well as assessing potentiality for a much wider use in fostering the collaboration between staff in service centres and branches. Similar considerations motivated the introduction of video conferencing in the technology centre and was a central element in the IT strategy proposing to use electronic means to support the use of expertise between remote sites of the company.

In what follows we present fieldwork materials to illustrate the video technology in use in both the bank and the technology centre. Our aim is to show how larger organisational issues can interact, in complex ways, with the use of the technology under consideration.

5 INSTANTANEOUS ACCESS TO EXPERTISE

5.1 Strategic Context

The role of the Telehelp team is, in line with the strategy of the bank to centralise specialised services in order to reduce costs, to give insurance advice to customers from branch offices. The following are integral to this strategy. Firstly, increased routinisation of cases brings the cost down. Not only are exceptional cases more time-consuming to evaluate and record, but the decision making process itself requires costly expertise. By offering a standardised product, the bank can rely on less educated, younger staff. This is traditional hierarchic organisational design and, as long as the exceptions are easily dealt with, eg. by referring 'difficult' customers to other companies, it works well and the risk profile is maintained. Secondly, centralisation of expertise is one of the bank's explicit organisational goals. Service centre staff used to work in the 'back offices' of the branches. By bringing these 'back office' staff together, many more branches can be served as well as reducing managerial and training costs. Finally, increasingly international and competitive markets, alongside a more mobile customer base, have forced the bank to abandon its traditional 'administrative' focus. Not only has the business expanded and taken up new areas, such as insurance, but reduced profit margins have made the product focus paramount. Banking is now the in the business of 'selling' a wide range of financial products.

The 'macro' organisational context for the introduction and use of the Video Link was, therefore, a complex scenario of implementing and evaluating a new technology whilst responding to changing market, managerial and organisational pressures. Like other financial institutions, the bank was involved in improving profit margins by cost reduction through the centralisation of 'back office' processing and 'deskilling'; both requiring heavy investment in IT. At the same time the bank was attempting to defend its 'market share' by endeavouring to change from an organisation that had traditionally been concerned with administration to one that focused on selling.

5.2 The use of the Video Link and Workflow system

One integral part of the Video Link system was the Workflow package designed to be used alongside it. From the managers' perspective, workflow systems are valuable because they enforce the business rules. In this case it was intended to ensure that all the accepted home insurance covers issued complied with the risk profile of the unit. Equally important was the normative effect on the behaviour of the workforce, making control easier and reducing the need for training. With a well-designed workflow system, people with little or no background in banking or insurance could be brought in to sell policies, because all the rules would, ideally, be maintained by the system. On the other hand, the workflow system was also expected to make better sales' people out of 'back office staff' by displaying on the screen the right responses to negative customer reactions, alongside a suite of effective selling expressions. There was a general belief that the customer needed to feel that they were speaking to an 'expert' capable of providing a service *above that* offered by the branch staff, thereby building confidence in bank services which, it was hoped, would then be extended to the purchase of other bank products and services.

The first releases of the Video Link package included document sharing and a whiteboard, but was later reduced to a simple Video Link and screen transfer of completed documents.[1] At the time of the study customers were only shown the finished form and asked to confirm details.

This fieldnote extract displays a 'typical' session:

1. ... using video link - intro - host at branch; customer...using headset (problem of feedback when using speakers) - customer using speakers.
2. Using screen - filling in details on form - asking customer questions - name; date of birth; initials; occupation; post code - then tells customer address - street/rd - (say that this impresses customers) asks for house number
3. Transfers info over - explains that this will take a few seconds and will make her image break up/go fuzzy a bit asks to check if its OK.
4. Goes through policy - filling in form on screen - and asking customer questions - building and contents; rebuilding costs; contents; accidental damage; away from home.
5. Transfers quote over - explains again about the image breaking up.

---

[1] Initially customers had 'shared' the documents as they were being prepared by staff, but spelling mistakes had tended to erode customer confidence. The managers also felt that if they made the customer focus on the document-oriented nature of work, they would miss out on the most important part the interaction from the bank's perspective, namely the non-verbal communication and facial expressions of the specialist, thus making up the 'sales pitch'

6. Goes through the figures - gives details on policy - what it covers in addition - cycles; frozen food; £ 2 million owners liability; - and outlines repayment details .
7. "Do you know roughly what you are paying at the moment?"
8. Offers to print out quote - to take away and compare.
9. Takes daytime telephone number - "in case we need to contact you for any reason"
10. Gives 'official data protection script - on card in front of screen.
11. Transfers 'features and benefits' of policy (a list of other items covered by the policy).
12. Customer does questionnaire in branch - operator has headset on - can hear
13. Gets printout.

5.3 The nature of work and management

At the time of the study the Video Link was set up between the Insurance Centre and ten branches. Staff, selected for their insurance expertise, had been trained to use the Video Link. The training had to a large extent been presentation-oriented, and the specialists had also received instructions about how to use the workflow system. The branches would 'prepare' the customer for the Video Link emphasising the expert status of the person at the other end.[1]

The Telehelp team was managed in a process-oriented way with a light panel keeping them continuously updated on average service, waiting time, calls answered and calls in the queue. The panel also showed how many of the group's members were 'not ready' and performance sheets for each period were displayed. Company policies were implemented both as a set of managerial sanctions as well as socially through various forms of peer pressure. The emphasis on 'sales points', a metric assessment of the commercial value of each transaction, can, not surprisingly, create conflicts. It is in this context of intense pressure to perform that the Video Link would eventually be evaluated.

5.4 The work that makes technology work

The fieldwork reveals the considerable amount of 'work to make the Video Link work' both in the immediate context for the operator and, in the context of 'micro-organisational politics', for the Manager of the Telehelp team. For the operator this consists of demeanour and 'face' work to make the customer feel at ease, as well as the articulation of Video Link work with other aspects of the organisation of insurance cover; work that takes place away from the 'video booth'.

Throughout the 'Video Link process' the operator is engaged in extensive and skilful 'demeanour work' consisting of exaggerated smiling, nodding and facial gestures as well as varied conversational asides and 'jokes', maintaining a sensitivity to the customer's reception of both the technology and the information on insurance. This is accomplished whilst the operator is simultaneously completing the insurance details; a not inconsiderable task since in order to 'look' at the customer the operator has to orient herself to the camera on top of the screen and cannot actually see much of the screen - containing the customer's image and the document - in front of her. There is also a considerable amount of 'talking through the technology' - explaining to the customer what is happening, or is about to happen on the screen; explaining, for example, that *"the image will go fuzzy for a moment because of the amount of information I am transferring"* and so on, giving an 'account' of the ongoing transaction in a manner that will be easily understood and accepted. This 'account' includes conveying an impression of the bank's policies as 'quality' policies, (and therefore not the cheapest). That this is not a simple or straightforward process is illustrated in the next fieldwork

[1] The interesting point to observe is that the Insurance Centre's specialists are not really supposed to be *insurance* experts; they are, on the contrary, trained to follow procedures and either ask their supervisor to sanction exceptional or difficult cases, or plainly reject them. Their expertise lies in being able to use the system effectively.

extract when the operator suddenly finds herself dealing with an 'awkward customer' - in this instance the operator effectively 'freezes' her 'body language' but begins to engage in extensive explanation and justification of the details of the policies, thereby displaying her 'expertise'.

1. Phone - 'live' call
2. Puts on headset - brings up screen of branch and assistant.
3. "Hello ...(looking at camera)..turn the screen slightly"
"My name is...I need to take some information (gives standard script on information)..is that OK?" (Some problem here - later emerges that the customer said "No" and "if you send me details of any insurance I'm going to contact my PFA (Personal Financial Adviser) (At this stage the operator 'freezes' and becomes very formal and exact in what she says)
"Obviously that's why we ask at the beginning"
4. Explaining about transferring information and picture freezing
5. Asking for details and filling in screen - surname; initials; date of birth; occupation (mature student "what subject are you studying"); postcode - gives street; number of house.
6. Explains what the insurance is - not connected to Life Insurance Department.
7. Transfers information over - "Can you just check that that's correct?" - explains about postcode and address - stores it at this end.
8. Going through details - rebuilding costs; buildings and contents; accidental damage; items taken away over £1000; total taken away from home at any one time - "we have a minimum sum of £2500 - I'll quote you for that" "I'll transfer that - its just a premium indication and may be subject to future ..(Interruption - asked question - answers "not at the moment")
9. Paying the policy - "I can print off the quotation - put some details on the screen in front of you - some of the benefits..
10. Going through screens - printing options.
11. Asked question - answers "what do you mean? - if you have an alarm - if its an alarm with a service contract you can have a 5-10% discount..Is it approved by NACODS? - then you can have a 10% discount. There is an endorsement you must sign - that the alarm must be switched on - then there is a theft excess of £250 - some people don't like it.."
12. "I'm going to amend your quote to have the discount for having an alarm"
13. Customer asks question about letting out another property - "Is it let to professionals?"
14. Gets details of properties.
15. Customer asking questions - operator explains about going back to amend policy.
16. Asked question - "There is another one I can use." - using screen - cover choice - for house that is let.
17. Transferring data.
18. General chat about video link - "You wouldn't want to see me full size"
19. "Printing off quote for you now"
20. Answering questions - "H.(branch assistant). will give you one of our information packs.."
21. "Good-bye" - call ends.
22. "What a prat" Explains what the customer (a Physics postgraduate) was saying about the kit - that the mike was too big; the picture too small; he didn't like the delay; felt it was outdated. "I didn't like him..I let my feelings get the better of me.."

For the Manager there is a need to balance his resources between the telephone and video lines; to ensure staff support for the Video Link and to attempt to encourage branch utilisation of the link. The comparative infrequency of calls had reduced the manning level of the video booths so that at the time of the study branches were phoning the Telehelp section in order to get the booths ready and manned for incoming calls. Again this was a product of the 'micro-organisational' politics of the office. The selection and training of an 'elite task force' for the Video Link was a process which, in its identification of *expertise* had, apparently, created some tension within the section. The Telehelp team worked under intense pressure to answer calls and besides the manager's concern to keep the 'response rate' high (at an average of 6 seconds wait). There was some resentment that the RATE team were not 'pulling their weight', the Video Link sessions taking considerably longer to complete than the telephone interviews.

6 'GLOBAL' DIFFUSION OF EXPERTISE

Fieldwork at the technology centre occurred at a time when the organisation of the company to which it belonged was undergoing major restructuring, indeed these changes were frequently mentioned as taking place 'more or less all the time at the moment'.

Essentially what was taking place was a move away from a hierarchical 'divisional' and 'national' organisation towards what company members referred to as a 'global footing'. This new organisational configuration bought with it new requirements for the work of those in the technology centre. Competition between sites within the company was fostered and, as a result, technology centre staff were no seen as serving only the production sites within their UK division. Instead, they were to serve the 'entire company', taking part in the internal competitive process and seeking funding for new research and development in partnership with sites from various units in the 'global organisation'.

This new organisational configuration was explicitly underpinned by an IT strategy fostered by senior management; in particular the use of electronic communication technologies was encouraged as a means of supporting the kinds of contact required between staff at widely distributed sites within the company. In particular, video conferencing was introduced as a means of holding meetings with other sites, in an attempt to maintain the 'richness' of interaction typical of face-to-face meetings.

A number of these video conferences were observed between members of technology centre staff and members of the company based at other sites. These latter are the 'customers' of the centre's work, and are considered very much in these terms, rather than as members of the same company, and the need to maintain appropriate formal relationships, as with any 'external' customer, is a strong one. The importance of such meetings has increased considerably since the organisation's reconfiguration took place. Since Centre staff no longer directly serve other sites within their 'division' of the company, they must establish collaborative relationships with others on an *ad hoc* basis, as contracts are gained and lost throughout the wider company. As a result, on many occasions, such meetings are increasingly to do with establishing the precise nature of an offer of collaboration, negotiating and confirming funding details and a whole range of similar tasks. As a result of the more 'competitive' basis of the organisation's configuration, ('basically a kind of internal market' said one member of staff) these meetings were characterised by participants from the Centre as 'less to do with working with people you know and trust', and more to do with establishing and maintaining important new working relationships for the Centre.

There were two Centre staff taking part in each conference that was observed. Meetings were arranged over the phone in advance, with parties to the meeting specifying suitable, mutually convenient times for the conference. The majority of our discussion here will be based upon some detailed observations of one of these video conferences[1]:

6.1 Working Through the Technology

At the outset of each conference, time was spent ensuring that the software was functioning appropriately and that the image at each site was of a sufficient standard. This process typically took a few minutes, and was also treated as 'warm up' time, with 'jokey' interaction taking place between participants at both sites, before the business in hand was tackled in the meeting proper. The video camera placed on top of the PC monitor had, on most occasions, to be tilted downwards by wedging a book underneath its base in order that it could pick up those sitting on the low chairs found in that room.

The meeting discussed here is not one in which Centre staff are dealing with unknown parties, but it is nevertheless of importance. It is illustrative of many of the

1 While this is not necessarily representative of the possible range of video conference meetings it does provide insights into the types of interactions and practices that develop around such technology.

issues arising out of the exploration of this type of technology. This meeting had been called to discuss a document that had been produced and circulated by members of the Quality Management team at the technology centre which dealt with the reporting procedures connected to joint projects between the Centre and the Production Site. The particular concern is with consistency across a group of documents. As is clear from the following transcription extract from the meeting, the point at which the assembled conferees are called to order to begin the meeting proper is one which is not entirely clear to all:

A (a member of Technology Centre staff), B & C in the production site, D & E in the Technology Centre

A: You really need an inset of your own image don't you? [He appears to be switching between the technology centre's camera and his own - this is not clear to the Centre]

D: Eh?

A: I wasn't talking to you!

C: Hahaha

[All laugh]

B: I can't see you D ... sit up

E: Simultaneous {Shall we start?

D: {Am I OK now?

[Pause]

A: Yeah, OK, OK do we want to start?

D: Can you see me?

[Pause]

E: Can you see him?

B&A: Yep, yep no problem

[Pause]

A: Let's start ...

E: OK ... have you all got the agenda? it's only going to be brief?

C: Yes (holds it up to camera)

As the business of the meeting continues it becomes clear the difficulties the participants are experiencing with the video conference: there is a very clear echo of each individual's words a second or two after they speak, which impacts on the ways in which the participants talk to each other: there are abnormally long pauses between sentences, as participants seem to leave sufficient time for the echo to die down, and to be sure that the conversational cues being offered are ones that imply turn-taking to be appropriate. Furthermore, throughout the meeting all individuals enunciated their words extremely clearly, adding to the 'stilted' or 'unnatural' feel of the conversation. The slow frame refresh rate meant that the images of the other participants on the screen appeared jerky and somewhat blurred, this seemed to make following visual cues particularly difficult to follow. The following transcript illustrates these kinds of issues:

A: [Finishes sentence]

[Echo]

[Pause]

E: [Leans forward] [Speaks loudly and slowly]Can I say something?[Echo - appears to wait for echo to fade, checks those at Production Site on screen, all three nod vigorously] [Starts to speak]

C: [Simultaneously] Go ahead

[Pause]

C: Sorry go ahead

E: OK

What is clear here is the amount of 'work' that has to be done by conference participants to maintain some form of conversational 'flow': the exaggerated nature of turn-taking cues, and the highly demonstrative use of body movements are all made use of to compensate for the crude image and sound quality provided by the video link.

As the meeting progresses they discuss sections of the document to hand and all participants appear to focus more particularly upon the discussion document rather than upon the screen with the other participants upon it. Wrapping up the meeting is also bounded by a certain degree of overt demonstration on behalf of the participants.

E: Is there anything else we should discuss?

[Pause]

D: Did you get the package?

B: From 'X'?
D: Yeah
B: Yes, the panel was fine, thanks
[Pause]
E:[Breathes in loudly, slaps side of chair] Shall we wrap it up?
[Pause]
B&C: Yeah
B: Nice talking to you [Waves]
[All laugh]
D: See you soon, see you later A
[Pause]
A: OK
E (to D): Can we hang up?
[D nods]
E: Bye! [Clicks 'close call' on screen] [Monitor greys out] [To D] I presume the call's hung up.

Clearly many of the problems being experienced in this video conference are related to the developing state of the technology. The staff are well aware of the limitations of this technology, and swap stories of their experiences with it. After the conference discussed above, D tells E of the time that he had faxed a document for discussion through to the external site, started the meeting, confirming that the fax had arrived - which was confirmed by holding it up to the camera - and entered into a discussion of the document in hand. It was five minutes before they realised that there had been a mix-up of faxes and they were discussing different documents. There was a clear need for a facility, argued D, for 'proper' desktop conferencing, where electronic versions of documents might be discussed and updated effectively. The appropriate software had been ordered, stated E, and it was just the need for the 64k bandwidth that was holding things up. He added:

> *"You can't really see what they're doing, but you know that they're doing something and you can't really say "What are you doing?" It makes it difficult to keep up a steady flow of conversation."*

As the technology currently stands then, there is little or no scope for the 'added value' of a visual dimension to the conferencing set up, as was made clear by A on his return to the technology centre:

> *"I'm saying nothing! I don't like it .. I don't like it at all. Until the technology improves you can't really achieve anything that you can't do on the telephone.*

The description of the organisational context within which the video conference facility has been introduced, makes clear the expectations possessed by the policy-makers within the company with regard to this technology. However, as the fieldwork shows, the introduction of the technology has not kept pace with these policy decisions and, accordingly, fails to come up to expectations.

The crucial nature of such meetings for the Centre's personnel meant that, for many staff, such experiences with the technology were discouraging. On one occasion, serious problems were emerging with an overseas subsidiary of the company, and a meeting at directorial level was required. The Centre's head accountant explicitly ruled out the notion of holding a video conference with these individuals, since they would need to "Stare the buggers in the eyes and see which way they twitched". There was a real sense that the video-based technologies could not support such boardroom subtleties, and as such were not appropriate for the kinds of tasks they were intended to support. Thus, the perhaps hasty introduction of these technologies over a slow link has led to somewhat negative impressions of the role of the technology within the crucial working practises of the Centre staff, and subsequent scepticism regarding the policy behind such introduction:

> *"Little boys with new toys ... they don't play with soldiers anymore, they play with technology"*

The implications of this scepticism reach beyond a straightforward 'dislike' of the technology, and highlight a range of important issues associated with the introduction of new technologies within an organisation.

In this example from the technology centre a new organisational configuration has been supported by the introduction and exploration of the potential of video technologies for holding meetings. At the same time this reconfiguration has generated new requirements of the work of staff at the Centre concerning, in particular, the nature of the meetings in which they participate. Whereas previously a more stable set of established collaborative relationships underpinned the majority of meetings with other sites within the company, the Centre now operates within a competitive 'internal market' and staff increasingly find that meetings are the occasions at which delicate negotiations are carried out with those who cannot necessarily be 'trusted'.

Thus the role of meetings within the organisation has shifted as well as the means by which they take place: the organisational reconfiguration has implications both for the technology being explored as part of this reconfiguration (the introduction of video conferencing) and the working practices this technology is intended to support. Increasingly, the need to 'stare the buggers in the eyes', for example, and other such boardroom manoeuvres is emerging in these meetings as a result of the more competitive basis of the company's organisation.What has emerged here, then, is the fact that the technology under exploration cannot support the new practices related to the same sets of organisational concerns.

7 DISCUSSION

In this paper we have looked at two attempts to introduce video-based communication technology into commercial organisations, both of which have not been entirely successful, although the technology is still under evaluation. A number of complex and contradictory organisational pressures are involved here. For example, the bank's emphasis on 'customer service', on being "first choice for customers" might be regarded as fundamentally conflicting with the heavy emphasis on centralisation, standardisation and routinisation of procedures. These same pressures can be seen in the introduction and evaluation of the Video Link – the customer service it provided, of individual, personal 'remote access to expertise' had to be balanced and judged against commercial considerations of time and sales produced. The advice and sales arguments can be better formulated if the advisor recognises the type of person on the other end, managers claimed. This is presumably easier across the video link compared to the phone. This means that they expect the specialist to be able to detect and interpret, but also respond in a meaningful way to concerns like: "What turns the customer on?", "Does the customer ask many questions?", and "Is he concerned?". This is strongly in contrast with the fact that the current trend is towards integration of all support with workflow systems, an efficient way of enforcing the plan and standardising the process, as illustrated in figure 1.

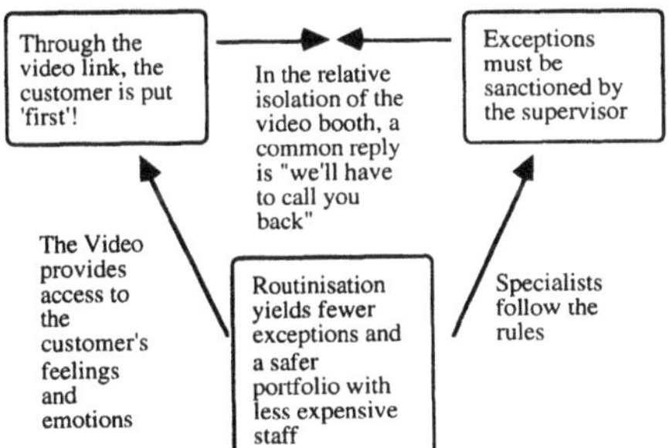

Figure 1. Routinisation-Sanctioning-Access

In the bank, a complex picture emerges since the Video Link provided the requisite remote access to expertise, albeit the 'normal' commercial pressures of time and sales completion and 'value added' suggested the inadequacy of the link in this particular context. Part of the explanation of why this particular introduction failed, is the tension between strategic expectations and local implementations for fulfilling these expectations. For example, the video based interviews are longer, they are hosted by two people instead of one, and they put the specialist as well as the customer in a situation in which "it is difficult to say no". Clearly, while the bank was hoping to benefit and learn from its experiment with the Video Link, it also held certain expectations of the technology focusing on its extension into other areas of bank services and the possibilities it offered of improved profit, market share and 'added-value'. While there was a recognition within the bank of a need to 'embrace the future' and experiment with different forms of multi-media and communication technology, there was also a contrasting, and day-to-day, pressure on 'generating results yesterday' and clearly demonstrating profitability. One aspect of the local culture is the importance of achieving sales points and meeting the bank's expectations. One consequence is that whilst the branches would be keen not to 'hand over' a VIP customer to the Centre, they would try not to spend resources, eg. host a video conference, on people that they did not expect would 'buy the product'. It was into this complex organisational 'culture' therefore, that the Video Link was introduced and evaluated, as illustrated in figure 2.

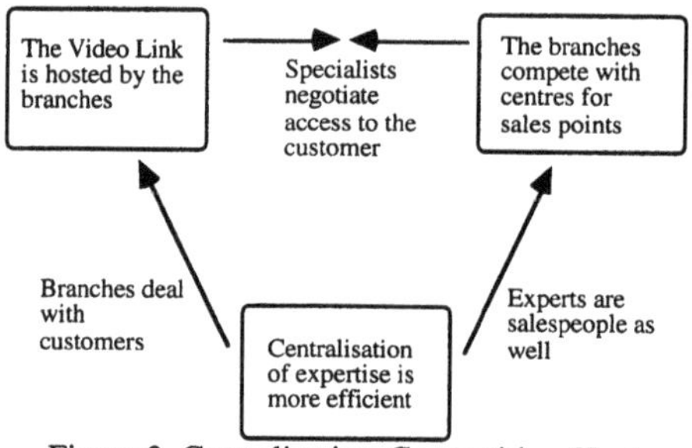

Figure 2. Centralisation-Competition-Host

In the technology centre, changes in the organisational context within which its staff have to operate to one which is more 'global' in nature, working in partnership with those not necessarily co-located, as they were previously, within the division of the organisation, has brought about changes in the nature of the meetings which are needed. One element of the company's policy has been to use video-based communication in order to facilitate meetings between distant sites; in the example discussed here, however, the policy-makers' expectations of the technology have not been fulfilled, since the slow link has prevented personnel holding meetings in a manner appropriate for the organisational importance of such meetings. As a result, both the technology and policy have become seen as inappropriate for dealing with the broader organisational changes with which they are designed to cope.

The studies reported here support the argument that the implementation of new technologies needs to attend to the complex interactions between corporate philosophy and, particularly, how this, in the local settings of the organisation of the work, can affect the introduction and adoption of new technology. In both these cases, the introduction of video-conferencing technology was ill-suited to the organisational politics engendered by wider organisational changes. The technology was offered as a way of 'fixing' organisational problems but, in the event, created further problems for those who had to use the technology and, through this, induced no little scepticism not only about the technology but also about the general strategy of reorganisation.

9 ACKNOWLEDGEMENTS

Support for this work was provided by the UK's Engineering and Physical Sciences Research Council under the DTI/EPSRC programme on CSCW, the Research Council of Norway as part of project 100268/410 and Norsk Regnesentral. We are grateful for the constructive criticism given to us by the anonymous reviewers and to all those who kindly allowed us to observe their work.

10 REFERENCES

Abel, M. (1990). Experiences in an exploratory distributed organization. In Galegher, J. et al. (eds). *Intellectual Teamwork: Social Foundations of Cooperative Work*, Lawrence Erlbaum Associates. Hillsdale, New Jersey.

Andersen et al. (1986). *Professional Systems Development: Development, Experience, Ideas and Action* (in Danish). Teknisk Forlag. Copenhagen.

Dennis Alan R., Jay F. Nunamaker, and Douglas R. Vogel. (1990) A comparison of laboratory and field research in the study of electronic meeting systems. *Journal of Management Information Systems*, 7(3).

Egido, C. (1988). Videoconferencing as a Technology to Support Group Work: A Review of its Failure. In *Proceedings of ACM CSCW'88 Conference on Computer-Supported Cooperative Work.*

Francik et al. (1991). Putting Innovation to Work: Adoption Strategies For MultiMedia Communication Systems. In *Communications of the ACM*, 34(12).

Geertz, C. (1983) *Local Knowledge*. Fontana. London.

Grudin, J. (1994). Groupware and social dynamics: Eight challenges for developers. In*Communications of the ACM*, 37(1).

Greenberg (1991). Personalizable groupware: Accommodating individual roles and group differences. In *Proc. European Conference of Computer Supported Cooperative Work*, Amsterdam, September 1991.

Keen (1981). Information systems and organizational change. In*Communications of the ACM*, 24(1).

Kling, R. and Iacono (1984). The control of information systems development after implementation. In *Communications of the ACM*, 27(12).

Malone, Thomas W., Kenneth R. Grant, Kum-Yew Lai, Ramana Rao, and David Rosenblitt. (1987). Semistructured messages are surprisingly useful for computer-supported coordination. *ACM Transactions on Office Information Systems*, 5(2).

Orlikowski (1992). Learning from notes: Organizational Issues in Groupware Implementation, In *Proceedings of ACM CSCW'92 Conference on Computer-Supported Cooperative Work.*

Pagani, D. S. & Mackay, W. Bringing Media Spaces into the Real World. (1993). In *Proceedings of the Third European Conference on Computer-Supported Cooperative Work.*

Root, R. W. (1988)., Design of a Multi-Media Vehicle for Social Browsing. In *Proceedings of the ACM CSCW'88 Conference on Computer-Supported Cooperative Work.*

Tang, J. C. & Isaacs, E. (1993). Why Do Users Like Video? Studies of Multimedia-supported Collaboration. In *Computer Supported Cooperative Work (CSCW)*, 1 (3).

Yates, J (1989). *Control Through Communication: the Rise of System In American Management*, Baltimore, The John Hopkins University Press.

Professor John A. Hughes, b. 20.3.41 in Sheffield. BA (Birmingham) Class I, Ph.D. (Lancaster) 1982. Taught at the Universities of Birmingham, Exeter, Lund : teaching and researching at Lancaster since 1970. Visiting Scientist at Interval Research Corporation, Palo Alto. Since 1986 has been the recipient of Research Council grants on air traffic control, and technological change in the police, Tri-Council support for collaborative research with computer scientists on air traffic control and software development, Deputy Director of ESPRIT Basic Research Project, COMIC, and DTI/EPSRC projects Sycomt and VirtuOsi.

Steinar Kristoffersen b. 25.9.66 in Namsos. Cand. Scient. from Dept. of Informatics, University of Oslo in1993, Researcher at Norsk Regnesentral from 1993-1994, PhD student at Lancaster University 1994-

Jon O'Brien b. 13.11.70 in Cambridge. BA (Lancaster) Human Communication, Class I, PhD student 1993 - , Research Assistant, DTI/EPSRC VirtuOsi Project Apr '94 - Oct '95, responsible for ethnographic study of technology centre in manufacturing industry.

Mark Rouncefield b. 10.6.52 in Bristol. BA(Exeter), MA(Durham), MA (Lancaster) - Research Assistant DTI/EPSRC SYCOMT Project Oct '93 - , undertaking ethnographic studies of a financial institution.

6

Comparison and Analysis of Diffusion Models

Hannu Jaakkola
Tampere University of Technology, Information Technology (Pori)
P.O.Box 30, FIN-28601 Pori, Finland; E-mail: hj@pori.tut.fi

Abstract

A *real diffusion process* consists of a huge amount of interrelated variables. This complexity can be modelled by *diffusion models building* a *simplified mathematical representation* of the main features of the process as a time series of indicators describing the phenomenon in interest. *Mathematical models* are mostly used for technological forecasting purposes; forecasting is based on the *best fit* of the empirical data to the model formula and trend extrapolation outside the empirical period. The fit gives numeric values to the parameters of the model. Some of the models include also *explanative factors* - values of parameters describe behavioral properties of the process. The paper *concentrates on mathematical diffusion models*. The variety of models derived from the literature is introduced and analyzed. As an application of mathemat ical approach to the diffusion the diffusion of mobile phones is discussed. The focus of this paper is to point out problems in mathematical analysis and to discuss about alternative approaches.

Keywords

Diffusion models, diffusion process, technology management, mobile phones

1 INTRODUCTION

The *diffusion of an innovation* is a process, in which the innovation spreads through certain channels in the social system (target population) in time (Rogers 1983, p.5). According to Ayres (1969, p. xii) *diffusion* (of a new technology) is the evolutionary process of replacement of an old technology by a newer one for solving similar problems or accomplishing similar objectives. In the literature the term *innovation* appears typically in a context. By definition, *innovation* is the introduction or application of a new idea or invention; it is a change in the existing order. Essentially, diffusion or innovation concerns changing and managing a new technology by a *model* for predictive (or explanatory) purposes. An essential part of the model is presented by the *diffusion effect*, which has been defined by Mahajan et al. (1990, p. 38) as the cumulatively increasing degree of influence on an individual to adopt or reject an innovation.

Measuring the diffusion can be done either on *qualitative* or on *quantitative* level or *combining* these two approaches. *Quantitative analysis* is based on the time series of a selected variable or a group of variables representing the whole complicated process of the diffusion.

Qualitative analysis is based on the methods crystallizing a united view from the collection of more or less intuitive standpoints on the diffusion. Martino (1993), in his book, has classified the following methods (for technological forecasting purposes):

- Delphi method (qualitative)
- forecasting by analogy (qualitative; semiquantitative)
- growth curves; figure of merit (quantitative; proportional to trend analysis)
- trend analysis and extrapolation (quantitative)

This paper concentrates on *quantitative modelling* of the diffusion.

A *real diffusion process* consists of a huge amount of variables and interrelations between them. This complexity can be modelled and managed by *diffusion models*. The primary purpose of diffusion models is to manage the *regularity* encountered in the process. Traditionally the model is a *simplified mathematical representation* of the main features of the process as a time series of indicators describing the phenomenon in interest. *Mathematical models* are mostly used for technological forecasting purposes; forecasting is based on the *best fit* of the empirical data to the model formula and trend extrapolation outside the empirical period. The fit gives numeric values to the parameters of the model. Some of the models also include *explanative factors* - values of parameters describe behavioral properties of the process.

An optional approach called *heuristic (loose) modelling* is derived from the principles of mathematical diffusion models and introduced by the author of this paper in several publications (Jaakkola 1994;1994a; 1993; 1992; 1992a; 1991; 1991a). The heuristic modelling means the *intuitive* approach to the analysis of the complex process. All the knowledge the *analyst* has on the process is used first to *understand* the changes of the process in the past and then to *reason* the future improvement. The principles used in the analysis are collected in the heuristic diffusion model, which is a generic model (collection of analysis principles) supporting the *feature analysis*.

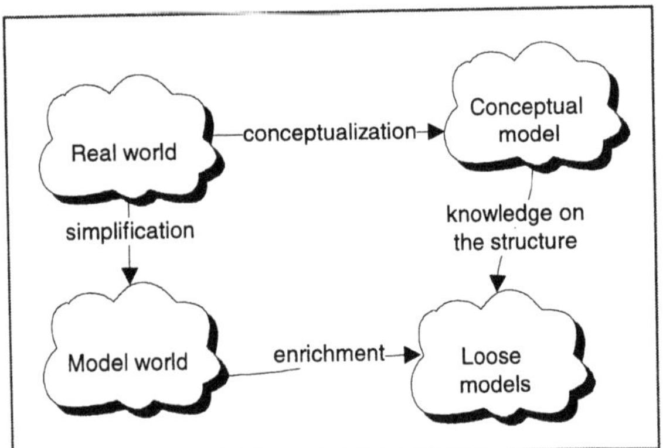

Figure 1 Modelling the diffusion process

This paper *concentrates on mathematical diffusion models*. The models are tools for *diffusion analysis*. Using the models in the right way consists of two factors: understanding the *modelling principles* and understanding the *assumptions* behind the model. Chapter 2 concentrates in the basic principles of the diffusion process. The variety of models derived from the literature is introduced and analyzed in chapters 3 and 4. As an application of mathemathical analysis the diffusion of mobile phones is studied in chapter 5. The main result of this paper is the critical analysis of the properties of mathematical models used in diffusion analysis. The study will argument the need of *improved mathematical methods* and/or *loose and a more heu-*

ristic approach in analysis to improve the usability of the models in practical problems (Figure 1); the simplified world of mathematical models requires structural knowledge on the real world. The special problems in connection with the analysis of IT diffusion are discussed. This critique is included in the conclusions in chapter 6.

The paper is one of a *series of papers* discussing the principles of mathematical diffusion models. In the paper (Jaakkola 1995) the general principles of mathematical models and their scope are discussed. The paper (Jaakkola 1995a) concentrates on the flexibility features of mathematical diffusion models.

2 HISTORY AND THE ERAS OF DIFFUSION MODELS

In the literature, the theory of diffusion models has its roots in the 19th century: a sociologist, *Gabriel Tarde* (1890) applied mathematical models in the spread of political ideologies. He noticed the power of *imitation* as the explanation factor in the diffusion. Since the beginning of 20th century there exists a wide variety of models of the same kind applied in different fields, e.g. epidemiology, sociology, marketing, learning, anthropology, biology, technology diffusion and substitution; more about the history of modelling see e.g. (Jaakkola 1993a; 1993b).

The active period of technology diffusion research starts in the 1960's. The period from the beginning of the 1960's until now can be divided into three eras:

- the era of basic models (1960's and the beginning of the 1970's)
- the era of expanded models (1970's and the beginning of the 1980's)
- the era of new applications (from the 1980's)

In the *era of basic models* the research concentrated on the development of mathematical basic models. The models were simple mathematical formulas (statistical distributions) used to fit in the empirical time series data. The main thing in the use of models was *forecasting by extrapolation*: the parameters of the model were estimated by regression analysis methods.

In the *era of expanded models* the research work concentrated on the shortages of basic models: the fixed structure, inability to take into account the changes in the environment and inability to handle competitive innovations. A basic method was to add the flexibility of models by joining together two or more basic models. This kind of modifications focused in the dimensions of the changing environment, competitive innovations, multi-phase adoption, interaction between innovations etc. The main purpose in the use of models was still the forecasting by extrapolation. Most of "umbrella models" are created in this era.

The *era of new applications* has expanded the scope and flexibility of models. Typical new features are unbundling of the population of potential users, critical analysis of the adoption decision, improved capability to take into account the effect of environmental factors and the use of feedback mechanisms to adapt the behavior of the models to fit better in the behavior of the real world phenomena. The most meaningful is however the *transition from the forecasting towards more complicated use of models*:

- *descriptive use*: testing hypothesis to get information on the effect of different operations in the diffusion process
- *normative use*: the use of models to optimize the estimates of factors affecting in the diffusion process

In the same time period the complexity of models has grown and they have come nearer to simulation models than the models of former eras.

This paper concentrates on the analysis of the models of two first eras; the purpose of this paper is to analyze the properties of mathematical diffusion models to become acquainted with the functional power of typical forecasting models. The complicated "simulation type" feedback models do not include essential new information from that point of view.

3 BASIC MODELS

3.1 The Use of models

General model and the pressure function

The diffusion process is typically modelled by using components described in Figure 2. Symbols in the figure denote the following:

f(t) non-cumulative adoption function; *diffusion function*

F(t) cumulative adoption function; *adopter (distribution) function*

$\overline{F}$ *potential adopter population* (most of the models presuppose a fixed potential of adopters during the adoption period

{1} *the whole population* in which the potential adopter population is a subset

{2} the l*ower threshold level* of penetration; if a substitution has progressed to this level it will proceed to its completion; practically, the threshold level is 10% of the potential, and the behavior of the diffusion process before this point is irregular (Fisher and Pry, 1972)

{3} *on the inflection point* $t=t^*$, f(t) has its maximum value and the first degree derivative of F(t) will change from positive to negative

{4} the upper threshold level, *maturation level*; after reaching this level of penetration, the process is practically finished and the behavior of the rest of the population is not regular and exactly modellable

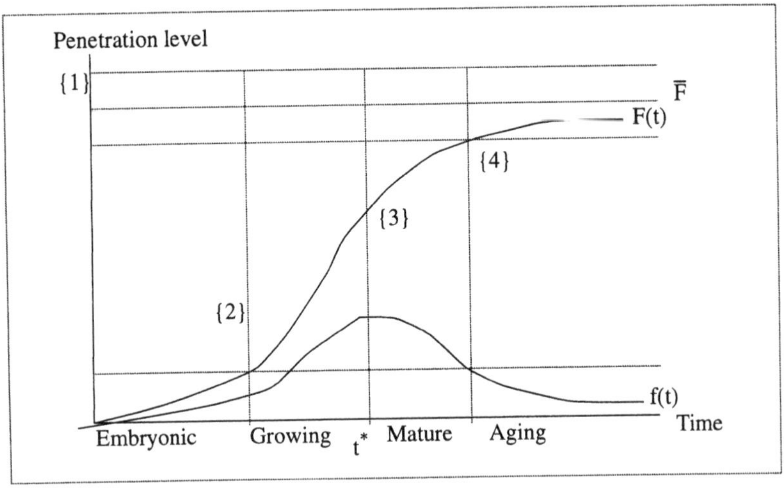

Figure 2 The components of diffusion models

The *fast growth phase* between points {2} and {4} is the focal point of most diffusion models. Some of the models are valid only in this area because of the irregular behavior in the beginning and at the end of diffusion, or because they are limited only to some part of the process (e.g. the models presuppose a symmetry relative to the inflection point and they describe only the area before or after that point). The whole period of diffusion can be divided into four phases with characteristic features of their own. These features are discussed in detail by Jaakkola 1993; 1993a).

A general form (see e.g. Majahan 1977; 1985), of the diffusion process can be presented according to the following formula:

$$f(t) = a(t)\,(\bar{F} - F(t))$$

in which a(t) is called the *pressure function*. The growth is proportional to the remaining user potential. The pressure function of a diffusion model describes the factor affecting the growth in the use of the innovation analyses. The pressure function a(t) characterizes the structure of the diffusion model and it is defined:

$$a(t) = \frac{f(t)}{\bar{F} - F(t)}$$

The pressure function specifies the behavior of the model in the following way:

- *internal model*: the internal interaction (imitation) of the user potential directs the adoption; the value of a(t) approaches the value zero in the early beginning of the adoption process
- *external model*: adoption process is controlled by the external effect only (innovation effect); the value of a(t) approaches a positive constant in the early beginning of the process
- *mixed model*: the diffusion process is a sum of internal and external effects

The growing value of the pressure function means a growing interest in the adoption of the product, and descending value a reduced interest.

Table 1 Properties of some diffusion models

Model	Pressure function a(t)	lim a(t)	Analytic form of a(t)	Class
Logistic distr.	bF(t)	0	Growing	I
Gompertz distr.	$\frac{-bF(t)\ln F(t)}{1-F(t)}$	0	growing	I
Floyd	bF(t)(1-F(t))	0	inverted U	I
Sharif-Kabir	$\frac{bF(t)(1-F(t)}{(1-(1-\sigma)F(t)}$	0	σ=1:inverted U σ<>1: growing	I
v.Bertalanffy	$\frac{bF^{\theta}(t)(1-F^{1-\theta}(t)}{(1-q)(1-F(t))}$	0	θ<1: growing $\theta\geq$1: decreasing	I
NSRL	$bF(t)^{\alpha}$	0	α=0: constant α<>0: growing	I
Bass	p+qF(t)	p	growing	M
NUI	$a+bF(t)^{\alpha}$	a	α=0: constant α<>0: growing	M
Exp distr.	a	a	Constant	E
Weibull distr.	kpt^{k-1}	k>1: 0 k<1: inf.	k>1: growing k<1: decreasing k=1: constant	k>1: I k$\leq$1: E
Normal distr.	-	0	growing	I

Pressure function is an optional way to introduce the *analytic form* of the model; the cumulative and non-cumulative diffusion functions can be derived from the pressure function representation solving the differential equation. Pressure functions of some diffusion functions described later in this paper are introduced in Table 1 (Jaakkola 1991, p. 83), indicating to the analyst the driving force of the adoption decision of the adopters.

Analytic form of the models

A typical use of the model is to fit the predefined mathematical function in the empirical time series data describing the spread of the product or the innovation; the data is used to estimate the parameters of the predefined mathematical models (either cumulative or non-cumulative diffusion function; best fit is based on simple regression analysis, e.g. least square sum). The parameters in the model are the parameters defined in the pressure function and the expected potential user population $\bar{F}$. The predefined mathematical functions (distributions) used in models are e.g.

- logistic distribution (Blackman, Fisher-Pry, Dodd)
- derivatives of the logistic distribution (Floyd, Sharif-Kabir, Mansfield, Bass, Easingwood, Sharif-Ramanathan)
- flexible logistic (FLOG) distribution
- Gompertz distribution
- exponential distribution (Coleman, Fourt-Woodlock)
- normal distribution (Stapleton)
- lognormal distribution
- v. Bertalanffy distribution
- Weibull distribution (Sharif-Islam)

A common feature for the distributions is the *S-shaped cumulative and bell-shaped non-cumulative adoption curve*; the curves having a different shape (exponential, decayed exponential etc.) actually have a head in the beginning or a tail at the end out of the modelling period (Jaakkola 1995). The distributions differ from each other regarding the *symmetry*, the location of the *inflection point* and the amount of *parameters*. Both logistic and normal distributions are symmetric regarding the inflection point; Gompertz distribution is not symmetric but it has a fixed inflection point depending on the user potential ($\bar{F}$); Weibull distribution has the inflection point depending on the parameter. A detailed analysis of mathematical properties of the distributions is not worth doing in this paper. Details are given by Jaakkola (1991, pp. 243-252), Kumar&Kumar (1992, p. 162) and Majahan et al. (1990, p. 12).

The *reliability* of the modelling differs in models and it is based on the length of the time series of empirical data regarding the basic assumptions of the model. The areas outside the fast growth phase are usually *unstable* and left out of the analysis in most models. There are also presumptions of reaching a certain penetration level to allow the use of models for forecasting purposes. These features will cause problems especially in the case of fast changing technologies, which diffusion typically can be described as a series of exponential growth curves; the analyst's interest in the older generation curves decreases after the appearance of the newer one. The most serious problem in the use of mathematical models is the need to *fix the values of model parameters* in the beginning of the analysis: the result model is as good as the parameter "guess".

3.2 Some basic models

Fisher-Pry model

This model is perhaps one of the most known diffusion models. It is based on the idea of using Pearl's formula (epidemic model) to describe the diffusion process. This model is a derivative of the logistic model and introduced by Raymond Pearl (1925). The epidemic model was applied by Fisher and Pry (1972) in the replacement of the old technology by the new one. The model is based on the following expectations:

- when the diffusion has reached a certain penetration level (lower threshold), the process will progress until full penetration
- the *lower threshold* level is $0.1*\overline{F}$ and the *upper* one $0.9*\overline{F}$; the process is *regular* between these points and symmetric regarding the *inflection point* in the middle (time when the penetration $0.5*\overline{F}$ is reached) of the process
- the proportional growth of the user population is constant regarding the remaining potential until the inflection point; the user potential is expected to be fixed (not changing as a function of time)

The model is based on the *imitation effect*: the adoption decision is based on the experiences of the earlier adopters. Because of that there is the expectation that the diffusion process has its beginning in the "spaceless past" which guarantees the reaching of the lower treshold level and symmetrically it continues in the "spaceless future" reaching the full penetration somewhere after the time where the upper threshold level is reached.

Blackman and Mansfield

The Blackman model (1972) is a derivative of Mansfield's model (1961). The interrelation between these models also describes the interrelation between *two typical uses* of the models: the use to describe the diffusion of a product (Mansfield) and the use to describe the changes in the performance of the product (*figure of merit*; Blackman). In the *Blackman model* the changes in the adoption depend on the

- ratio $F(t)/\overline{F}$ (the proportion of the users in the potential amount of users); the user potential is expected to be fixed
- the expected benefit that can be achieved
- the magnitude of the investment

The adoption function is based on the Taylor polynome introduced by Mansfield: the function is built by combining all three parameters in the form of Taylor transformation. Blackman expects that the *environment of the diffusion is unchanged* in the diffusion period; this assumption simplifies the function to be a derivative of the logistic distribution and gives *semantics to the parameters* of the pressure function. The values of the parameters describe the power of the factors mentioned above to the process and are useful e.g. in comparing the similarity of two different diffusion processes (forecasting by analogy). By the characteristics the model belongs to the class of *imitation models* and it is *symmetric* regarding to the inflection point ($0.5*\overline{F}$). In his own evaluations Blackman has noticed that the biggest shortcoming in the model is the assumption of the static environment; it will cause too optimistic short run and too pessimistic long run forecasts in the use of the model.

Bass' first purchase model

Bass' model (1969) is one of the oldest and most modified (see e.g. Majahan 1977; 1990) diffusion models. The original application of the model is the forecast of the first purchase of consumer durables; the effect of new generations and multiple purchases is eliminated by shortening the analysis period. The model is improved to take into account the interaction between product generations by Norton and Bass (1987).

The pressure function in Bass' model has two parameters: the other one describes the *innovator* effect and the other one the *imitation* effect in the diffusion decision. The structure of the potential user population is analyzed by Rogers (1970) in his well-known book "Diffusion of Innovations" and further developed by Majahan e.g. in papers (1990; 1990a).The imitation effect describes the amount of adopters deciding the adoption independently (internal pressure). The rest of the user potential is controlled by external pressure - imitating the earlier adopters (innovators and imitators already made the positive adoption decision).

The Bass' model has following properties:

- the model is *asymmetric* and the inflection point (varies in the area from 0 to $0.5*\overline{F}$) depends on the parameter values
- in the analysis, the model assumes the availability of *empirical data exceeding the inflection point* (compare e.g. Fisher-Pry assumes exceeding the lower treshold only)

The model assumes static environment of the diffusion and is useful for first-purchase analysis only; it can be used in the empirical data reaching the inflection point.

4 ADDING FLEXIBILITY

The critique against the usefulness of basic diffusion models concerns on the factors causing *inflexibility* in models. The inflexibility is caused by the fixed analytic form of the model: in forecasting the use of the mathematical model is based on the "best fit" evaluation of parameters of the model and the inflexibility will cause the growth of error factor in the fit process. An complementary approach to the development of diffusion models is based on the concept of "*umbrella models*". An umbrella model joins the properties of two or more basic models having different behavior and is based on the assumption that the characteristics of the diffusion process are changing in the run of the diffusion. This approach will

- increase flexibility (and leads to better fit than fixed models)
- add new (non explanatory) factors to the model

Two examples of the dedicated umbrella models are the Sharif-Kabir model (1976) and Sharif-Ramanathan model (1981).

Sharif-Kabir Model

Sharif-Kabir model is the technology replacement model, in which three models having different behavior are combined together. The basic models are

- Blackman model
- Fisher-Pry model
- Floyd's model (1968) for non-competing technologies

The two first models were introduced earlier in this paper. Floyd's model is nonsymmetric (inflection point $0.333*\overline{F}$) derivative of the logistic distribution. According to Sharif and Kabir, the two first models lead typically in too optimistic and the last one in too pessimistic forecasts. Combining the models results a *generalized model*, that is more reliable than any of the component models alone.

The combination of models is created by joining the two first models (Fisher-Pry model can be interpreted to be a special case of Mansfield model) and combining this with Floyd's model by using a coefficient (value 0..1, specifying the power of the component models in the combined result model). The values of the *delay coefficient* describe the delay of the adoption compared to the most optimistic estimate (logistic distribution). The value of the delay coefficient depends on the

- data scattering (DS)
- data extent (DE; the time span of the empirical data in reflect to the time span of the analysis)
- the last value of F(t) in empirical data (fl)
- the effective life span (the time from the penetration level from $0.1*\overline{F}$ to $0.9*\overline{F}$

In the early diffusion DS and fl are dominating the value of the delay coefficient. The scattered empirical data increases error level; the abundant portion of the *empirical data under the lower threshold level* (10%) causes pessimistic forecasts. The *life time of the innovation* also has an effect on the value of the coefficient: the shorter is the life time of the innovation the smaller its effect in the coefficient. The length of the time series of the empirical data increases the value of the coefficient. The flexibility of the model is illustrated in Figure 3.

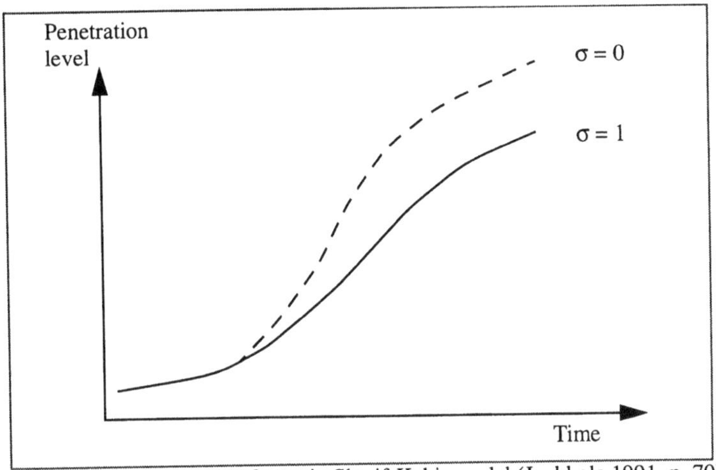

Figure 3 The effect of the delay factor in Sharif-Kabir model (Jaakkola 1991, p. 70)

Sharif Ramanathan Model

Sharif and Kabir combined the models havingthe same kind of basic properties but different behavior in different parts of the diffusion process. In his newer study Sharif has used an alternative approach by joining two component models having different behavior. Sharif and Ramanathan have combined *Coleman's model* (1964) and *Dodd's model* (1953) which both belong to the early history of the diffusion studies. *Coleman's model* is an *innovator model* (the amount of new users in time *t* is independent of the amount of existing users *F(t)*. The analytic form of the diffusion function is *reversed exponential* function and the adopter distribution a *decayed exponential* function describing the fast decrease of the external pressure in the adoption decision. The assumptions of the model are:

- fixed user potential
- full penetration will be reached during the diffusion period
- the source of innovation is fixed it effects all adopters in the same way

In the original article Coleman has a long discussion on the *interpretation of the parameters* of the functions (these interpretations are not in the development of Sharif-Ramanathan model)

In *Dodd's model* the diffusion function is a derivation of the logistic distribution and the assumptions in the model are the same as above. The arguments of the adoption decision are expected to be same during the whole diffusion period and the their effect in the potential user are expected to be homogenous in the whole population.

The purpose of Sharif and Ramanathan has been to create a model having both exponential and logistic behavior built in the model. The model is an innovator-imitator model having S-shaped diffusion function; its flexibility covers Blackman's, Bass' and Fourt-Woodlock (1960) model. The flexibility of the model is described in Figure 4.

Coleman's exponential distribution corresponds very well to the diffusion of *fashion products*; the adoption is very fast and the adoption period short. Dodd's model and logistic distribution is better suited to typical phenomena. Changing the parameters of the Sharif-Ramanathan model the behavior of the model can be varied inside these two ends.

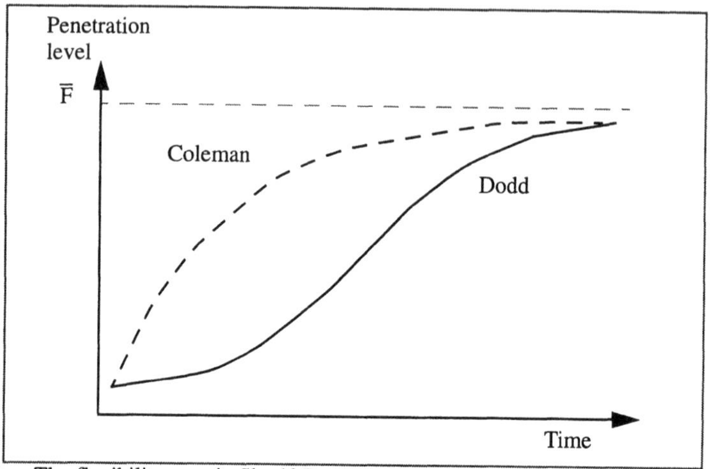

Figure 4 The flexibility area in Sharif-Ramanathan model

More advanced flexibility properties

The flexibility of the models described above are implemented by adding characteristics of two different basic functions in one model and varying the value of the coefficient describing the importance of the components. The flexibility in general is a concept including different means:

- a *flexible* model: varying inflection point and symmetry/asymmetry
- a *dynamic* model: values of parameters (user potential, imitation factor, the structure of the user potential, etc.), can be varied during the diffusion period as a function of time (or some other argument)
- an *adaptive* model: the model adapts in the empirical data (feedback property; e.g. error factor of the regression adapts the model)

Flexibility of the models is achieved by the selection of distributions having built in flexibility needed for the analysis. Such distributions are e.g. *Gompertz distribution* (changing inflection point) and *Weibull distribution* (changing inflection point and symmetry). The adaption is a *technical solution* to fit the model pattern in the empirical data. *Dynamic features* in the model are implemented by replacing the constant parameters by the functions depending on some variables controlling the process.

The models developed to implement high flexibility are e.g. NSRL (Non Symmetric Responding Logistic Model) introduced by Easingwood et al. (1981), NUI (Non Uniform Influence) introduced by Easingwood et al. (1983) and General Rationalized Models (GRM) by Skiadas (1985). A detailed analysis of these models is done by Jaakkola (1995a); the paper concentrates on the flexibility properties of diffusion models. The main finding in the paper is the parallel increasing flexibility and *inability to explain the process* features.

The problem of the increasing flexibility in diffusion models is the conflict between the needs to model the real phenomenon and to create flexibility. In principle, the high level of flexibility makes possible for a good fit of the model in the empirical data, but at the same time it obscures the understandability of the behavior of the model and decreases the opportunity to use the parameters of the model to interpret the properties of the process or in the comparison of two distinct processes. The flexibility becomes the end in itself and the primary purpose of the model remains in the background. The variety of the models developed for flexibility purposes are not handled here in detail.

5 DIFFUSION OF IT

About IT Diffusion Studies

A wide variety of diffusion studies are introduced in literature. Jaakkola (1991, pp. 113-122) analyses ten empirical studies. In the same book a deep analysis of the diffusion of IT in Finnish industry is introduced (see also Jaakkola 1992b; 1993b). An interesting review of IT diffusion studies is given by Fichman (1992); the study includes an overview of 36 research papers and articles. A wide spectrum of like studies can be found in literature.

The *diffusion of IT* can be measured in several different ways. Indicators used in diffusion studies are e.g.

- the amount of IT users among the employed people, time series based on that data and international comparisons; these indicators describe the level of utilization of new technology in different sectors of the society
- the relative amount of computers at homes; these studies are implemented by market research companies and results indicate the spread of computer culture as a part of daily life
- the utilization of IT in different sectors of the industry and business; these indicators describe the progress in the different user segments and application sectors of the society
- the structure of the computer base and the changes in the annual sales; these kinds of studies are implemented by market research companies and describe the technical improvements as a *quality dimension* of the use of IT
- the utilization level of a product indicating the process in the researcher's interest

In most cases there are two main problems causing uncertainty in the results of analysis: (1) rapid changes and (2) short time series. *Rapid changes* are realized in the analysis as the sequence of *product generations* meaning the replacement of the old generation product by the new one before the penetration reaches the level of reliable analysis; *short time series* are the consequences of rapid changes and do not allow the use of exact mathematical analysis, which typically expect the *break-trough point* to be reached to get the model reliable enough for forecasting purposes. The need of modelling comes from the *need to manage the changes* - predict the demand of products, predict the behavior of future generations of a product in markets etc. Understanding the power (and the lack) of mathematical diffusion models provides valuable information for the development of the subjective (heuristic) application specific combined methods for the bases of the change management.

The use of mathematical models follows the steps below

- decision cocerning the break point between empirical data and forecast (mostly all empirical data available is used); this decision means that the static environment of the break point is accepted to be the environment of the extrapolation period
- specificying the parameter values (e.g. user potential) not evaluable in the "best fit" phase (a new fixed value in the static environment)
- solving the values of model parameters (fitting the model to the empirical data; best fit gives values to the parameters; adding new values to the static environment)
- extrapolation (forecast) in the static environment

As an example of this process the diffusion of mobile phones is analyzed below.

An example of the mathematical analysis

An example of mathematical analysis and an introduction to the problems included in the analysis is given below. The empirical data analysed is the number of mobile telephone licenses in Finland. *Mansfield's model* (see chapter 3) is used in the analysis:

$$F(t) = \frac{e^{c_1 + c_2 t}}{1 + e^{c_1 + c_2 t}} \bar{F}$$

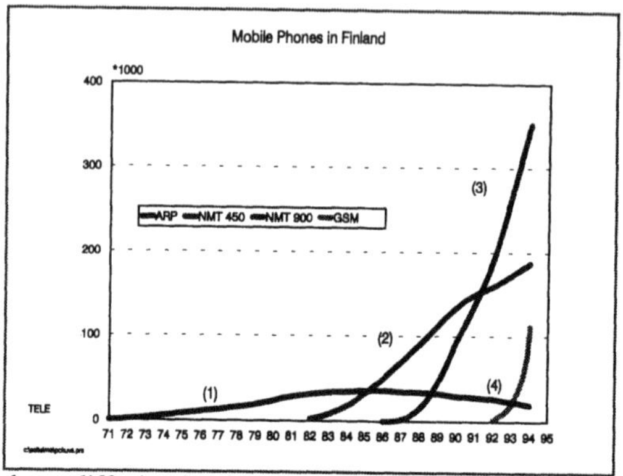

Figure 5 Mobile phone diffusion in Finland

Mobile phone diffusion in Finland is an interested application for analysis for several reasons:

- the history of mobile phones in Finland includes four generations following each other allowing generation based analysis in addition to the analyses of the total phenomenon (Figure 5); manual (today semi automatic) ARP network (1) started to operate in 1980 has 19.000 licences (highest 35.000 in 1986), 450 MHz analogic network NMT-450 (2) started to operate in 1982 has 187.000 licences, 900 MHz analogic network NMT-900 (3) started to operate in 1986 has 352.000 licences and two competing digital GSM networks (4) started to operate in 1992 have 110.000 licenses; the growth rate in NMT-450 is 8%, NMT 900 has the rate of 30% and GSM hundreds of percents
- Finland is the leading country in the adoption of mobile phones, which means that the experiences in Finland can be used in the plans concerning less penetrated countries; the penetration rate in August 1995 is 18% (900.000 licenses in the population of 5 Million), which has almost reached the level of the EUTELIS (1993) forecast by the year 2010 in Europe (penetration rate 30-50% in business user and 15-35 in private user segment); the most positive Finnish forecasts expect the penetration level of 100% of the population to be reached by the beginning of next decade
- there seems to be a trend towards *private sector* dominance in the new mobile phone licences; today almost 60% of new licences are registered for private people and this share is increasing all the time; the share of the private sector seems to grow several percents in a year; there is a good reason to believe that in the static situation the share *90% private, 10% business* will be reached in the beginning of next decade (i.e. the static situation in fixed line telephones today)

There are some other indicators but the number of licenses that can be used in empirical analysis, e.g. the number of calls in mobile telephone network. According to Telecommunications Statistics (1995, p. 38) the number of calls in whole network was 292.8 Million (12.5% in digital networks and 87.5% in analogic ones). The forecast is that the number of calls in two digital networks is increasing from 36.7 Million in 1994 to 100 Million in 1995.

The behavior of the four diffusion processes includes a huge number of explanative factors not modellable in the model: changing user potential, network coverage, network capacity problems, pricing of the licenses, pricing of the calls and monthly fee, services etc. Short time series make impossible the mathematical analysis of individual processes, which seem to fill the properties of the theory of competing and replacing technology generations. The purpose of the following example is to show the difficulties rising up in practical analysis of fast changing technologies. Mansfield's model is selected; the model used could be some of the other ones introduced earlier in this paper.

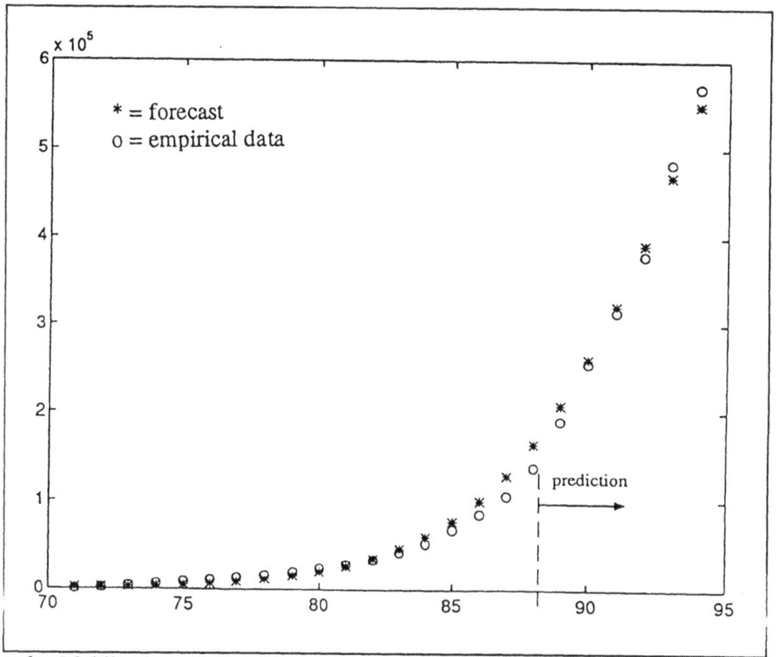

Figure 6 Mobile phone diffusion - empirical data 1971.. 1988, forecast 1989 .. 1994

The Analysis on mobile phone data is done in two phases:

1. *sensitivity on empirical data* was tested by moving the break point of empirical data and forecast in the area 1985. 1988; the rest of the curve was built by forecast, which was compared to the real empirical data in the period from break point to 1994
2. *sensitivity on user potential* was tested and forecasts based on different expectations on user potential were produced

Table 2 Parameter values in the break point analysis ($\overline{F}$=1.2 Million)

Year	C_1	C_2
1985	-6.97	0.30
1986	-6.92	0.29
1987	-6.89	0.28
1988	-6.86	0.28

Sensitivity on empirical data was tested by moving the *break point* between empirical data and forecast in the area from 1985 to 1988; the purpose of the test was to find the minimum proportion of the empirical data needed to produce reliable forecasts (in the existing empirical data). The change of values of model parameters is represented in Table 2. In the analysis, a short empirical data period seems to produce too *optimistic forecasts* and the break point in 1988 seemed to produce stability in the model (Figure 6). In the analysis the number of licenses in 1988 was 105.860 which represents the share of 8.8% of the expected user potential (1.2 Million).

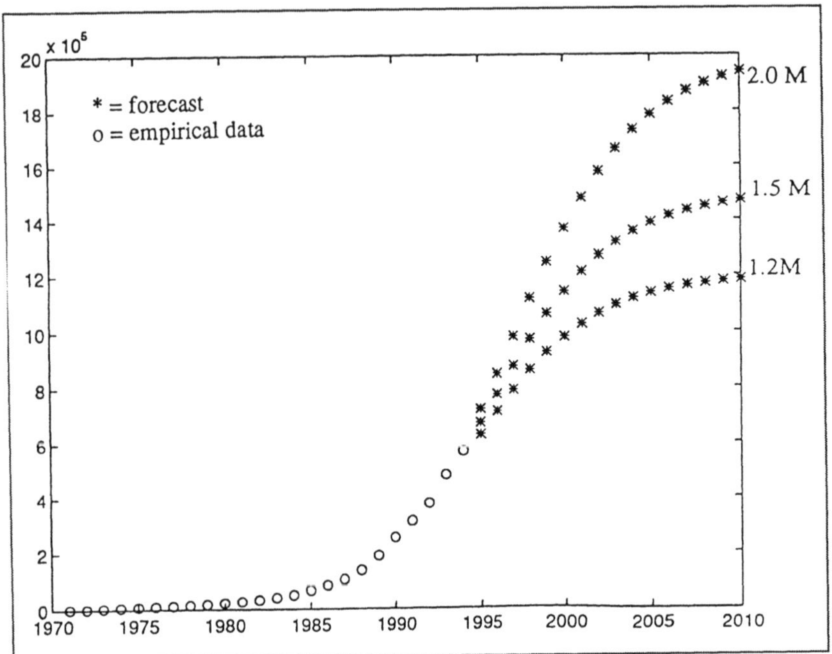

Figure 7 Mobile phone diffusion - empirical data 1971 .. 1994, varying potential

The second part of the analysis tested the forecast sensitivity to expected user potential. The results of the analysis are shown in Figure 7and Table 3. In the analysis the empirical data in the period 1971 .. 1994 was used and the user potential was varied as shown in Table 3.

The user potential variations are based on the EUTELIS (1993) study. The number of licenses at the end of 1994 was 676.000 (in the population of 5 Million the penetration rate was 13.5%).

Table 3 Parameter values in the analysis

$\overline{F}$	$F(1994)/\overline{F}$	C_1	C_2
1.2 M	24%	-6.86	0.29
1.5 M	30%	-7.05	0.27
2.0 M	40%	7.31	0.27
5.0 M	100%	-8.18	0.26

The tests above point out that the models are very sensitive to the factors that are not predictable Each of the sensitivity analysis made above did not lead to the stabilization of model parameter values (in this case because of too short period of empirical data). Stabilization the environment with these unstable parameter values adds unreliability in forecasts. All the models expect the *static environment.* In the case of mobile phones "static" means fixed telephone and service prices, fixed services available, fixed economy etc. Another point is the user potential: in the models having imitator effect built in the model the driving force is the gap between the number of existing users and the user potential. In the case of mobile phones the user potential is growing as a function of huge amount of factors, among those the ones mentioned above. In fact, the analysis above is based on a compromise between two requirements: length of the time series and exactness built in the data of components. In this case the analysis of component curves is not reliable, however all the component curves have different factors controlling the changes. The effect of these factors may not be joint in the joint curve of its components.

The analysis points out the difficulties in mathematical analysis. The discussion in the beginning of this chapter includes information, that can not be built in the exact models. For an analyst having need to manage the changes of a technology mathematical models are excellent tools to be supplemented by heuristic information available. For exact analysis purposes the models can be used only in very limited applications in the static environment, without rapid changes.

6 CONCLUSIONS

For a forecaster there exists a wide variety of mathematical models that can be used in the analysis. The forecaster must be *familiar with the properties* of the models and *especially the restrictions and assumptions* in the background. If these details are not taken into account the analysis is unreliable and useless or has *negative value* to the analyst. This paper has described the background of some mathematical diffusion models - the basic models and some more complicated ones. The purpose of the introduction of the models has not been to explain their properties in detail but to focus on their restrictions and limitations. The existence of tens of basic models and hundreds of variations and still more studies - more or less reliable - in which these models are applied in wide variety of applications does not give facts enough for the beginner analyst to find the right tools for his purposes.

The main findings of this paper are

- the availability of the wide variety of diffusion models and variations of them; it will cause a problem the choice of the right model
- the *"unrealistic" assumptions* restricting the usability of the models; to be exact there exists no real diffusion process that fills the presumptions of any of the models
- the symmetry - are the diffusion processes really symmetrical
- in most models - especially in the models including advanced flexibility - the parameters of the model do not describe any of the real process; the situation is the same in the case of comparing two processes and in the evaluation of a single process
- in all models there is a need to fix such parameters of the model that will have a revolutionary effect in the results of the analysis
- the model is always a simplified presentation of the real phenomenon; this polarization hides huge amounts of important information that should be known in the management of technological changes

Most of the models expect the *knowledge of the potential user population* - in some cases we don't know it and in most cases it is changing as a function of time. The behavior outside threshold levels is *irregular* - how do we really know *what is the threshold level.* These are the problems of the practical analysis.

In the world of the *exponential growth* of information technology the usefulness of the models is still more questionable. The rapid flow of generations and short life cycles of the products do not allow exact mathematical analysis. The models are at their best when they provide interpretable parameters and include the knowledge of the behavior of the process either in its parameters or in the modelling principles itself. This way the analyst learns to understand the behavior of the product in the market and based on this deeper understanding is able to use the information available from the models carefully enough and with the critical grip. A big problem is the misconception of exactness which is caused by the strong belief in mathematical models. The analyst must remember that at its best the models are informative - not exact. Adding the results of mathematical modelling in intuitive knowledge of the process will give the best results. In the literature, the cases analyses are "post ante" analysis giving exact results to show the usefulness of the model. In the real analysis the analyst deals with problems of uncertainty of more parameters that the analysis is able to solve.

REFERENCES

Ayres, Robert U. (1969) *Technological Forecasting and Long-Range Forecasting*. McGraw-Hill Book Company, New York.

Bass, F.M. (1969), A New Product Growth Model for Consumer Durables. *Management Science* **15**, 215-227.

Blackman, A.W. (1972), A Mathematical Model for Trend Forecasts. *Technological Forecasting and Social Change* **3**, 441-452.

Easingwood C., Majahan V., Muller E. (1981), A Non Symmetric Responding Logistic Model for Forecasting Technological Substitution. *Technological Forecasting and Social Change* **20**, 199-213.

Easingwood C., Majahan V., Muller E. (1983), A Nonuniform Influence Innovation Diffusion Model of New Product Acceptance. *Marketing Science* **2**, 273-296.

EUTELIS Consult (1993) *Scenario Mobile Communications 2010: Study on Forecast Development and Future Trends in Technical Development and Commercial Provision up to the year 2010*. Report to the Commission of the European Communities. CEC Contract No. 48166.

Fichman, R.G. (1992), Information Technology Diffusion: A Review of Empirical Research. In De Gross, Becker, Elam (Eds.), *Proc. of the 13th Internatonal Conference on Information Systems*, Dallas. pp. 195-206.

Fisher, J.C., Pry, R.H. (1972) A Simple Substitution Model of Technological Change. *Technological Forecasting and Social Change* **3**, 75-78.

Floyd A. (1968), Trend Forecasting: A Methodology for Figures of Merit. In Bright J. (ed.), *First Annual Technology and Management Conference*. Prentice Hal Inc.

Jaakkola, Hannu (1991) *An Analysis of the Diffusion of Information Technology in Finnish Industry*. Tampere University of Technology, Publications 70 (In Finnish, English Summary), Tampere.

Jaakkola, Hannu (1991a) Managing By Modelling - How to Manage the Diffusion of a New technology. *Proceedings of the Portland International Conference on Management of Engineering and Technology*, IEEE.

Jaakkola, Hannu (1992) Modifications and Integration of Diffusion Models. Proceedings of the Joint EURO XII/TIMS XXXI Conference, Helsinki.

Jaakkola, Hannu (1992a) Data Models from Theory to Practice - Modelling the Adoption of New Data Models. In Ohsuga S. (et al.), *Information Modelling and Knowledge Bases III*, IOS Press, Amsterdam. pp. 675-690.

Jaakkola, Hannu (1992b) The Diffusion of Information Technology in Finnish Industry. In Vuori S., Ylä-Anttila P. (eds.), *Mastering Technology Diffusion - The Finnish Experience*. ETLA Serie B82-1992, Helsinki. pp. 379-432.

Jaakkola, Hannu (1993) Diffusion Models for Technology Management. In Clark J.D., Troxell

W.O. (eds.), *Design for Competitiveness*. Proceedings of the International Conference on Technology Management (April 4-7, 1993), Manufacturing Excellence Centre Press, Denver, Colorado. pp 351-366.

Jaakkola, Hannu (1993a) Toward the Heuristic Model of Technology Diffusion. In the *Proceedings of the IFAC World Congress, Preprint Vol. 3*, Sydney Australia, International Federation for Automation and Control (IFAC). pp. 441-446.

Jaakkola H., Tenhunen H. (1993b) The Impact of Information Technology on Finnish Industry: A Survey of Two Studies. *OECD STI Review* **12** (April), pp. 53-80.

Jaakkola, Hannu (1994) The Heuristic Model of Technology Diffusion. In Khalil T.M. et al. (eds.) *Management of Technology IV: The Creation of Wealth*. Proceedings of the Fourth International Conference on management of Technology (Miami Feb. 27 - March 4, 1994). Industrial Engineering and management Press, Institute of Industrial Engineers, Norcross, Georgia.

Jaakkola, Hannu (1994a), The Heuristic Analysis of the Diffusion. In *Management in Transition: Engineering a Changing World*. IEEE Proceedings of the IEEE International Engineering Management Conference 1994 (Oct. 17-19, Dayton, Ohio). IEEE, New Jersey, 1994. s. 123-130.

Jaakkola, Hannu (1995), Technology Management with Mathematical Diffusion Models. Working Draft, not published.

Jaakkola, Hannu (1995a), Flexibility in Mathematical Diffusion Models. Working Draft, not published.

Kumar, U., Kumar, V. (1992), Technological Innovation Diffusion: The Proliferation of Substitution Models and Easing the User´s Dilemma. *IEEE Transactions on Engineering Management* **39**,2 (May), 158-168.

Lavaraj U.A., Gore A.P. (1990) On Interpreting Probability Distributions Fitted to Times of First Adoption. *Technological Forecasting and Social Change* **37**, 355-370.

Majahan, V., Schoeman, M.E.F. (1977) Generalized Model for the Time Pattern of Diffusion Process. *IEEE Transactions on Engineering Management* **EM-24**, 1 (Feb.), 12-18.

Majahan, V., Peterson, R. (1985) *Models for Innovation Diffusion*. Sage Publications, Beverly Hills.

Majahan, V., Muller, E., Bass, F.M. (1990) New Product Diffusion Models in Marketing: A Review and Directions for Research. *Journal of Marketing* **54**, 1-26.

Majahan V., Muller E., Rajendra K., Srivastva K. (1990a), Determination of Adopter Categories by Using Innovation Diffusion Models. *Journal of Marketing Research* **27**, 37-50.

Mansfield E. (1961), Technical Change and the Rate of Imitation. *Econometrica* **29** (October), 741-765.

Martino J. (1993), Technological Forecasting for Decision Making. McGraw-Hill Inc.

Martino J. (1994), An Approach to Balancing the Risks f R&D Performance Goals. In *Management in Transition: Engineering a Changing World*. IEEE Proceedings of the IEEE International Engineering Management Conference 1994 (Oct. 17-19, Dayton, Ohio). IEEE, New Jersey, 1994. s. 164-167.

Norton J., Bass F. (1987), A Diffusion theory Model of Adoption and Substitution of Successive generations of High Technology Products. *Management Science* **33**, 1069-1086.

Pearl, Raymond (1925), *The Biology of Population Growth*. Knopf, New York.

Rogers, E. (1983) *Diffusion of Innovations*. The Free Press, New York.

Sharif M.N., Kabir C.(1976), Systems Dynamics Modelling for Forecasting Multilevel Technological Change. *Technological Forecasting and Social Change* **8**, 353-364.

Sharif, M.N., Ramanathan, K. (1981) Binomial Innovation Diffusion Models with Dynamic Potential Adopter Population. *Technological Forecasting and Social Change* **20**, 63-87.

Skiadas C. (1985), Two Generalized Rational Models for Forecasting Innovation Diffusion. *Technological Forecasting and Social Change* **27**, 39-61.

Telecommunicatons Statistics (1995). Painatuskeskus, Helsinki (in Finnish).

BIOGRAPHY

Hannu Jaakkola is a professor of information technology at Tampere University of Technology. He received his Ph.D. (Eng.) degree from Tampere University of Technology in 1991; MSc (computer Science) 1974, BSc (Business Economics) 1979, Licentiate degree (computer science) 1982 in University of Tampere. His research interests cover wide variety of topics in technology management, especially the problems concerning the adoption of new technologies. Additionally he has research activities in the area of software engineering methods and networks. Before present position since 1992 he has been working in different academic positions at Tampere University of Technology, University of Vaasa and University of Tampere.

7

Information technology transfer and implementation: The introduction of an electronic mail system in a public service organization

Karlheinz Kautz
Norwegian Computing Center
POBox 114 Blindern, N-0314 Oslo, Norway, Karl.Kautz@nr.no

Abstract

The organizational implementation of information systems is an important and problematic issue of information technology transfer. The case study presented in this paper deals with the introduction of an electronic mail system in a public service organization. An interpretive framework is used to understand the interplay of the different elements which influence the introduction process. It comprises three main components: the content of the introduction, the context in which it takes place, and the social process of the introduction. This involves both a cultural and a political perspective of the process. The analysis of the case is used to present some broader implications for understanding and managing introduction processes.

Keywords

Information technology and organization, organizational implementation

1 INTRODUCTION

The organizational implementation of information systems, and in a broader sense information technology, has been subject of research for nearly 30 years. Most of the studies relate a set of factors and dependant variables to each other. It has been stated that although this research has produced some valuable information about a number of implementation characteristics, it has only led to little of a unified, coherent body of knowledge (Kwon & Zmud, 1987).

A demand for research aiming at understanding the complex process of implementation and the linkage between its various elements has been put forward by different researchers (see, f. ex,. Markus & Robey (1988), Wastell (1992)) and a growing number of studies strives for satisfying this request (see Borton & Brancheau (1994), Montealegre & Applegate (1994), Walsham & Waema (1994) for more recent efforts). The study presented here contributes to this line of research. However, while organizational implementation is often considered as a stage in a development process, this article describes and analyses the introduction of a ready-made information system purchased on the market. The article deals with the introduction of an electronic mail system in a public service organization. An approval of this technology is highly dependant on reaching a critical mass of users within the different departments of an organization (Marcus, 1990).The paper uses an interpretive framework to understand the interplay of the different elements of this particular introduction process which despite of problems and weakness - at least at the time of writing - has led to a certain acceptance of the system among the employees of the organization.

The remainder of the paper is structured as follows: The next section contains the research background and framework. Section 3 comprises a presentation of the research method. The case description and analysis is included in section 4. Some broader implications for understanding and managing introduction processes are subject of section 5. The paper finishes with some conclusions in section 6.

2 RESEARCH BACKGROUND AND FRAMEWORK

Research on information technology is performed on the background of different world views. Dahlbom and Mathiassen (1993) see basically two different philosophies which have moulded the field: positivism and hermeneutics. Orlikowski and Baroudi (1991) identify three research philosophies. They distinguish between positivist, interpretivist and critical research. In their survey of contemporary IS research however, they do not find any contributions performed according to the critical paradigm.

Positivistic research is interested in general knowledge, in collecting empirical, unilateral cause-effect laws and factors that can serve as guidelines for action in all situations that seem to be alike. The aim of knowledge is explanation and prediction. This paradigm is the leading one in information technology research. Wastell (1992) points out that such research has produced very little knowledge of apparent benefit to the field. The correlations obtained by rigorous and controlled factor and survey studies contain little divergence and in terms of actual answers, they are often worthless. No real advice for specific work settings can derive from studies seeking general laws.

In hermeneutics, there is an interest in understanding actions by interpreting, not explaining or predicting them. The aim of knowledge is edification and enlightenment. Knowledge is not a general object that can be collected; knowledge is individual. Phenomenological research is based on a view that knowledge of reality is socially constructed by human actors. There is no objective reality that can be discovered by researchers and replicated by others. Different perceptions of reality are ways of making sense of the world. Meanings are shared through an ongoing process of communication and are forms of intersubjectivity rather than of objectivity.

The struggle between positivism and hermeneutics can not be settled. As Dahlbom and Mathiassen (1993) formulate it, it expresses the fundamental and antagonistic difference between technology, the objective, stable, controllable, and people, the subjective, unsteady, and hardly controllable. This might be seen as a simplistic and extreme position, important however is their argument that understanding and respecting the relation between information technology and people is a valuable source for developing and managing information technology in organizations. The introduction of information technology is not just a process of technical change, but also, or first and foremost, means organizational development.

Hirschheim et al. (1987) argue that systems development which aims at the use of computer technology is a social process which relies on technology. Bjerknes (1992) describes this social process as a dialectical reality of mutual reciprocating influences and contradictions in which organizations are seen as diversified structures. There, many points of view and interests exist. This makes the introduction of information technology a complex, social and political phenomenon. This political dimension is also stressed by Markus (1983) and Franz and Robey (1984). Pluralistic research is requested. A research that comprises all vital aspects of introducing information technology, namely the technical, the social, the cultural, the organizational, and the political.

Walsham (1993) puts forward such an approach with his interpretive approach to systems development. He advocates research that counterbalances and complements not only positivism and its concerns of technology and technological control, but also hermeneutics and its desire for increased understanding through mere description. He includes issues such as power, control, conflict, and contradictions as raised by critical social theory in his framework.This approach combines elements of interpretivist and critical research as presented by Orlikowski and Baroudi. Walsham has used his framework successfully for studying the development and implementation of computer-based information systems as well as for the formation and implementation of IT strategies.

Here, the framework will be applied to study the introduction of a software system that was purchased ready-made on the market. The framework comprises three main components for understanding organizational change. The content of the modifications is naturally an important element of any change processes. With respect to the organization, this comprises planned alternations of products and services, business process, and formal organizational structures and roles. With respect to the associated information technology hardware, system software, and application software are all constituting parts of an information system that have to be considered. The second component is the context in which the introduction takes place. Elements of this component include the history of previous undertakings in connection with computer-based systems as well as the social relations and the social infrastructure of those involved in and concerned by the information technology. On a broader level the context comprises also the sectorial and national environment of the organization. The third component of the framework touches the social process. It involves both a cultural and a political perspective of the introduction. The cultural perspective takes into account the role and interaction of different subcultures; the political perspective stresses the role of information technology in processes of control and power. The cultural and the political perspective are not independent of each other. In the following description and analysis of the case, emphasis has been put on the dynamic interlinking between these components

3 RESEARCH METHOD

The research presented here is part of a larger project investigating the introduction and use of existing technologies in public service organizations. The researcher himself was involved in the project as a supporting external consultant. The aim of the study is to contribute to a broader understanding of the introduction processes of information technology.

For this purpose case studies are, according to Zmud et al. (1989), highly appropriate, in that they offer a holistic view of the processes involved as well as a high level of richness of worldly realism.Yin (1989) discusses case studies and ethnographic studies. Case studies are structured and purposeful from the start, whereas ethnographic studies are less structured and open. The approach of the study presented here has elements of both types with a tendency towards case studies. Although no explicit hypotheses are stated, the study is based on a clearly expressed perspective. A similar approach is advocated by Carstensen et al. (1995) in their research on the work of software testers. The purpose here is to investigate how standard computer-based communication technology is introduced and used in large organizations.

There are disadvantages with a case study oriented approach like the lack of control and a corresponding difficulty in generalizing the results. Knowledge gained through case studies is not formally generalizable, but this does not mean that it does not contribute to the collective body of knowledge of a discipline (cf. Eisenhardt (1989) and Flyvbjerg (1992)). Any research approach is inevitably a trade-off between tightness of control and richness of worldly realism. Here the latter has been chosen, because whilst it may be compromising the ability to generalize, it offers valuable insights about the specific process under discussion.

The research started in summer 1993 and was carried out during a period of 18 months. The study and the data analysis is based on qualitative as well as on quantitative data. The principle method to collect data was semi-structured interviews. In total 12 formal interviews with management personnel, project members and related clerical officers and consultants were conducted. These were supplemented by many informal conversations.The interviews were recorded in writing and a resulting report was acknowledged by the organization. It is known that interviews are verbal reports and as such subject to problems of interview bias, poor memory, and inaccurate statements. Kidder (1981) argues however that many critics tend to exaggerate the significance of interview bias. They overlook the fact that scientists interested in social and organizational issues are dependent upon data which have been collected by means of oral or written reports. The reports are, no matter how collected, invariably subject to essentially the same bias than those based on observations, experiments, or survey questionnaires. One must nevertheless be aware of the fact that interview subjects have a tendency to rationalizing their behaviour and acts. The interview material has therefore been substantiated with document studies. Strategy documents, internal reports and memos as well as the organization's internal newspaper served as additional sources. Finally a survey concerning the use of the system was performed among all employees of the headquarters half a year after the system was technically available for everyone. This survey had a high response rate as half of the employees answered the questionnaire.

4 THE CASE DESCRIPTION AND ANALYSIS

Subject of the case study are the headquarters of a public service organization which delivers communication services to the citizens of Norway. After a reorganization the headquarters now consist of 8 business departments and 10 accompanying service centres. In total 600 people are employed there, the majority are clerical officers, consultants, and case workers.

In 1992 a project group consisting of 3 full time project members was established in the support department for technical services and internal administration to introduce electronic mail into the organization. In line with the organization's official strategic document, both top management and the project leader stated that the project pursues two aims. These are (1) to increase the efficiency of the organization by improving office work, and (2) to gather experience with electronic mail (email) as a basis for the development of new customer services. The group's assignment was to take care of the necessary infrastructure, to supply system software and to install the email system for the employees of the headquarters. Along with the technical tasks, the group is responsible for providing information about the system and to prepare training material.

In 1993 much of the product-independent infrastructure work had been finished, but no decision had been made about the email system to be purchased. This was due to discussion about a common system with the two subsidiaries of the main organization which also were planning to use email. Finally after negotiations which did not lead to a common solution an email system was bought for the headquarters. In May 1994 it was announced in the organization's newspaper that all employees of the headquarters had access to the new email system. At this point in time the project was half a year delayed with regard to the original time schedule and it was only then when all employees were officially informed about the introduction of the system. Furthermore, no formal training was provided. Besides a very short on-line document explaining the system's main features, a booklet was distributed that should serve as a user manual.

The user survey half a year later showed that 90% of those who answered the survey used the system. A third of them considered themselves as people who utilized the system to a great extent and 50% considered the system as beneficial for their work. On the other hand, also 50% mentioned that they had problems with the system and that they did not know enough about it to really take advantage of all its possibilities.

4.1 Contextual aspects of the case

According to market surveys during the last years the organization is ranked among the most popular in the country concerning customers' satisfaction with the services delivered. In parts of its business the organization enjoys a monopoly on the market. However, lately, the organization has been exposed to growing competition, a trend which probably will increase in the future.To meet this challenge and to become more market-oriented, the headquarters have undergone a reorganization process in 1993 which ended up in the above described organizational structure. One effect of this process is that departments and service centres have to work more result-oriented. They have to sell their services to each other, which also means that they have to compete with other providers on the open market.

A momentum which is more directly related to the email project, is its origin. The idea of introducing electronic mail into the organization goes back to 1990 to a technical consultant who worked in the then existing computer department of the organization. At that time however his ideas were not severely considered. An event of some significance is an ensuing attempt to introduce email rather informally. The system chosen was regarded as very user-unfriendly and technically unstable. What counts more, however, is the fact that it was mainly used to send around long circular documents which were not of direct interest for daily work. In general the number of messages was very low and only few employees looked into their post boxes every day on a regular basis. Many employees did not even know that they could send messages themselves, they thought that the system was a tool for management only to distribute notes and information. All this lead to a situation were the system was not used very actively and the introduction was widely considered to have failed.

Finally in connection with the new departmentalization of the headquarters it is worth mentioning that the project leader who had held a leading position in the technical support department when the project idea emerged, left this department short after the official start of the project to join a more traditional business-oriented department and took the project with him.

All these features had an important influence on the direction of events the project took in the course of time. Further contextual features are closely related to culture in the organization and will be taken up in the subsequent section.

4.2 A cultural view at the introduction process

The organizations culture as a whole is moulded by the original product which the organization provides, namely the delivery of communication services. The predominance of this culture is mirrored by the fact that the email project was moved to the department which develops products for the national information exchange market and not to the department which has as its task to develop and maintain physical and electronic net services and the internal infrastructure of the organization. Management in the product-oriented department expressed that they like to control the speed of the introduction such that email on the commercial market does not outlive the traditional products too fast.

Another characteristic of the culture is its technique-orientation. The employees are open for technical innovation and many new technical systems have been introduced into the organization in the past. This openness provided the ground for acceptance of the email system. The technical orientation has however also apparent disadvantages. Success of the project is measured in number of installations. It has not yet been monitored, and it is so far not planned to do so, whether the project is reaching its aims, to increase efficiency and to gain new knowledge.

The organization is hierarchically structured. Work, officially, has to be performed following formal rules. This leads to a diffuse picture concerning the informal and formal communication patterns. As no directive has been issued, it is not clear whether, and for which tasks, the use of the email system is mandatory or optional. Today, the system is not used to exchange documents as the employees are insecure about its formal status. They wait for official rules for the use of the system with the effect that one important potential of the system is not exploited at all.

Hierarchical thinking and rigid communication patterns had direct consequences for the cooperation in the project. The project group informally notified the user support group and the training center about a need to include them in the project. None of the groups, which are both understaffed, reacted to the informal request. They waited for an official call while the project group was waiting for being contacted by them.

However, besides the formal communication channels, informal ones exist which are viable for the organization. A good example here is user support's network of key persons in all departments who actively support the introduction of information technology. Although no direct evidence can be presented for the introduction of the email system, the assumption can be made that this informal network also worked in this case.

Hierarchical thought and the idea of centralisation is also expressed in management's attitude towards the project. By and large, management believes that to get the employees to adopt the system it is sufficient that they themselves use it. The project has only been paid little attention and only comparable little resources have been provided. Management's aims with the introduction have not been communicated to the employees clearly and for a long time uncertainty prevailed whether the introduction had more the character of a technical experiment or whether a new support for daily work was provided. Both aims are not contradictory, but as mentioned above they have not been explained enough.

Another attribute of the culture is the fact that many of the employees have spent their whole professional life in the organization. This leads to a enormous loyalty, a strong corporate identity, and an esprit de corps concerning the values the organization stands for. One example for loyalty towards the own department has been described earlier. Another instance exhibiting the relationship between loyalty and communication can be presented here. The project team did not want to jeopardize the organization's image in the public and the project leader, by all means, wants to avoid another failed introduction. Therefore the group did not inform the employees about the introduction before they were fairly certain about the technical stability of the system. This, however did not only have positive effects. It also contributed to rumours and uneasiness concerning the change of working routines in the headquarters.

The esprit de corps shows to be important when the settled distinction between those who are "internal", who have spent their working life in the organization, and those who have been hired from the outside is considered. This is manifested when a look at the role of two external consultants in the project is taken. The consultants are welcome as a reinforcement of the approach chosen by the project group, but their proposals are only taken up hesitantly and they are more or less confined to a passive role. Another example in this respect is the way the ideas of a manager who was recruited from the outside are treated. His plan to integrate email with other office systems was met with resistance. It was interpreted as an attempt to change working routines with a "big bang" approach and responded with a suggestion to start with a smaller stand-alone solution. Integration however is not conflicting to a stand-alone start given that an incremental approach and a design are chosen which take into account future extensions.

Besides the cultural-associated scepticism towards the outside proposal, this example also has a political dimension pointing to a power struggle between a top manager and middle management. This will be described in more detail in the following section.

4.3 Some political elements of the introduction process

The future of the email project is subject to ongoing discussions in the headquarters. The debate about a stand-alone or an integrated solution has led to some delays and some uncertainties about the further course of the work. The considerations are not only about an organizational and a technical approach to the utilization of technology. They also have a political momentum.

This momentum is concerned with the control over the project. One possible consequence of following the top manager's proposal to strive for integration will be a loss of control for the actual project leader. The project team might be changed and experts on office work in general as well as experts on existing office support systems might be included. Ultimatively the leadership of the project might be placed into hands of a person who is more sympathetic to the ideas of this top manager.

Besides a power struggle between top management and middle management, another interdepartmental conflict can be uncovered here. The mentioned top manager also wants to move the project away from the product, communication service-oriented department. As explained before, until now the project lies in the responsibility of this traditional department where management wants to control the introduction of email to protect its own products. In this department top management shows little understanding that email is a supplement, and not a replacement of existing products. In addition, not much sense can be found here for the possible benefits of email for internal work. Moving the project to another department and going for an integrative solution will change the power relationship in the headquarters which historically was dominated by the product-oriented department. The conflict has not been settled yet and negotiations are still going on.

Another example how the introduction process has been used politically, can be demonstrated by the cooperation problems between user support and the project team. User support has been understaffed. Not reacting upon the project teams' request for help, gave them another opportunity to demonstrate their personal situation with the aim to get additional staff.

But also on a higher organizational level political processes are involved: the decision about what email system to purchase by the headquarters and two of the organization's subsidiaries, was on the surface a debate about opting for a local product which is in line with a chosen standard or a product from an international vendor which fits into a larger product line. The technical argument that no interface between these systems exists is only of minor significance, because the development of such a gateway is not a big technical challenge. The discussion is much more about who is controlling the whole organization. The two comparably new subsidiaries who operate on the financial market are contributing the major part to the organization's financial success, whereas the original parts of the organization which still control the organization are financially less profitable.This control is now challenged in decision making processes like the described one. For the introduction process under consideration, no compromise could be found. Different systems have been bought, further delays occurred and lately the two subsidiaries have been separated from the mother organization and operate now independently.

5 IMPLICATIONS FOR IT INTRODUCTION AND TRANSFER

A discussion which aims at some more wide-ranging implications for the introduction of information technology has to take into account to what extent the described case presents a success story or a failure. This is however not such a simple task as different success criteria may be applied.

The introduction of the email system can be considered a success as the system in the initial phase is used by approximately 40% of all employees and the majority of them experience the system to be beneficial for their work. Yet, the project has not been finished within its original time constraints and many people report problems with the use of the system. In this respect, the project has not been successful. No judgement can be made whether the project is a success or a failure in relation to the objectives pursued by senior management. Nonetheless, it is important to note that the introduction process has at least partly been performed as a project that was mastered in a controlled way, in contrast to other introduction processes which evolve totally uncontrolled. Some disagreements like the political considerations described which were related to the selection of the email system just need time to be settled or resolved. Other obstructions might be cleared out of the way when handled appropriately. Therefore, in the following a closer look is taken at some specific aspects of the case presented.

Project mission and project goal.

According to the majority of senior management and the project leader, the introduction of the email system has two goals. On the one hand, an aim is to carry out office work more productively. As possible gains, more efficient communication and saving man power were named. The other aim is to learn about the technology for the development of future products for the market. As mentioned, these aims are in line with the official strategy of the organization.

These are strong and unambiguous objectives which are clearly related to the business needs of the organization. They are not determined by short-sided and seasonal demands, but by enormous and pressing requests in a competitive situation, but in a long-term perspective. Such a context has shown to be stipulating for the introduction of technology in other areas (cf., Roberts & Barrar, 1992).

However, it is unclear in how far these aims are known in the headquarters. They have not been communicated to the employees. Communication between the directly involved groups and general information seems to be a problem in this project. The misunderstandings resulting from this situation make it difficult to introduce and promote technology which is supposed to support integration, coordination, and cooperation. The embodiment of the project within the organization is questionable and the role the technology should play in the organization is not obvious for the employees either. This resulted in an uncertainty and a hestitant and limited utilisation of the system.

Little can be said whether the mission has been accomplished. No measurement programme concerning increased efficiency and a higher level of knowledge has been initiated. The basic lesson learned here can be formulated like this: Defining clear goals is not enough, they have to be communicated and their accomplishment has to be monitored and evaluated.

Senior management involvement and support.

Senior management's attitude towards the introduction of email gives no uniform picture in the headquarters. The spectrum ranges from fear of a competing product and doubts about the usefulness of the system to absolute enthusiasm about the operation and the possibilities of the technology.

Most of the management shows an enormous interest in using the system themselves and are convinced about its benefits for their work, but also for the organization as a whole. Within this group, no consensus has been reached so far how to combine email with the existing technical office environment. Integration versus stand-alone are the alternatives discussed among the leaders.

There is a consensus in the group that the most important support they can provide for the introduction process is that they themselves use the system and nearly all of them describe themselves as eager users. There is little doubt that such symbolic acts have some significance for the introduction process. It is more likely that the employees will not use a new communication channel which is supposed to support information exchange between all groups, if management does not use it.

But besides this contribution management's effort for supporting the introduction process has to be characterized as quite passive. Management did not appear really committed. Sound engagement like active participation in introduction arrangements and courses or public appeals motivating the usage of the system have not taken place. Support in form of provision of resources has been fairly modest. Management was not willing to participate in a proposed extended project group 'organizational introduction' and were quite hesitant in providing personnel for such a group. Some of them thought the group to be a good idea, but did not want to delegate staff from their own department. Extra resources for training where not considered at all. Here lies a reason why the introduction process struggled for a while and for the uncertainty about the system's purpose and the problem's of use which were reported.

We get another confirmation that mere interest and passive involvement is not sufficient when it comes to senior management 's role in change processes in the context of technology introduction. Lack of support can slow down and jeopardise the process, but in the presented case, so far utilisation has not stopped or faded away because a technology-friendly community has created the critical mass which is necessary for the meaningful exploitation of a communication medium.

Education and training.

The headquarters have an own consultancy and competence center. Two persons there are responsible for organizing education related to the use of information technology. A detailed procedure exists for arranging training which can be adjusted to specific events like the introduction of an email system. The IT training consultants partly prepare courses and handbooks themselves, partly they take care of hiring lecturers and buying courses on the market.

One of them was quite early informally notified about the email project. Formally their support was requested very late and in a very restricted form. They were never officially members of the project group.

The organization got hold of the original course material issued by the email supplier. This material comprised a one day tutorial with exercises for every major feature of the tool. The project group published however only a one page on-line help and used the competence center only to produce a small brochure explaining the most important functions of the system. This brochure presented a subset of the original documentation and no exercise tasks were included. No formal training was provided.

More than half of those employees who reported problems with the system argued that this was due to a lack of training in combination with a lack of time for self-study. The more general message here is that formal education and training which go beyond studying a handbook and provide hand-on use experience are important components of a successful introduction strategy.

Organizational validity and usefulness.

The headquarters are part of a formal department where work to a large extent is rule-governed. Half of the user survey respondents agree that email is a significant tool for the organization. Only 10 employees disagree strongly. A third of the staff who answered consider themselves as intensive users, many report that the system makes it easier to exchange messages and they state that it has replaced many yellow stickers. Some say that they save many telephone calls now.

Concerning document exchange the situation is more complicated. Although again half of the respondents think that email is useful for the exchange of documents, 25% share the opinion that there are many documents which cannot be sent by email and only few formal letters and notes have been replaced by email transmissions.

One reason why the email is less applied than desired lies in the fact that there has been little information about the use of the system. There exists a lack of guidelines about what should be sent and to whom. The established steering mechanism and the reporting rules concerning formal management and the treatment of cases are violated by the system. There is no possibility to properly trace a document through the organization and so far no announcement has been made whether email documents are considered as official documents. One respondent even meant that files which have been sent by email are neglected and handling them is more often postponed than the work with physically received papers.

In general it is felt in the organization that the work procedures and regulations and the technical support are not adjusted to each other. This is regarded as a major obstacle for a more far reaching utilisation of the email system.

This leads to a broader implication: The information technology to be introduced has to fit the structure of the organization and the work patterns of the departments, groups, and individuals. If this is not the case, the necessary adaptation should be part of the introduction process.

6 CONCLUSIONS

The presented case describes the introduction of an email systems. It demonstrates the relationship between organizational change and technology transfer. Despite a number of problems, it looks as if in this case the technology is on the way of being accepted and used by the staff of the organization.

The interpretive framework which was used broadened the analysis and comprised not only the technical content of the email system to be implemented, but also its context and the dynamics of the introduction process. Such a perspective uncovers cultural and political elements. These are interdependent and influence the transfer of the technology.

On this basis four broader implications for the introduction of information technology were discussed. These concerned the definition, communication and monitoring of project goals, the role of senior management and education and training, and the relationship between organizational structure and work patterns and information technology.

The case appears to be quite typical and does not provide many surprises and new theoretical insights. It is rather a further piece of evidence for the usefulness of the interpretive approach to understand the implementation of information technology as a social process. Introduction of standard, computer-based communication technology, in this respect does not differ more tailor-made information systems.

Although the broader implications might not offer much novelty, they can be put into concrete terms. This concretization can be of benefit for the organization in question as the introduction process is not finished yet.

A project group "organizational introduction" still seems appropriate. Such a group needs real support by top management, both in form of resources, but also by active participation.

Besides management and technical-oriented staff, the involved units user support and training should take part as well as delegates from the clerical officers and case workers from different departments.

The group should

- use the existing communication channels like the organization's new magazine or the email system itself to explain the project
- establish a measurement scheme to monitor the accomplishment of project goals by e.g. recording
    - the labour hours used on work cases
    - the number of telephone calls and paper-based messages
    - the number and degree of customer satisfaction
    - the number of ideas for new products
- develop or initiate the development of procedures and regulations for the use of the technology for reporting and official document handling
- provide for short training courses and comprehensive paper-based and on-line manuals.

These recommendations do not offer a guarantee for success, but they have some value in that may help minimise the risk of failure for the introduction of information technology and in that they can serve as a starting point for the formulation of introduction strategies in other technology transfer projects.

Finally, the question remains, why, if we accept that these guidelines are fundamental, does it still occur that introduction of information technology happens the way as described in this case: If this "knowledge" is not known, the question is, why is this so; and if it is known, the question is, why is it not applied? These are questions open to further investigation in technology or to be more precise knowledge transfer research.

7 REFERENCES

Bjerknes, G., (1992). Dialectical Reflection in Information Systems Development. In Scandinavian Journal of Information Systems, Vol. 4, pp. 55-78.

Borton, J. M., J. C. Brancheau, (1994). Does an Effective Information Technology Implementation Process Guarantee Success?. In Levine, L. (ed.), Proceedings of the IFIP TC8 Working Conference on Diffusion, Transfer and Implementation of Information Technology, Pittsburgh, PA, USA, 11-13 October, 1993, North Holland, Amsterdam, London, New York, pp. 159-178.

Carstensen, P. H., C. Sørensen, T. Tuikka, (1995). Let's Talk about Bugs. In Scandinavian Journal of Information Systems, Vol. 7, No. 1, pp. 33-53.

Dahlbom, B. & L. Mathiassen, (1993). Computers in Context - The Philosophy and Practice of Systems Design. Cambridge & Oxford:NCC Blackwell.

Eisenhardt, K. M., (1989). Building Theories form Case Study Research. In Academy of Management Research Review, Vol. 14, No. 4, pp. 532-550.

Flyvbjerg, B., (1992). Rationality and Power - The Science of the Concrete (In Danish). Akademisk Forlag. København.

Franz, C. R., D. Robey (1984). An Investigation of user-led System Design: Rational and Political Perspective. In Communications of the ACM, 27(12):1202-1209.

Hirschheim, R., H. Klein, M. Newman, (1987). A Social Action Perspective of Information Systems Development. In DeGross, J. and C. Kriebel, eds., Proceedings of the 8th International Conference on Information Systems, pages 45-56.

Kidder, L. H., (1981). Selltiz, Wrightman & Cook's Research Methods in Social Relations. Holt, Rinehart and Winston, New York.

Kwon, T. H., R. W. Zmud, (1987). Unifying the Fragmented Models of Information Systems Implementation,. In Boland, R. J., R. A. Hirschheim (eds.), Critical Issues in Information Systems Research, Wiley & Sons, New York.Winston, New York, pp. 227-251.

Markus, M. L., (1983). Power, Politics, and MIS Implementation. In Communications of the ACM, 26(6):430-444.

Markus, M. L., (1990). Toward a "critical mass" theory of interactive media. In Fulk, J., C. Steinfield (eds.), Organizations and Communication Technology, Sage Publications. Newbury Park, Calif., USA, pp. 194-218.

Markus, M. L., D. Robey, (1988). Information Technology and Organization Change: Causal Structure in Theory and Practice. In Management Science, Vol. 34, May 1988, pp. 583-598.

Montealegre, M., L. M. Applegate,(1994). Information Technology & Organization Change: Lessons from a Less-Developed Country. In Levine, L. (ed.), Proceedings of the IFIP TC8 Working Conference on Diffusion, Transfer and Implementation of Information Technology,Pittsburgh, PA, USA, 11-13 October, 1993, North Holland, Amsterdam, London, New York, pp. 99-131.

Orlikowski, W. L., J. J. Baroudi, (1991). Studying Information Technology in Organizations: Research Approaches and Assumptions. In Information Systems research, Vol. 2., No.1, pp. 1-28.

Roberts, H. J. and P. R. N. Barrar, (1992). MRPII implementation: Key Factors for Success. In Computer Integrated Manufacturing Systems. 5(1): 31-38.

Walsham, G., (1993). Interpreting Information Systems in Organizations.Wiley Series on Information Systems, Chicester.

Walsham, G., T. Waema, (1994). Information Systems Strategy and Implementation: A Case Study of a Building Society. In ACM Transactions on Information Systems, Vol.12, No.2, pp. 150-173.

Wastell, D. G., (1992). The Social Dynamics of Systems Development: Conflict, Change and Organizational Politics. In S. Easterbrook, S., (ed)., CSCW: Cooperation and Conflict?. Springer Verlag, London, pp 69-91.

Yin, R. K., (1989). Research Design Issues in Using the Case Study Method to Study Management Information Systems. In Cash, J. I., P. R. Lawrence (eds.), The Information Systems research Challenge: Qualitative Research Methods. Vol. 1. Havard Business School Research Colloqium, pp. 1-6.

Zmud, R., M. H. Olson, R. Hauser, (1989). Field Experimentation in MIS Research. In Benbasat, I., ed., The Information Systems Research Challenge: Experimental Research Methods, Vol. 2, Harvard Business School Research Colloquium, pp. 97-112.

8 BIOGRAPHY

Karlheinz Kautz is employed as a research scientist at the Norwegian Computing Center. Before joining this research institute he was a researcher and lecturer at universities in Germany, England, and Norway. Kautz's education includes a MSc in computer science from the Technical University of Berlin, Germany and a doctorate in systems development from the University of Oslo, Norway. He is vice-chair of IFIP TC 8 WG 8.6 on Diffusion, Transfer, and Implementation of Information Technology and a member of ACM. He has published in Information Technology & People, Information and Software Technology, and the Scandinavian Journal of Information Systems and co- authored a book on prototyping. His research interests are in technology transfer, organizational impacts of information technology, evolutionary systems development, participatory design, prototyping, software quality and software process improvement.

8

On the diffusion of software technologies: technological frameworks and adoption profiles [1]

G. León
Dep. of Telematics Engineering
Universidad Politécnica de Madrid
Ciudad Universitaria 28040-Madrid (Spain)
Ph.: +341 336 7334
Fax: +341 336 7333
E-mail: gleon@dit.upm.es

Abstract

This paper presents an analysis of the forces that constrain the diffusion of software technologies in the organizations from the perspective of the technological frameworks exhibited by individuals and the social groups to which they belong.

In the adoption process, stakeholders are organized as circles of diffusion; each group possesses different reference frameworks that constrain the way that information technology is accepted and diffused. These constraints are explained in terms of the lack of congruence between the technological frameworks exhibited by the different groups.

After characterizing the transition groups in terms of the adoption profiles we postulate a set of actions to decrease the risks of failure in the adoption of software technologies. Finally, the ideas are applied to the analysis of a technology transfer case with FDTs in the telecommunication domain.

Keywords

Technology transfer, Technological frames, Software technologies, Formal methods, Adoption profiles

[1]This work has been partly sponsored by the Spanish Research Council under project EMEDAS

1 INTRODUCTION

It is well known that the introduction of a new technology in one organization not always produces the intended benefits (Levine, 1994). In many cases, either the receivers do not reach the intended level of use or simply the technology is rejected because it does not match with the expectations (true or false) and the accepted psychological effort to use it. The case of formal methods is a paradigmatic example of continual failures.

The published cases with problems or failures only constitute the visible part of a large iceberg of adoption cases. It is difficult to get companies to openly express the problems they had; however, from the experience of the author, failure cases are very common and they include any type of company. Many reasons to explain the failures (and in some cases the successes) could be postulated; however, the experiences are not structured enough and it is difficult to extract from them useful guidelines for avoiding future problems.

Generally speaking, there is a trend to find the root of the problems in the technology itself and in its adequacy with the preexistent technological context. Technocratic technology transfer models describe the problems in terms of these aspects. Although it is true that those factors limit the probability of success, there is another source of explanations linked to the individuals and working teams and how they perceive the technology.

Before entering into the analysis of the problem, the concept of software technology as used in this paper [2] will be presented.

Software technology is understood as a set of integrated notations, tools and methods, based on sound principles to develop and maintain a software product in a given organizational context.

A software technology is composed of the following elements (see figure 1): a set of textual or graphical notations (semantically related); a reasoning framework to analyze the notations and to validate properties; a set of tools (more or less integrated) to support the notations and the reasoning framework; methods for developing large systems by using the notations, tools and reasoning framework and industrial guidelines where the know-how in one application domain is structured (in (León et al., 1994) a more detailed definition of these concepts can be found).

When we address technology transfer and diffusion (technology diffusion is the process of making available a mature technology in a community of users and technology transfer refers to the process of inserting a technology into an organization that adopts and probably adapts it), the technology cannot be considered in an isolated way if we wish to understand the associated problems. Following the above mentioned concepts, figure 1 depicts the relationships between technological components and the adoption context.

We postulate that the adoption success depends on the way that the components of the technology interacts with the adoption context. This interaction is strongly de-

[2] Although the reference is on software technology, most ideas and concepts can be applied to any type of information technology.

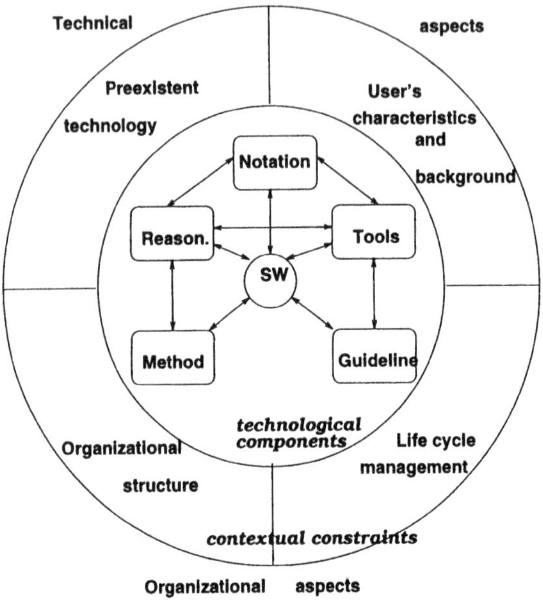

Figura 1: Technological components and adoption framework

pendent on the technological frameworks exhibited by people (individuals and groups) involved in the process.

The rest of the paper is organized as follows: section 2 presents the idea of technological frameworks and how it affects the perceived technology. Section 3 describes the concept of technology transfer profile and its relation with technological frameworks. Section 4 will present the idea of circles of technology diffusion where the identified stakeholders enter into contact. Based on those concepts, section 5 will describe an integrated model to speed up the diffusion of software technologies. In section 6 the model is applied to understand the diffusion problems found in one case study concerning the adoption of formal methods in the the telecommunication sector. Finally, from this experience some conclusions are summarized in section 7.

2 TECHNOLOGICAL FRAMEWORKS

Reference frameworks are defined in cognitive psychology field as predefined structures of mental patterns that facilitate any experience or conduct. Reality is valued or interpreted with reference to these patterns.

Although the definition applies to individuals, it is possible to extend it to large social groups when they are composed by individuals sharing some relevant aspects concerning the reference framework. Orlikowski and Gash (1994) borrowed this idea to define the

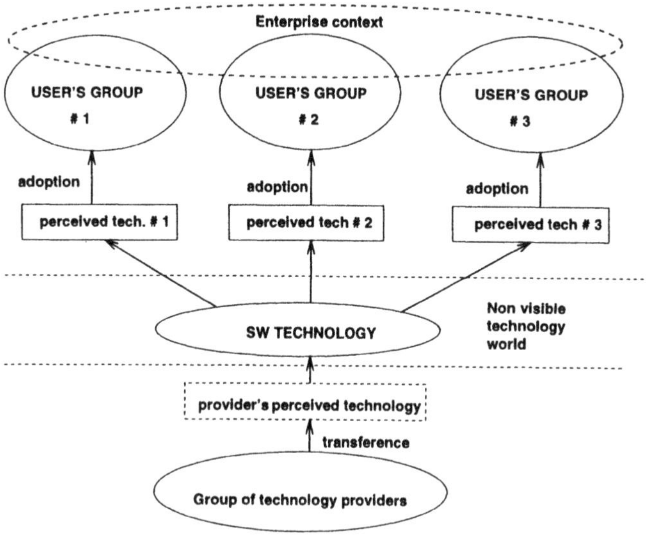

Figura 2: How the technology is perceived

technological frameworks as a subset of cognitive elements related with the technology (in their case, groupware technology).

In the above mentioned article, both authors establish the hypothesis that the inconsistency of technological frameworks (ambiguous, incomplete or incorrect concepts) is responsible for the reported problems of introducing a predetermined technology in a given industrial context. It explains why technology produces such a different reaction among people involved in different organizations even when the differences between current and target technology were the same in all of those organizations.

It is interesting to mention that when a technology is adopted by a community of users, they do not see the technology "as is" but as perceived technology.

A technology is the result of the description of its technological components and its relationships. Nevertheless, each receiver has a different lens that modifies this real technology in some of its specific components or inter-relationships as a function of its reference framework. Figure 2 expresses this idea. It also suggests that many people can share the same perceived technology although they were completely isolated (the idea of social group does not mean that they are working together; when it occurs, it will be termed a team) or different perceived technologies even when they belong to the same company (the case represented in figure 2).

Differences in observable behaviour of two communities with respect to the same technology are associated to the way that the perceived technology is evaluated (interpreted) in relation with a preexistent technological framework. In other words, the actual technology is filtered and perceived under a limited scope.

Obviously, it is not a static process. The (new or old) inter-relations among individuals, the use of the technology and the modifications of the perceived technology are inputs for modifying the technological framework and, hence, the observable behaviour. Notice that providers also manage a perceived technology. This fact is even more important when the target technology is not completely stable. In this case, not only perceptions change with time; the technology itself is also a moving target.

The consequence of this analysis is that the adoption of a technology cannot be isolated from the adoption context and this fact avoids speaking of any technology in its pure form.

3 ADOPTION PROFILES

In order to assess the barriers for the adoption, we intend to identify a small number of features that globally permits us to understand the inherent difficulties of technology transfer and to serve as a comparison grid to evaluate a given adoption case with respect to well documented reference cases. The value of these features, define the so-called **adoption profile**.

Features were chosen to capture the most important aspects related with the technological framework. They come from three main sources:

- From the people involved, taking into account the freedom and reactions they have with respect to the technology transfer project. We assume that one of the main criteria to understand the difficulties of one specific technology transfer case comes from knowledge of the people's attitude and profile involved in the process.
- From the technology transfer context, to measure the way that the transference is carried out. Even with very motivated and free people, transference is constrained by the conditions associated with the adoption process itself.
- From the technology to be transferred. Here, the main aspects of the technology that affects the adoption (although we are not interested in the technology in itself) are considered.

The following subsections will present the chosen features.

A more general process to assess the innovative climate has been proposed (Bergman and Ohlund, 1995). They consider variables such as: challenge, freedom, idea-support, trust, dynamism, playfulness, debates, conflicts, risk-taking and idea-time to characterize an organization as innovative or stagnant. Globally, those aspects indicate the organization's attitude. We will follow in this paper a different approach in which the three different views are combined.

3.1 Receptor's attitude

This takes into account the attitude of receptors during the adoption. Although it is true that in every case, many user's profiles participate in the process (from top management to administrative support), we prefer to take a global view of the receptor's value. The value to be included in the adoption profile is an average of the situation at the company level.

Three main cases are relevant:

- **Passive.** Organizations receive the new technology as an order taken outside them. In fact, decision about the technology to adopt, when, and where is taken outside them. This lack of motivation has been reported as a main barrier to a successful end of the transference (Fowler and Levine, 1993).
- **Active.** Receptors envision technology transfer process as a necessary personal decision. They assume the responsibility for choosing the technology and how it is used. It is usually adopted for mature technologies.
- **Cooperative.** Receptors cooperate with providers in the design of the technology transfer case. In this way, technology is adapted to the internal requirements at the company. We postulate that cooperative transferences are more suitable to cope with technology transfer of immature technologies by increasing the success probability.

3.2 Formality of the adoption process

This feature is intended to measure the degree of formalization in the process. If technology transfer is considered as a project, we are interested in knowing if a model is or is not used and if it is adjustable to the specific needs of the case. Three main points are relevant:

- **Informal.** Technology transfer is not a project. Activities are invented for receptors during the adoption. It relies on a naive view of the adoption process and is responsible for many of the reported failures.
- **Planned.** The project is conceived as a sequence of defined steps (phases and activities) following a predefined model.
- **Progressive.** Technology transfer project is conceived under a progressive model adapted to the evaluation of the technology transferred.

Notice that it is a complementary perspective of the receptor's attitude. We postulate that a progressive transference model is better adapted to cope with the problems behind the adoption of complex technologies. Probably, it is also a signal about the maturity of the processes at the company according to any model like CMM. Recently reported problems in accepting CMM from the receivers' standpoint (Saneidian, Kuzaro, 1995) can be also interpreted under those premises.

3.3 Interdependency of receptors and providers

This perspective measures the relation between receptors and providers completing the view obtained from the above coordinates. Three main cases could be mentioned.

- **Independent**. Receptors act by themselves as a completely independent unit. They can freely decide on the technology to use and how it should be transferred.
- **Subsidiary**. They depend on the technology providers and probably the technology cannot be changed; however, they can decide about how the technology should be transferred and when.
- **Chained**. Receptors are strongly linked to the decision of providers. They should accept the new technology without further discussion. Technology transfer process is decided by providers.

3.4 Pressures to start the technology transfer process

Pressures are defined as any aspect that forces the adoption of a new technology. Although pressures have many sources (internal and external pressures to initiate the technology transfer project) we have preferred to collapse them into a single perspective to pick up the feeling on the process as a whole.

In other words, if receptors start the process because they cannot wait any longer, we will say that they are receiving huge pressures. Three cases are relevant:

- **No pressures**. If TT process starts it is because they would like to do so. I do not think that this naive situation can be found in practice; even innovative companies use very advanced technologies as a part of their role.
- **Moderate pressures**. Probably, receptors should start a technology transfer process although it is not mandatory to start now. They can accommodate the adoption pace to the severity of the problems.
- **High pressures**. TT should inevitably start ... and soon, before competitivity decreases under a predefined threshold.

3.5 Impact of the technology

Impact measures the effect of the technology in case of adoption on the user's organization and working procedures. Large impact technology means that many things should be changed to take advantage of the potential benefits offered by the technology under adoption. Three situations are representative:

- **Low**. Technology only affects specific individuals in one of the development activities (included in one phase of the life cycle) and it could be mastered in a short time.
- **Moderate**. Technology affects a working team during a phase of the development life cycle and it takes weeks to months to be mastered.
- **High**. Technology affects the whole project team, several phases of the development are affected and it takes months to years to be mastered.

3.6 Maturity

Maturity is a measure of the effort required to use the technology for its main purpose. Mature technologies also means that they have reached a stable situation where providers have experience, transference material and know how to help receptors during the adoption process. Three cases could be considered:

- **Stable**. Technology was developed some time ago and nowadays it is stable and well known.
- **Progressing**. Although the technology was developed some time ago, it is undergoing improvements (some components were not completely mature) or usability in one application domain is not yet assessed.
- **Unstable**. The technology is very immature and its transference will need cooperation between providers and receptors. This is a high risk situation.

Maturity is one of the basic parameters considered by organizations where risk is a basic factor for decision-making.

3.7 Adaptability

It measures the capability of the technology to be customized to the user's requirements. In principle, a customizable technology allows an easier integration into the user's environment.

- **Fixed**. Technology is used on an "as is" basis. Receptors cannot modify any of its components; then, technology transfer is devoted to master its use.
- **Customizable**. Several elements of the technology could be changed to accommodate them to the user's requirements or to the application domain.
- **Open**. Technology is not completely defined and it needs to be completed (defined) by the user.

3.8 Distance with respect to the current technology

This coordinate measures the differences between source and target technology. We would not like to enter in this paper on the metrics associated with the distance, but it is easy to identify relevant aspects of the technology and to concentrate the effort on them. The effort required to complete the transference depends on the distance to be covered.

- **Short distance.** No specific problems should appear. Target technology could be considered as an improvement of the current one and technology transfer can be embedded in continuous process improvement activities.
- **Medium distance.** Some components of the current technology significantly change while others remain in use. This is the typical case of technology transfer within information technology because there are not many new software technologies available that remove all components of the old one. Medium distance advises the convenience of using a planned process.
- **Large distance.** This is the most problematic case because the differences between source and target technologies are so large than the probability of failure is very high. Probably, it is necessary to use another technology (to a shorter distance) as an intermediate step.

3.9 Graphical representation of the adoption profile

Although we have tried to describe them as separate views, it is common to find in practice some interdependences among them in order to ensure a successful project. Figure 3 summarizes most probable relations found in practice. Notice that two clusters clearly appear: one of them related with the technology and another one related with the context. The gap between both clusters reveals that the barriers against the adoption of a technology could be separately analyzed.

In order to obtain a global view of the technology transfer situation, we have depicted the coordinates in the diagram represented in figure 4.

The area covered by each profile is a sign of the difficulties and simplicity or complexity of the technology transfer considered. In figure 4, as a wider area is covered the situation is improved. Thus, it allows people involved to focus the attention on specific aspects where risk of problems are more probable just looking at the profile's shape.

We have used interdependencies between coordinates in the table to distribute them along the circumference. In this way, when the interdependence is high they are placed closer. As a consequence, profiles can be easily understood at a first glance.

4 CIRCLES OF DIFFUSION

In software development companies, more than isolated individuals, technologies are transferred to teams composed of people cooperating to perform a global activity (then,

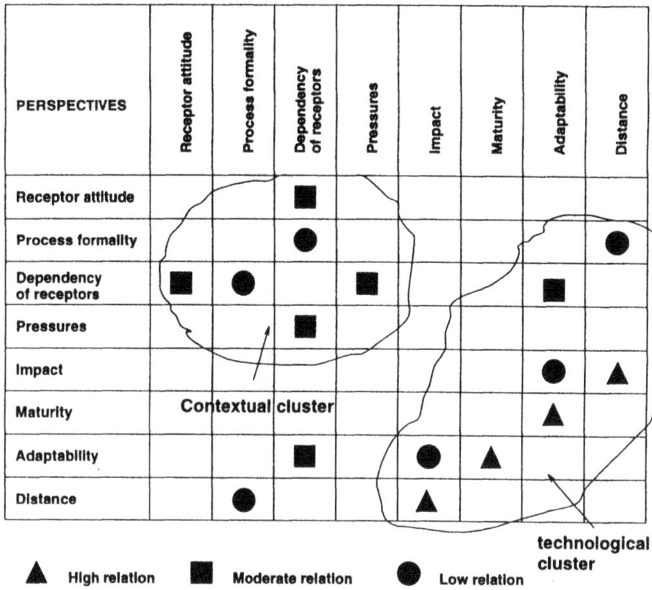

Figura 3: Dependencies between coordinates

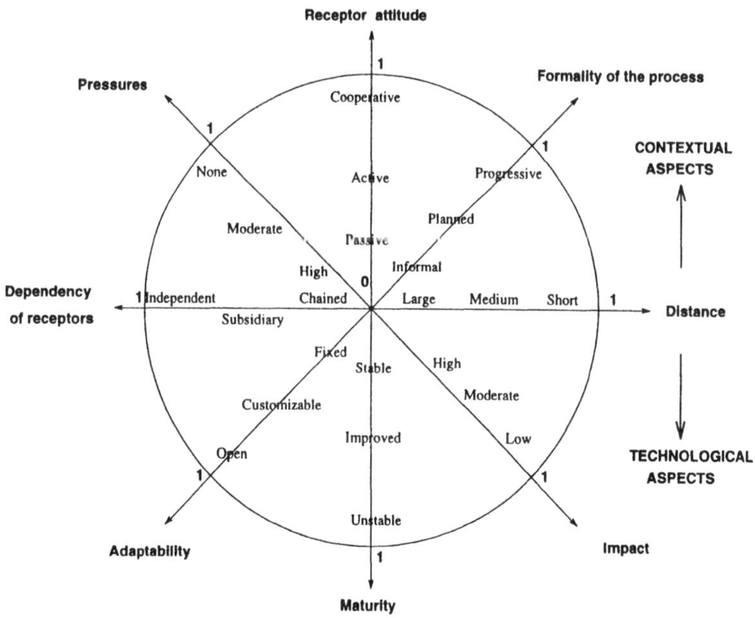

Figura 4: Graphical representation of TT profiles

impact is, at least, moderate). In some cases, they use the same set of tools (conceptual or machinery-based); in others, they perform different tasks with a specific set of tools. As a consequence, the view of the technology is not the same.

When top management decides to start a technology transfer process, several groups related with this process are created. We postulate that the way that these groups interact during the adoption process significantly affects the success or failure of the process as a whole. For us, the company as a whole should be involved in the adoption process as the only way to increase the probability of success. This idea was also expressed by Shuster (1994) under the concept of "mobilizing the whole company".

4.1 Identification of stakeholders

In order to put in practice the circles of diffusion, the following stakeholders were identified:

- **Top management**. They constitute the reduced management core defining the strategy to adopt the technology. More than to evaluate or to define the transition process, this group is focused on maintaining the support for the entire process. It is common that top management makes an initial decision to stimulate the transition. Then, a top down approach to technology diffusion as the most common case found in practice. Only SME's can rely on a more bottom up approach due to their flattened structure.
- **Transition group**. It constitutes the group of people with the basic responsibility of selecting, evaluating and adopting the technology. It is composed of a group of people coming from the different areas of the company that cooperate in the diffusion of the technology as its main role. Providers could also participate when immaturity or adaptability becomes crucial.
- **Pilot project development groups**. In most cases, adoption of a new technology implies the development of some pilot products to test the adequacy of the technology to the typical products developed in the company. Development teams receive the technology from the transition group which incorporates some of its members in the development of pilot cases.
- **Dissemination groups**. Initially passive, these groups are the basis for the diffusion of the technology to the rest of the company. They periodically receive some information about the experiments (pilot cases), the technology and its potential advantages and disadvantages and offer feedback to the pilot and transition groups.
- **Entreprise staff**. The rest of the technical staff at the company. They appear when a decision about the technology has been adopted but they will be affected by it.

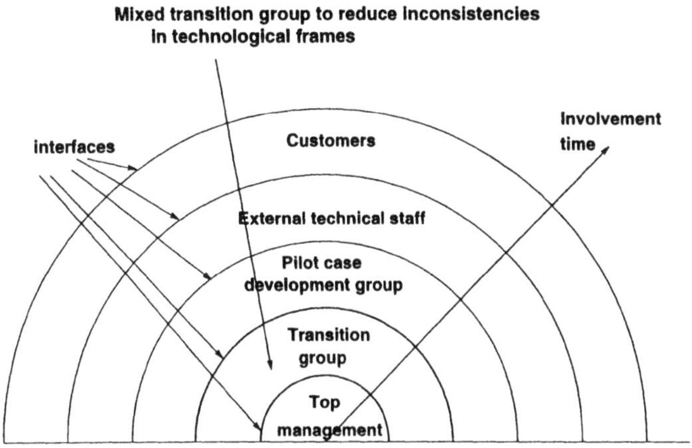

Figura 5: Circles of diffusion

- **External customers.** They are the receivers of the products developed with the new technology. Customers can belong to the same company or to others. In all cases, they should understand the effort made by their providers to adopt a new technology as a long-term benefit for them. Links should be enforced through marketing departments.

At each level, several profiles (project managers, developers, implementers, etc.) from the company and academia populate these groups. Figure 5 details the relation among people working at different circles of diffusion.

Interfaces between the different stakeholders as suggested in figure 5 are also filters of the technology. Each stakeholder possesses a technological framework generating different perceived technology. It explains the difficulties found traversing the interface (i.e., explaining the goals and roles with respect to the adoption process and the difficulties in interpreting the results). Figure 6 depicts this idea where two types of interfaces are shown. External interface between adjacent levels and internal interfaces within the components of the group.

From the discussion presented in this section, we postulate that the lack of congruence between technological frameworks used within the organization is primarily responsible for provoking the difficulties in the technological innovation process. Nevertheless, in spite of the creation of diffusion circles, the lack of common reference frameworks impedes the smooth exchange of information and, more importantly, the assessment of the technology and its impact is undermined.

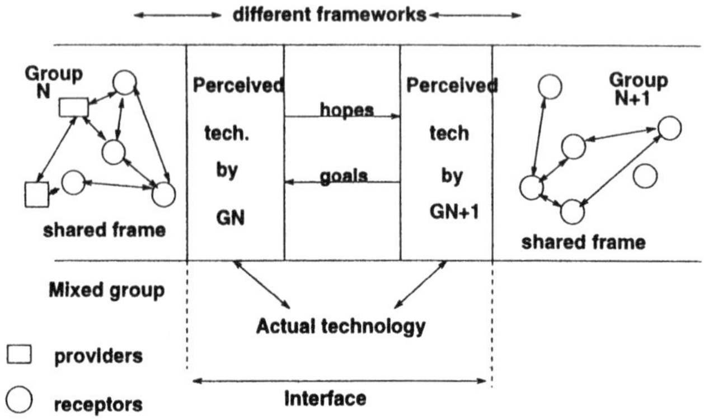

Figura 6: Perceived technology through the circles of diffusion

4.2 Integrating concepts on diffusion of software technologies

Until now, we have developed the concept of adoption profile as a mechanism for facilitating the global understanding of the adoption problems. Furthermore, the structure of circles of diffusion offers a layout to organize the process facilitating the interaction between people with different profiles and responsibilities. Interfaces have been presented as filters when technological frames between adjacent groups are very different. Now, all these concepts will be integrated to speed up the adoption of a new technology.

Time required to diffuse a technology in a company is strongly dependent on the mechanisms used by stakeholders to perform their work and to communicate information with other stakeholders through the defined interfaces. If both receivers and providers do not share the same framework, two possible positions could be held by people involved: to devote much more time to set it up or to ignore the differences; in this last case, the consequence is that the potential benefits are not realized.

The next table reflects the common elements of technological frameworks and the relation with the stakeholders defined above (the number of stars means the relative importance of the common element).

Columns reflect the stakeholders and rows the technological elements (in terms of the technology and its context) that constitute the technological frameworks in terms of expectations of the perceived technology. Items were extracted from the author's experience as the most important in technology transfer projects (other factors were found by Akao (1990) and Linton et al. (1992)).

Element	Top manager	Transition	Pilot	Staff	Customer
Motivation	+++	+++	++	+	
Responsibility	++	++	+		
Background	+	+++	++	++	+
Cost	+++	+			++
Competitiveness	+++	+++	+	+	+
External image	+	++	+	+	++
Full use		++	++	++	
Range of products	+++	+++	+	+	++
Resources	+	++	++	+	+
Effort		++	+++	++	+++
Adoption time	++	+++	++	++	
Total values	19	26	17	13	12

The analysis of the table reflects several important facts:

- Motivation and responsibility decreases from inner to outer circles. The consequence is that only a reduced group of people considers the adoption process as a problem. In fact, the use of top down approach always makes difficult the involvement of lower levels (outer circles). Specific measures to increase consciousness of it should be created.

- Several aspects that managers consider important to evaluate the success or failure of the process are not considered relevant for customers or staff. The consequence is that decision making is not understood by outer levels that perceive an erratic behaviour in its management staff. Information on goals and progress should be available to the whole company.

- Initial perception of problems is different. Thus, expectations are also different. Customers only perceive visible aspects of the technology although internal staff are worried about how the technology is adopted. The use of QFD techniques (Akao, 1990) can help in the creation of a common understanding.

The knowledge of the differences in technological frameworks and their impact on the adoption process is the basis for setting up policies to reduce them. They should be enforced in the management of the transition.

5 EXPERIENCES FROM A CASE STUDY

Following the ideas expressed above, we can try to understand the problems found in technology transfer when two different institutions with very different frameworks interact in the transference of an immature technology: a department at the University as

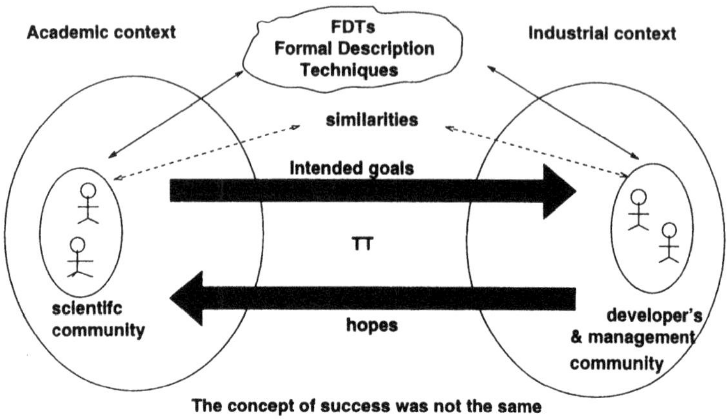

Figura 7: Scenario of FDT technology transfer

provider of a new technology based on formal methods and an industrial development group belonging to a large company adopting the technology provided by the university department. Technical aspects of this project have been recently reported ((León et al., 1994), (Yelmo et al., 1994)) and they will not be considered here.

We only mention that the involved technologies were LOTOS and SDL for the description of communication systems. The project spent three years under a controlled scenario. Figure 7 depicts the general framework of this experience.

Our experience relied on two basic assumptions: the technology was not mature enough to avoid feedback from providers; thus, an incremental model was used (León et a., 1994). On the other hand, to close up providers and receptors, a mixed transition group was created (both groups had similar technical background).

First of all, we will extrapolate several characteristics of the diffusion of new technologies in academic and industrial environments. Then, a preliminary analysis of technological frames and adoption profile will be summarized. Finally, some conclusions are presented.

5.1 Diffusion in academic environments

Academic environments are very complex social structures where faculty members perform very different tasks. We focus our attention on the R&D activity. It is usually characterized by a very free and poorly organized scenario. Professors have a large influence on the activities carried out in the departments by other people working there. In this sense, professors act as supporters of a new technology usually linked to their own professional careers. PhD or master students are more focused upon technical work with little or no motivation for technology transfer. In fact, they do not know industrial wants and needs except when they are filtered by their supervisors.

Typical problems found in this case concerning technological frameworks are:

- The use of the new technology does not appear as a consequence of problems in the development capability. The reasons are related with the publication of papers in congresses or journals or with PhD thesis related with the new technology.
- Costs are secondary. The use of a new technology is made because it has high potential to be developed, good research image or other causes.
- Poor understanding of industrial needs and wants. In some cases, the problem to be solved is idealized addressing symptoms and not causes.
- No motivation for diffusion except in professors when it is linked to funding research activities.

5.2 Diffusion in industrial environments: software development companies

Industrial environments are characterized by the adoption of new technologies in a top down manner triggered by losses of competitivity or by strategic objectives to increase user's satisfaction. In software development, failures in the introduction of formal methods are very well known and to reduce them was the basis of the commented case study.

Typical problems concerning technological frameworks in this case are:

- Software engineers on the receptor accept a top down approach and they feel that decisions are very far from their daily activity. Motivation is not evident.

  The consequence is that formal methods should be adopted through systematic planning of the adoption process because it cannot rely on the motivation of people. Motivation must be explicitly created.
- Managers trigger the process with a very limited knowledge of the technology involved. They trust in the experience of other companies in the same field or in academic or industrial champions.

  This situation forces us to consider managers as a very important target in the activity of transition groups. Obviously, they play a key role in the motivation of people.
- Technology is not only evaluated with respect to its technical soundness. For instance, verification capabilities of formal methods are not fully exploited in industrial practices. Main factor relies on its applicability and friendliness.
- The dynamics of the enterprise is based on the development of projects. Thus, people involved overvalue pilot cases and demos, and undervalue evaluation activities. It is related with the lack of clear rewarding mechanisms. This situation becomes crucial in project-driven organizations.

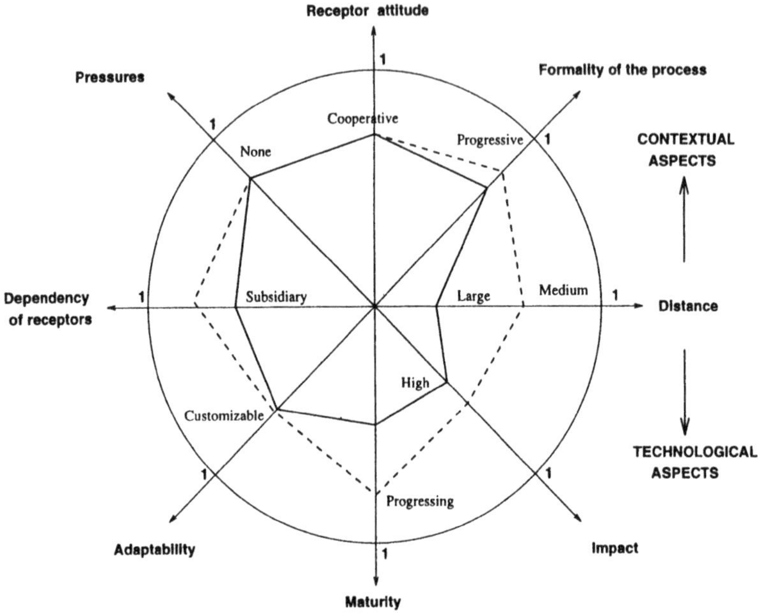

Figura 8: Adoption profile of FDT technology transfer case

5.3 Analysis of the adoption profile

It is interesting to compare the different contexts for adopting the **same** technology found in both cases. It is also interesting to comment that the background (telecommunication engineering) in both cases was practically the same.

The transference was done by creating a joint effort where circles of diffusion were composed of people belonging to both institutions. Figure 8 depicts the adoption profile of this case. SDL and LOTOS were considered separately.

A short rationale behind the coordinates follows:

- Receptor attitude. It is considered cooperative. Both providers and receptors participate in the transition group to transfer the technology.
- Process formality. An incremental multicycle model was used to adopt and to adapt the technology to the company's requirements.
- Dependency of receptors. During the first phase, receptors were subsidiary to providers. This role changed in the last stages of the adoption when knowledge of the technology was very similar between providers and receptors. With SDL no dependency appeared. In some sense, the borderline between providers and receptors was transparent.

- Pressures. This was a rather free experiment in the sense that no deadline to adopt the technology was required. In fact. evaluation could be positive or negative; then, progressive commitment strategy was followed. The industry participated with a horizontal division where exploratory actions could be carried out as a part of its mission.

- Impact. Formal description techniques have high impact on the development life cycle. They take months (or years) to be mastered and they affect development projects as a whole.

- Maturity. Although the theoretical basis for LOTOS and SDL was known before starting the transference project (notation is a standard, prototypes tools were available and the capabilities of the reasoning framework have been extensively published), no industrial experience was available nor the applicability to large communication systems properly assessed. In this case, FDTs were in a progressing stage. Maturity degree of LOTOS and SDL is not the same (LOTOS is clearly less mature and provided by the academic group).

- Adaptability. FDT can be adopted in many ways. In this case, links with preexistent software development technologies were considered crucial. Then, customization of the technology was a very important goal.

- Distance. The industrial partner was using SDL (although automatic code generation was not used). Good implementation support and project management was available. LOTOS was not used at all.

The analysis of the shape exhibited by the profile indicates a good case for technology transfer with high probabilities of success. No special problems were anticipated except those derived from the technology itself (i.e. impact and distance). Risks with LOTOS were clearly higher than with SDL.

5.4 The analysis of technological frameworks

In spite of the relatively good adoption profile presented in the above section, the technological frameworks were not the same. This situation offers a complementary perspective to interpret the difficulties found.

Figure 9 summarizes the different perceptions of both institutions on FDT (Formal description techniques) and the role they played during the adoption process.

These incongruities made it difficult to obtain a common view of the degree of success or failure. As an example of the problems in the interfaces, the transition group (a mixed working group) needs to dialogue with top management (from the industry). Their motivations were very different and the concept of success was also different.

To the transition group, FDTs is a valuable technology to gain confidence in the quality of software products based on the powerful reasoning framework. Top management

ACEDEMIC GROUP	INDUSTRIAL GROUP
Most important aspect is the verification &validation	Important aspect is to increase the formality in the process
Emphasis on tools	Emphasis on methodology
Tool integration	Method integration
Pure use of FDTs	Complementary use of FDTs
Interest in academic outputs	Interest in internal dissemination
Overoptimisic mentality	Overpessimistic mentality
Recognition by the scientific community	Recognition by top management
Experimentation know-how	Consolidation practices
Emphasis on quality advantages	Emphasis on cost/time savings

Figura 9: Inconsistencies between providers and receptors

considered that this is also a way to increase the quality but relying on its merging with current practices.

6 CONCLUSIONS

Diffusion of technology cannot be understood without considering the technological frameworks exhibited by all stakeholders involved.

As this paper has analyzed, they could be very different and not shared. The consequence is that the technology perceived by each stakeholder group differs. We have postulated that this is one of the most important causes in order to understand the failures in adopting software technologies.

Several mechanisms were proposed in this paper to address these undesirable effects:

- Analyze the technology transfer profile exhibited by the receptor organization before starting the adoption process. From them, the planning of the adoption process trying to reduce the identified inconsistencies could be done.
- Create circles of diffusion with well defined technological frameworks. In other words, define the technologies perceived by all them. The problem is not that people have different conceptions about the same technology, the problem is that they do not consider it as an input for reducing the problems.
- Share the technological frameworks among all people involved. It does not imply building up a single one; this is not possible. The goal is to be sure that everybody can understand the others before starting the adoption process itself. Interfaces should be clearly stated. At the end of the process, frameworks will be closer.

- Adapt the transition process to the characteristics of stakeholders by defining reachable goals. Incremental technology transfer models seem appropriate to have time to re-create new technological frameworks when technology is not stable.
- Create observatories to evaluate how the technological frameworks have changed and to propose restructuring of circles of diffusion. This is the basis for being ready for future adoptions.

The experience used as an example demonstrates that technological frames are very important to understand the reasons and problems in accepting a new technology and a basis for reducing those problems even when adoption profiles do not present bad shapes. Nevertheless, much more experience should be collected to be able to extrapolate the results to other scenarios. This will be our future work.

7 REFERENCES

1. Akao, J. (1990): *Quality Function Deployment. Integrating customer requirements into product design.* Productivity Press. Cambridge, Mass.

2. Bergman, L., Ohlund, S.E. (1995): Development of an assessment tool to assist in the implementation of concurrent engineering. *CE 95 Conference.* Mc Lean Virginia. USA.

3. Fowler, P., Levine, L. (1993): *A conceptual framework for software technology transition.* Technical Report CMU-SEI-93 TR-31. December 1993.

4. León, G. Carracedo, J., Yelmo, J.C., Sanchez, C., Moreno, J.C., Gil, J.J., Carrasco, F.J. (1994): An industrial experience of using an incremental model of technology transfer of formal development methods. In (Ed. Levine) *Diffusion, transfer and implementation of information technology.* IFIP Transactions A-45. North-Holland, 1994.

5. Levine, L. (Ed.) (1994): *Diffusion, transfer and implementation of information technology.* IFIP Transactions A-45. North-Holland, 1994.

6. Linton, L., Hall, D., Hutchinson, K., Hoffman, D., Evanczuk, S., Sullivan, P. (1992): First principles of concurrent engineering. A competitive strategy for product development. *CALS/Concurrent Engineering Working Group. Electronic Systems.* May 1992.

7. Orlikowski, W.J. and Gash: Technological frame: making sense of information technology in organizations. *ACM Transactions on Information Systems.* Vol. 12. April 1994. pp 174-207.

8. Saneidian, Kuzaro (1995): SEI capability maturity model's impact on contractors. *IEEE Computer.* January 1995. Vol. 28. No. 1. pp 16-27.

9. Shuster, H.D. (1994): The mechanics of cultural change: mobilizing management transformation theory and putting into practice. *2nd International Conference on Integrated Logistics and Concurrent Engineering.* Montpellier. Feb. 1994. pp 23-33.

10. Yelmo, J.C., Carrasco, F.J., Sanchez, C., J.J. Gil, Ramos, C., Felipe, M.I. (1994): FDT based development of an interworking unit between LANs and X.25 networks. *FORTE'94.* Bern (Switzerland). October 1994

8 BIOGRAPHY

Prof. Gonzalo León received a phD in Telecommunication Engineering in 1982 from the Technical University of Madrid where he is full professor in the Telematics Department since 1990.

His experience and interest in technology transfer is focused on models for the introduction of immature technologies, basically formal methods, from academia to industrial companies in the telecommunications sector. He is the author of several papers in this field.

He has lectured on technology transfer in graduate courses and he was also responsible for the design of a course on technology transfer in the COMETT programme of the EU. He belongs to the IFIP WG8.6 on Diffusion, Transfer and Adoption of Information Technology where he serves as vice-chairman.

9

Implementation planning for information systems: promoting the transition with a communication strategy

T. McMaster & R. T. Vidgen
Information Systems Research Centre
University of Salford
M5 4WT
UK
Tel : +44 161 745 5000
Fax : +44 161 745 5559
Email T.McMaster@mcs.salford.ac.uk
R.T.Vidgen@mcs.salford.ac.uk

Abstract

Too many information systems fail, and sometimes this is due to poorly planned, or unplanned implementation procedures. We discuss the meaning of failure and the role of design in this context, and we propose an implementation planning model which takes soft human issues into account. Our model borrows tools and methods from the marketing domain, and particularly from marketing research disciplines which have a long tradition of investigating qualitative issues for the purpose of promoting new products and services.

Keywords

Information systems, implementation, technology transfer, design, failure

1 INTRODUCTION

Who can count the cost of Information Systems failures? If Lyytinen and Hirschheim (1987) are in any way accurate, at least half of all systems fail, and very likely an even higher proportion than that. At worst, these failures have resulted in the loss of lives, as was the case in the failure of the London Ambulance Service Dispatch System in

1992 (Robinson, 1994). Even in less extreme circumstances however, IS failures represent an enormous waste of an organization's resources. To quantify this in terms of hard cash is not easy if indeed it is possible or even desirable. However when we consider that the 500 or so Local Government Authorities in England and Wales for example, a mere pixel in the bigger cross-sectorial, trans-national picture, allocated more than an estimated one thousand million pounds to IT expenditure in 1993 alone (Miles, 1990), we can begin to see that globally we are looking at a problem of enormous proportion.

Some of these failures are due to poorly planned or unplanned implementation procedures (Lyytinen & Hirschheim, p. 291), though we recognize (and we caution others to do so), that viewing the implementation of information systems as a separate activity to information systems design (ISD), may well be inviting or inventing the very problem which it seeks to alleviate. Nevertheless despite more than two decades of observation and insight into the design and development processes of IS by researchers, consultants and practitioners, and in particular by those associated with what has come to be known as the 'Scandinavian Tradition' (cf. Bansler, 1989, Bjerknes & Bratteteig, 1989, Bødker et al., 1989, Ehn & Kyng, 1989, Grønbæk, 1990, etc.), where much emphasis has been placed on the importance of user-participation in IS design and development, still individual managers too often resolve to build or buy new systems without consulting or involving users and other stakeholders. When the subsequent implementation process fails, no one seems more surprised than they do

This paper proposes that including what we have chosen to call a *communication strategy* as a core component of an implementation plan, may greatly facilitate successful technology transfer into organizational settings. We believe that such a strategy can help to reduce the risks and propensities for such systems to fail. For one thing, it involves the would-be implementor developing a dialogical relationship with the intended user or other stakeholders (late in the process though this may be), and for another, it focuses the attentions of those involved on the implementation process itself. These may be the minimum requirements for the successful implementation of any new technology into the workplace.

We use the term 'implementation' in this paper rather broadly. This includes decisions and actions which are intended to lead to, and are directly concerned with the transfer and the adoption of information (and other) technologies into organizational settings. This may include the introduction of 'new' technology into technologically mature organizations, for example a new database application into a situation where database technologies have already been accepted, routinized and infused (Saga and Zmud, 1994). On the other hand it might also mean the introduction of new or even novel technologies into technologically naive organizations. We may speculate as to whether or not it may be easier to introduce new technical systems into the one rather than the other, but what we do know is that introducing new information technology, even into professional IT departments, can and does fail (Kautz and McMaster, 1994). Generally speaking therefore, it would appear that the technical competencies of stakeholders may have little direct bearing on the success or otherwise of the project, and it may well be that problems with new technology are more often than not, problems of a non-technical nature.

We make some references in this paper to a case study which has been reported in more detail elsewhere (McMaster et al., 1995, and Vidgen & McMaster, 1995). This concerns an attempt to introduce a new information and control system into the car parking arrangements in a British University. Clearly the wider organization consists of many highly-skilled individuals, some of whom enjoy a high level of technical fluency in their professional roles, though this is not necessarily true in their more fleeting roles in the abstracted car park organization. For the purposes of this paper, we regard the car park sub-system of the wider organization with its various stakeholders (managers, administrators, car park attendants, users, etc.) to be an 'organization' in its own right.

The main argument in this paper may be expressed quite simply: technical systems sometimes fail due to poorly planned or unplanned implementation processes. By failure, we mean simply that for one reason or another, the intentions for the system have been abandoned before it has become, in the words of Saga and Zmud (ibid.), embedded in the organization's work systems. We contend that system failures are sometimes due to a failure by the dominant coalition (this may be an individual manager) to recognize and take into account the fact that there are social consequences associated with introducing technical artefacts into organizations, and that these consequences can assist or impede, or even destroy the envisioned outcome.

We argue that a shift is needed towards a wider concept of design. The traditional IS design perspective reflects a rather narrow technical and 'product-oriented' view (such as that described by Floyd, 1987), while we propose that a 'customer-oriented' view which encompasses social, political, ethical, aesthetic and other issues (Stolterman, 1992), is both necessary and desirable. We present a prototype implementation model to assist this process, at the heart of which lies a communication strategy. To develop this, we borrow ideas from soft systems methodology (SSM), and from marketing disciplines. Since marketing has long been concerned with factors such as customer satisfaction, value and quality, we feel that the IS community might benefit from ideas imported from this domain. This work is formative, but some theory testing is currently underway.

2 IS FAILURE AND IS DESIGN

2.1 Information systems failure

Failure is a qualitative, subjective judgement, and just as difficult a concept to pin down as the notion of quality itself, with which it shares certain features. For example, failure is described by Bignell and Fortune (1984) as an assessment of the outcome of an activity which is based upon the values of the person making the judgement.

Service quality is similarly described by Parasuraman, et al. (1985) as a comparison between expectations and performance, and evaluations which involve outcomes and processes. Just as quality may mean different things to different people (cf. Garvin, 1984), so too, what is seen as failure by one person, may not be regarded as failure by another. Just to further complicate the issue, what may have been seen as failure yesterday, may not be regarded as failure today, highlighting the notion that failure needs to be viewed in a historical context. Like quality, failure is a construct which is both elusive and indistinct.

According to Lyytinen and Hirschheim (1987), IS failures can be classified into one of four types. These are *correspondence failure*, *process failure*, *interaction failure* and *expectation failure*. Correspondence failure means that design objectives have not been met (tending to reflect a management view of failure). Process failure relates to the ISD process where budgetary, time or other resource allocations have overrun to the point where any benefits expected from the proposed system have been negated, or where the allocated resources do not result in a workable system. Interaction failure is an argument that the low-level use of the system can be interpreted as failure, and expectation failure is simply that the system has failed to meet the expectations of at least one stakeholder group. On the basis that the expectations of *any* stakeholder group are not met, then the situation can be regarded as a failure. Lyytinen and Hirschheim (ibid.) take the view that the first three classes of failure may be subsumed by expectation failure, since this is essentially a superset of the others.

We now turn our attention to the relationship between design, and IS failures.

2.2 Design and IS failure

Design in the context of information systems has a variety of meanings. Clare and Stutely (1995) for example describe (system) design as a stage in the development life cycle which produces as its deliverable 'detailed system specifications' (pp. 213-214). These consist of input details (devices, screen layouts, forms etc.), output details (ditto), database details, and computer and associated manual procedures such as algorithms, program structures, process diagrams and data diagrams. This seems positively liberal when we read that programming - an activity stage in the IS development process, is about designing machine behaviour that can assist or even replace humans in intellectual tasks (Hoc et al, 1990, p.3). Design in formal structured methods such as SSADM for example, aims to construct modules which 'mirror' the real world (Downs et al., 1988, p. 7), the implication being that the designer is somehow a detached and impartial observer, skilled at making objective pronouncements on the nature of organizational reality.

Each of these examples reflects a hard 'product-oriented' view of information systems (Floyd, 1987) which is deeply rooted in the positivist traditions of Western European thought. From this perspective, design is reduced to a mechanistic, efficiency-driven set of choices related to machine components (including people), where system development projects are nothing more than solutions built to repair a malfunctioning reality (Stolterman, 1992).

We feel that we must reject such views which assume an objective reality 'out there' that can be measured using modern scientific techniques and methods. Instead, we subscribe to a constructivist philosophy, whose proponents, including for example Floyd (1992), Dahlbom (1992) and Burstall (1992) among others, acknowledge the active role which we bring to our perception and understanding of reality. The emphasis in constructivist thought, is on the observer constituting reality, and inventing suitable descriptions (Floyd, 1992). This means that 'choice' becomes an important ingredient in the process, and there is therefore greater scope for design, and design decisions. Stolterman (ibid.) uses the term 'design process' to describe a highly complex kind of human activity concerned with meeting the demands of factors such as economy, function, aesthetics, ethics, politics, environment and others, while Schön (1983) describes design as a reflective conversation with the situation.

We prefer this broader notion of design, because it allows us to consider stakeholder factors such as feelings, concerns and emotions, and to design systems and implementation strategies with much more care and consideration for humans. From such a perspective we view the classes of information systems failure detailed by Lyytinen and Hirschheim (ibid.), each as design failures. 'Correspondence failure' is admitted by those authors as design failure, but 'process failure' may also be seen as a design failure. If for example, we were to instruct a graphic designer to produce a letter-head for us, for £500 in one month's time, to be later told that it would cost £1000 and take two months, we may well consider this to be a serious design problem. Design should also incorporate resource constraints where these are previously specified and agreed.

'Interaction failure' may also be seen as design failure, since systems are not designed *not* to be used. The subsequent low use or non-use of the system may therefore be considered as falling short in certain design considerations. This is supported by Ovaska (1991), who argues that 'usability problems' can be solved by better design and development efforts, and Bødker (Bødker, 1987 quoted in Ovaska, ibid.) has stated that the user interface cannot be seen independently of the goal of the user, or of the other conditions of the use activity. Since information systems are designed to be used, then the failure to use them, is a failure in design.

'Expectation failure' suggests that no consideration was given to the needs of at least one stakeholder group. This may be due to a tendency for traditional system development approaches to consider users as a single homogenous group. A stakeholder perspective however, recognises that the system will affect and be affected by sometimes a large number of groups, each with their own sets of needs and concerns. Our model for designing an implementation strategy includes the explicit identification of as complete a set of stakeholders as possible, and one of its aims is to help each of them construct appropriate expectations for the proposed new system.

For us, design is a complex set of considered planning activities, whose interests include stakeholder concerns and other soft issues including the 'use' of information systems and their associated technologies. Any issue which can affect the success of technology transfer is for us a legitimate area for the application of design decisions, and we would argue that in these areas 'failing to design' may be 'designing to fail'.

3 RESEARCH MOTIVATIONS

In the introduction we stated that some at least of the many putative IS failures may be attributable to a failure to design (plan) the implementation process with sufficient rigour or thoroughness. We undertook a mini-survey to test this assumption, and we also draw on our recent experiences of a case study. These have served as motivators for this paper, and we present brief details in this section.

3.1 Survey

In January 1995, ten local authority IT managers were contacted, and of these eight agreed to discuss with us their IS/IT implementation practices. The ten contiguous District Councils used to make up what was Greater Manchester County, prior to its dissolution by a former Thatcher administration. This is significant, because the very close relationships which the various authorities in the conurbation once had have not disappeared, and there are still strong links, some informal, between the districts. One such forum is known as the Greater Manchester IT Group. This comprises the ten respective IT Department Managers, who meet approximately every three months to discuss issues of common interest. The importance of this as far as our purposes are concerned, is that because of such arrangements, there may be a tendency towards homogenous problem-solving strategies - a kind of 'groupthink' (Janis, 1971), which in turn is likely to limit our ability to generalize from observations and interpretations based solely on this group. On the other hand, it does provide us with some insight into practices in a specific type of organization.

A number of semi-structured interviews took place. Six of these were conducted by telephone, generally lasting not more than ten or fifteen minutes, and two were conducted face-to-face, with a duration of between twenty and thirty minutes. The interviewees are all senior managers within their respective Councils' IT Departments.

Our respondents confirmed our suspicions that traditionally little real planning for the implementation of new systems has taken place. The extent to which it had, was generally limited to a simple incremental stage model, where each step in the process represents for example a unit of time, a department in the organization, a module of the system, or some loose combination of these. This might take a form such as, implementing a module of the system in the accounts section by July, then into another section by August, for example. A product-centred view of the process prevails, with recognition that training may often be required by some 'users', prior to a new system going live. Training issues are possibly the only people matters to enter the equation, but even this has a technically-driven, positivist flavour to it, with managers deciding who receives training, and when..

All of our respondents were concerned about what they felt was a need to improve their traditional practices, as government legislation forces them to adapt to a competitive environment. Compulsory competitive tendering (CCT) will mean that they will no longer be the sole providers of IT/IS services operating in a monopolistic culture. Instead they will have to win contracts from their existing customers, very likely against highly professional and very determined competitors.

3.2 Case study

In 1993, an Institute of Higher Education in the UK purchased a new automatic access control system for each of its three main car parking areas. Despite winning a Gold Award, four weeks after becoming operational during which there were 4 accidents, the system was shut down. The system has a number of unconventional features, including proximity cards, retractable steel bollards, and an 'invisible' card reader which we briefly describe.

- *Proximity card technology*

These are cards that resemble 'magic wands' in the sense that they need only be waved around close to the 'reader', rather than inserted into a slot in order to operate the system. The cards each contain a unique code which has been allocated to the card holder. When this is presented to the system, a check is made against a database image which is downloaded periodically from a PC to the site computer, via modem links, for validation. The system also includes a more conventional 'slot' into which a token may be inserted, for casual users or visitors.

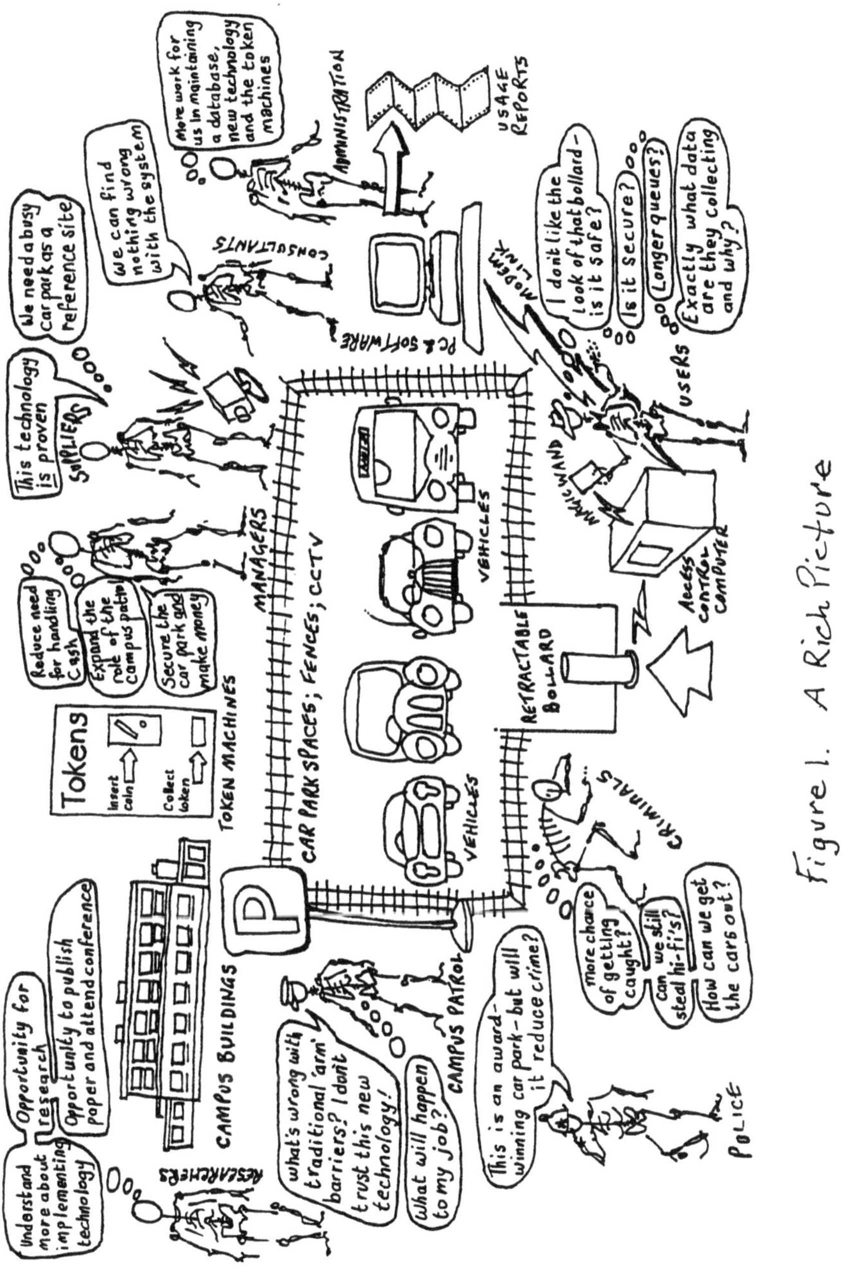

Figure 1: *A Rich Picture*

- *Retractable steel telescopic bollards*

These are unusual compared with the more conventional 'arm' type barrier with which most drivers are familiar. When retracted, these bollards are flush with the ground. Related to these, there are three induction loops embedded in each of the access roads, and these are designed to detect the presence of motor vehicles in the system. These are critical to the safe operation of the system, for if a vehicle were unfortunate enough to stall over the bollard for example, its detection on the loop ensures that the bollard remains retracted.

- *Hidden card reader*

The card reader is housed within a brick structure, and is therefore not visible to the user. There is a metal plate on the brick housing which indicates where the proximity card should be generally waved about, but there is no direct access to the reader, which picks up the code programmed into each card. The system has other unusual features, but those which we have described are most relevant for our purposes, since they form the main interface between the users and the system.

Within four weeks of implementing this system, there were four accidents which involved vehicles colliding with the bollards, causing damage to the vehicles. Following the final accident the systems were shut down by the organization's managers, and they have remained so, since. The system is almost universally regarded as a 'failure' by car park attendants (Campus Patrol), staff and student users, by administrators and by managers in the organization. We were curious.

Briefly, we found a number of interesting factors including:

- significant stakeholders had serious concerns about the system (car park attendants were worried how it would affect their jobs, users were worried about the safety of this novel (radically different) technology for example);
- no attempts were made to identify or address these concerns;
- stakeholders were not involved in design process;
- misgivings expressed by a campus patrol representative were ignored;
- no attempt was made to promote benefits of the system, nor was any explanation given for the choice of technical components;
- misuse of system (tailgating) by users was encouraged by Campus Patrol staff, and had become routine practice.

Since we advocate in our planning framework the use of rich picture techniques for stakeholder identification, we include a rich picture of the case (figure 1), which shows the principal stakeholders, and some of their feelings and assumptions, in speech and thought bubbles. From these, conflicts and other organizational relationships between stakeholders can be identified. No great significance should be made of the fact that in our illustration, the car park appears as the central focus of the situation. We do not suggest that the technical system is to be considered as more important than other components of the diagram, but this composition was helpful, since it allowed us to think about the situation using the car park as the focus for our study (Vidgen and McMaster, 1995).

4 IMPLEMENTATION PLANNING FRAMEWORK

4.1 Implementation planning

Implementing a new system needs to be a designed (planned) activity. Consideration needs to be given for example, to the installation of both the hardware and the software components, site commissioning, and system changeover processes (Yeates, et al., 1994). Yet, important as these things may be, they are not the only concerns, nor are they we suspect, overly-neglected aspects of systems implementation in any event. What we are interested in, are those elusive and unpredictable factors of human concern.

4.2 An implementation planning model

The model we propose (figure 2) by no means rejects incremental, staged introduction processes. We see it rather as adding a further, human dimension to it, through the process of developing and including a communication strategy.

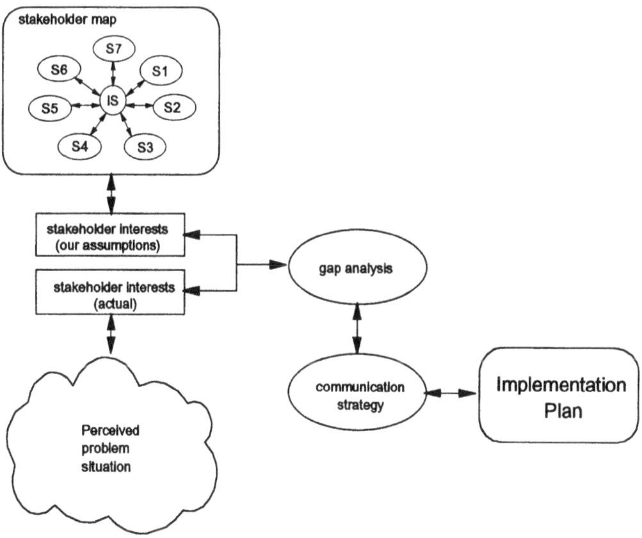

Figure 2: *An implementation planning model*

The purpose of the strategy is to promote the benefits, and eliminate or reduce fears and concerns about the system which may be unique to particular groups. This strategy aims to address the needs of all identified stakeholder groups, and in order to accomplish this purpose will give consideration to the content as well as to the mode of delivery. For example, the Campus Patrol officers were concerned about the effect of the technology on their jobs, and it would have been appropriate for management to address this issue. There was (and is) no intention that the technology should replace any of these staff, but that their roles might be extended to allow them to actually 'patrol' the campus, instead of confining them to car park access points. Since this is a relatively small group, direct briefings by senior managers may have been an appropriate mode of delivery, and may have allowed opportunities for concerns to be aired. Instead, there was no communication on the subject, and the group were left to speculate about the precise nature of the role of the new technology, and how it might affect their jobs.

The communication strategy might equally be called a 'marketing information strategy', since it performs a marketing function. Marketing, put very simply, seeks to identify consumer needs through research activities, and to influence the consumer's wants and demands by providing effective satisfactions for those needs. Similarly, the communication strategy in our implementation plan, seeks to provide satisfactions to emotional and informational needs related to the social impact of the system, which have been identified through a research process. Since each stakeholder group will have different needs, the communication strategy therefore consists not of a single plan, but a **set** of plans, each of which is targeted at a specific group.

We give a brief description of components in the model, starting with stakeholder identification and analysis.

Stakeholder identification

Stakeholders, according to Mitroff and Linstone (1993) are 'any individual, group, organization, institution that can affect as well as be affected by an individual's, group's, organization's, or institution's policy or policies'. In order to identify them, we propose the use of rich picture techniques. The rich picture is a Soft Systems Methodology (SSM) technique that allows a complex problem situation to be expressed informally, including relationships and value judgements, and they are helpful in gaining an heterogeneous understanding of the situation. It is intended to be a creative expression of possibly conflicting viewpoints rather than a representation of some 'objective reality'. In this respect it reflects a constructivist view, which is in line with our own standpoint. There is no formal notation for the technique, although some conventions (such as crossed swords to indicate conflict, for example), have been used. This representation of a situation assists us in identifying the stakeholders.

Stakeholder interest analysis (our assumptions)

Stakeholders are identified and represented diagramatically in a stakeholder map. This is represented in our model (figure 2) as S1, S2 etc. The analyst, together with project team members analyze stakeholder interests and surface the assumptions that the project team consider the stakeholders to have. These are the assumptions that need to hold if the IS implementation is to be successful. They are **not** necessarily the assumptions that 'real' stakeholders hold.

Stakeholder interest analysis (actual)

Mitroff and Linstone (1993, p. 144) provide a matrix against which stakeholder assumptions can be plotted. The vertical continuum maps the degree of certainty of the assumption, and the horizontal, the importance. For those assumptions which we think are important and uncertain, the project team might wish to undertake a deeper exploration of the problem situation. For instance, in our example of the car park, the project team might assume that car park users are a homogeneous group whose interests are personal security, and vehicle security. Investigation in the 'problem situation' (figure 1) might lead to the identification of a number of sub-groups such as car drivers, motor-cyclists, coach drivers, staff, students, and visitors. They may also have divergent interests. Membership of a stakeholder group is not necessarily exclusive, and individuals may belong to more than one sub-group.

Stakeholders may have beliefs and attitudes that are not congruent with the assumptions adopted by the project team. Problem situations tend to be messy since they are populated by individuals; our neat stakeholder map might prove to be a sterile and banal over-simplification. It is in this area that some of the techniques of marketing research, a mature discipline with a wide range of methods, might be fruitfully deployed.

Methods and Tools

Qualitative techniques used in marketing research provide a wide range of methods and tools, including 'depth interviews', and 'projective' techniques for example. These are particularly useful tools when the use of direct structured questionnaires may not be possible, either because the interviewee is unwilling, or is unable to respond. This may be because the questions adversely affect their self-perception or prestige, or concern motivations that they do not understand, or cannot verbalize (Tull and Hawkins, 1993, pp. 441-442). Such examples may be particularly relevant in circumstances where IS implementation is on the agenda.

Depth interviews may be conducted with individuals, mini-groups (4 or 5 people) or larger, 'focus' groups (8 to 12 people). Each has strengths. Individual depth interviews are useful when detailed probing of individual attitudes, behaviour or needs is required, where the subject matter is of an emotionally charged nature, or where the interviews are with people on the subject of their jobs (Tull & Hawkins, p. 443). Again, these are all issues of relevance to IS professionals. Mini-group interviews do not allow the detailed investigation of confidential or highly sensitive issues, but do allow detailed probing of 'fairly' sensitive issues to a substantial depth. Focus groups are particularly valuable in establishing the vocabulary as a preliminary step to questionnaire design, and in the determination of attitudes towards a particular issue.

Depth interviews make use of a variety of questioning techniques including 'laddering', 'hidden-issue questioning' and 'symbolic questioning'. Laddering involves respondents identifying attributes (usually of a brand, but of course we envisage a modified application to IS objects). Attributes are then probed to determine their meaning and significance. These reasons are then probed, and so forth. The purpose of this technique is to uncover the 'network of meaning' associated with the object or concept (Tull & Hawkins, p. 442).

Hidden-issue questions are designed to uncover individuals' feelings about sensitive issues, and the responses are analysed to determine whether or not there may be common underlying themes across a range of respondents.

Symbolic questions reveal feelings about issues by asking the respondents to describe the 'opposites' of the object under investigation. Feelings expressed about the opposite, tell a great deal about feelings toward the object itself, but which might be unlikely to emerge through direct questioning.

Projective techniques offer a repertoire of tools and methods which generally have been adapted from clinical psychology. These include association techniques such as free word association, and successive word association, and their value is often in 'positioning' the product (system). Completion techniques, such as sentence completion and story completion require the respondent to provide the finishing touches to an incomplete stimulus. The responses provide valuable attitudinal information.

Construction techniques are similar to completion techniques, except that less structure is provided to the respondent. These may include cartoon characters where 'thought bubbles' and 'speech bubbles' are filled in, in response to a stimulus. The rationale is that the speech bubble is likely to draw out the public stance the respondent would take on a particular issue, while the 'thought' bubble is likely to contain the private view.

There are many techniques available for qualitative research, and these few examples merely serve to illustrate the rich and varied source of tools available to IS professionals, from the marketing research domain. These may be especially useful when an understanding of the attitudes and the feelings of the stakeholders may be vital to the success of the introduction process.

Gap analysis

The 'gap' may be defined as the discrepancy between the implementor's assumptions about stakeholder attitudes in relation to the system, and the actual attitudes of the stakeholders which will be determined from the research activity. These differences may be substantial. Analysis of the gap will result in the identification of objectives for the communication plan. Gap analysis theory is reported to have originated with Weber (1976) for the purpose of guiding the search for growth and opportunity (Kotler, 1994, p.369). Gap analysis techniques have been used more recently for the purposes of improving communication and control processes in the delivery of service quality (Zeithaml, et al., 1988), which, it might be argued, is precisely the business we are in anyway. Our suggestion, is that the gap can provide the directions, the aims and the objectives for our communication efforts with the stakeholders.

Communication strategy

The communication strategy is a set of plans designed to eliminate, or at least reduce as far as possible, the gap in relation to each stakeholder. It does this by informing, influencing and promoting the benefits of the system in an appropriate and timely manner. It will seek to allay fears and concerns which the stakeholders may hold. In addition to the informational content of each plan, it will also consider the means of delivering that information to the target group, and the time frame for its delivery. Advertising, a mature sub-domain of marketing, offers a range of tools and practices from which IS practitioners might benefit.

5 CONCLUSIONS

We have indicated that this paper addresses a certain kind of problem, where decisions to acquire a new method or system have already been taken, and where intended users have not been participants in the pre-implementation processes, but how we might ask, can this happen?

Organization theory suggests that this kind of situation might easily occur where the personal interests of the decision-maker do not concur with the interests of the organization (Robbins, 1990), though it has been argued (Knights & Murray, 1994) that 'organizations' have no goals or interests, and that individual aspirations for power and prestige are sold under the guise of organizational direction. Divergent interests mean that the personal interests of individual manager are likely to take precedence over organizational interests (even if these exist), and that motivations behind at least some decisions may be therefore more closely related to issues of personal career enhancement, impressing superiors or peers, or simply plain 'technology pushing', than to organizational goal attainment. This tends to be particularly true in highly bureaucratic organizations such as local government, because excessive bureaucracy encourages 'goal displacement'; the substitution of organizational goals by sub-unit or personal goals (Robbins, ibid., pp. 314-315). In such situations we would hardly expect to see any great regard for users opinions or feelings. This may help to explain the seeming propensity for technology pushing without consulting intended users in some local authorities in the UK, (cf. Ramsey et al, 1992, Hales & O'Hara, 1993 and Kautz & McMaster, 1994), but we do not suggest that such practices are confined to this sector, nor indeed do we suggest that there are no good practices to be found here.

We believe our implementation model can help to reduce the risks of failure, even at such a late stage, because it requires dialogue with, and the involvement of stakeholders. So far however, our proposition is formative, and research is needed in the application of the model in order to illuminate areas that we have perhaps taken for granted, or that we assume are not problematical. The organization in which the case was interpreted, is about to attempt to re-implement the 'failed' car park system, and one of this paper's authors is providing advice to senior management who have agreed to employ a strategy based upon our model. It is too early to report on the process, except to say that stakeholder analyses have taken place and a number of briefing sessions have been undertaken with Campus Patrol staff, administrators and other staff so far. These have attempted to address the respective concerns of the stakeholders, and to educate and inform them about the role that the system is intended to play in the long term security strategy for the campus, and how they are likely to be affected by it. In addition, a draft document has been drawn up which will form the basis of the communications strategy with users, and the intention is that they will individually contacted through the internal mail system. An article has been prepared for the campus newspaper, and a help-line is to be set up. We are currently waiting for a number of physical modifications to be carried out, before the next stage of the re-implementation process can take place, and we look forward to reporting the process and outcomes in due course.

6 REFERENCES

Bansler, J., (1989) 'Systems development research in Scandinavia: three theoretical schools', in *Scandinavian Journal of Information Systems*, Vol. 1, pp. 3-20.

Bignell, Victor, and Fortune, Joyce, (1984), *Understanding Systems Failures*, Manchester University Press in association with the Open University.

Bjerknes, G., and Bratteteig, T., (1989), 'Florence in Wonderland: System Development with Nurses', in G. Bjerknes, P. Ehn and M. Kyng (Eds.) *Computers and Democracy, A Scandinavian Challenge*, Avebury, pp. 279-295

Bødker, Susanne, (1987), 'Through the Interface -- A Human Activity Approach to User Interface Design', Ph.D. Thesis, DAIMI PB-224, Aarhus University.

Bødker, S., Ehn, P., Kammersgaard, J., Kyng, M., and Sunblad, Y., (1989), 'A UTOPIAN Experience: On Design of Powerful Computer-Based Tools for Skilled Graphic Workers', in G. Bjerknes, P. Ehn and M. Kyng (Eds.) *Computers and Democracy, A Scandinavian Challenge*, Avebury, pp. 251-278.

Burstall, Rodney, M., (1992), 'Computing: Yet Another Reality Construction', in Floyd, C., Züllighoven, H., Budde, R., and Keil-Slawik, R., (Eds.), *Software Development and Reality Construction*, Springer-Verlag, pp. 45-51.

Clare, Chris, and Stuteley, Gordon, (1995), *Information Systems - Strategy to Design*, Chapman Hall.

Dahlbom, Bo, (1992), 'The Idea that Reality is Socially Constructed', in Floyd, C., Züllighoven, H., Budde, R., and Keil-Slawik, R., (Eds.), *Software Development and Reality Construction*, Springer-Verlag, pp. 101-126.

Dahlbom, Bo, and Mathiassen, Lars, (1993) *Computers in Context: The Philosophy and Practice of Systems Design*, NCC Blackwell, Cambridge, MA & Oxford UK.

Downs, E., Clare, P., Coe, I., (1988) *Structured Systems Analysis and Design Method: Application and Context*, Prentice Hall.

Ehn, P., and Kyng, M., (1989), 'The Collective Resource Approach to Systems Design', in G. Bjerknes, P. Ehn and M. Kyng (Eds.) *Computers and Democracy, A Scandinavian Challenge*, Avebury, pp. 17-57.

Floyd, C., (1987), 'Outline of a Paradigm Change in Software Engineering', in G. Bjerknes, P. Ehn and M. Kyng (Eds.) *Computers and Democracy, A Scandinavian Challenge*, Avebury, pp. 191-210.

Floyd, C., (1992), 'Human Questions in Computer Science', in Floyd, C., Züllighoven, H., Budde, R., and Keil-Slawik, R., (Eds.), *Software Development and Reality Construction*, Springer-Verlag, pp. 15-27.

Garvin, David, A., (1984) 'What does "Product Quality" Really Mean?' in *Sloan Management Review*, Fall, 1984, pp. 25-43.

Grønbæk, Kaj, (1990), 'Supporting Active User Involvement in Prototyping.', in *Scandinavian Journal of Information Systems*, Vol. 2, pp. 3-24.

Hales, Mike, and O'Hara, Peter, (1993), 'Strengths and Weaknesses of Participation: Learning by Doing in Local Government', in Green, E., Owen, J., and Pain, D., (Eds.), *Gendered by Design? Information Technology and Office Systems*, Taylor and Francis, pp. 153-172.

Hoc, J., -M., Green, T., R., G., Samurçay, R., and Gilmore, D., J., (1990), *Psychology of Programming*, Academic Press, London, San Diego, New York, Boston, Sydney, Tokyo

Janis, Irving, L., (1971), 'Groupthink: The Desperate Drive for Consensus at Any Cost', in *Psychology Today Magazine*, Sussex Publishers, Inc.

Kautz, Karlheinz, and McMaster, Tom, (1994), 'The Failure to Introduce System Development Methods: A Factor-Based Analysis.', in Levine, L., (ed.), *Diffusion, Transfer and Implementation of Information Technology*, Elsevier / North Holland, Amsterdam, London, New York, Tokyo. pp. 275-287.

Knights, David, and Murray, Fergus, (1994), *Managers Divided: Organisation Politics and Information Technology Management*, Wiley.

Kotler, Philip, (1988), *Marketing Management: Analysis, Planning, Implementation and Control*, 6th edition, Prentice-Hall International Editions.

Lyytinen, Kalle, and Hirschheim, Rudy, (1987), 'Information Systems Failures--a survey and classification of the empirical literature', *Oxford Surveys in Information Technology*, Vol. 4, pp. 257-309, Oxford University Press.
McMaster, Tom, Jones, Mark, C., and Wood-Harper, A., T., (1995) 'Implementation Planning: A Role for an Information Strategy?', 3rd Decennial *Computers in Context - Joining Forces in Design*, Aarhus, Denmark.
Miles, Ian, and contributors, (1990), *Mapping and Measuring the Information Economy*, Library and Information Research Report 77, The British Library Board, p.157.
Mitroff, Ian, I., and Linstone, Harold, A., (1993), *The Unbounded Mind: Breaking the Chains of Traditional Business Thinking*, Oxford University Press.
Ovaska, Saila, (1991), 'Usability as a Goal for the Design of Computer Systems', in *Scandinavian Journal of Information Systems*, Vol. 3, pp. 47-62.
Parasuraman, A., Zeithaml, V., A., and Berry, L., L., (1985), 'A Conceptual Model of Service Quality and its Implications for Future Research', in *Journal of Marketing*, Vol. 49, pp. 41-50.
Ramsey, Harvey, Baldry, Chris, Connolly, Anne, and Lockyer, Cliff, (1992), 'Computerizing the Council: IT, jobs and employee influence in a local authority', in Ramsey, H., and Beirne, M., (Eds.), *Information Technology and Workplace Democracy*, Routledge, pp.146-172.
Robbins, Stephen, P., (1990), *Organization Theory: Structure Designs and Applications*, 3rd edition, Prentice-Hall International, Inc.
Robinson, Bruce, (1994) 'Social Context and Participant Understanding of IS Failure', in *Proceedings of the 2nd BCS Conference on IS Methodologies*, Edinburgh, 1994.
Saga, V., L., and Zmud, R., W., (1994) 'The Nature and Determinants of IT Acceptance, Routinization, and Infusion', in Levine, L., (ed.), *Diffusion, Transfer and Implementation of Information Technology*, Elsevier/North Holland, Amsterdam, London, New York, Tokyo. pp. 67-86.
Schön, D., A., (1983), *The Reflective Practitioner: How Professionals Think in Action*, Basic Books.
Stolterman, E., (1992) 'How System Designers Think About Design and Methods', *Scandinavian Journal of Information Systems*, Vol. 4, pp 137-150
Tull, Donald, S., and Hawkins, Del, I., (1993) *Marketing Research, Measurement and Method*, 6th edition, Macmillan.
Vidgen, R. T., (1994), 'Information Systems: identifying customers and understanding quality requirements', in Proceedings of the 17th IRIS, Syöte, Finland.
Vidgen, Richard, T., and McMaster, Tom, (1995), 'Black Boxes, Non-human Stakeholders, and the Translation of IT through Mediation', *Proceedings of IFIP8.2 Conference on Information Technology and Organizational Change*, Cambridge, 1995.
Weber, John, A., (1976), *Growth Opportunity Analysis*, Reston Publishing Company.
Yeates, Don, Shields, Maura, and Helmy, David, (1994), *Systems Analysis and Design*, Pitman Publishing.
Zeithaml, Valarie, A., Berry, Leonard, L., and Parasuraman, A., (1988), 'Communication and Control Processes in the Delivery of Service Quality' in *Journal of Marketing*, April 1988, Vol. 52, pp. 35-48.

10

Integrating Diffusion of Innovations and Theory of Reasoned Action models to predict utilization of information technology by end-users

G. C. Moore
TRANSALTA Corporation
Calgary, Alberta, Canada
phone: (403) 267-4959
fax: (403) 267-3630
E-mail: moore.gary.c@transalta.ab.ca

I. Benbasat
University of British Columbia
Faculty of Commerce and Business Administration
Vancouver, BC, Canada V6T 1Z2
phone: (604) 822-8396
fax: (604) 822-9574
E-mail: izak@unixg.ubc.ca

Abstract

This paper reports on a field study investigating the adoption of an information technology (IT) by end-users. First, based on theories and empirical findings from research into the **Diffusion of Innovations** and the **Theory of Reasoned Action**, a model was developed of the factors influencing individual level decisions to use IT. The model was then field tested in a survey of 540 individuals in seven organizations. Results show that the model received good support and that it can be used for understanding the utilization of IT. Both one's own attitude and the expectations of others influenced the degree to which one used IT after adoption. Consistent with results from diffusion research, the most significant perceptions that had an effect on degree of use were *ease of use*, *relative advantage* and *compatibility*.

Keywords

Information systems adoption, diffusion of innovations, theory of reasoned action

1 INTRODUCTION

There has been increased interest in the information systems (IS) research literature recently on predicting and explaining the utilization of information technology (IT) by end-users (Hartwick and Barki, 1994). Most of these studies have been based on the Theory of Reasoned Action and its variants, such as the "technology acceptance model" (Davis, 1989) and the Theory of Planned Behavior (Ajzen, 1991; Mathieson, 1991).

This paper reports on a research study conducted to propose and test a model for understanding the different degrees of use of end-user IT by individuals. What distinguishes this work from previous ones is that it explicitly draws upon two distinct yet theoretically related bodies of research. The first is research into the **diffusion of innovations** (Rogers, 1983), which in general investigates individuals' reactions to new products or processes, and why some innovations diffuse and others do not. Our research was not intended to study the *diffusion* of IT *per se* (i.e., its rate of adoption over time), but rather the extent to which individuals use the technology. The second is research on the **Theory of Reasoned Action** (Fishbein and Ajzen, 1975) which is a general theory applicable to an array of behaviors, including the forces which influence the use of IT. Diffusion research applies to the behavior of accepting or rejecting an innovation. Thus, to the extent that personal use of IT can be considered as an innovation within the work place, certain concepts of diffusion research could be used to apply the Theory of Reasoned Action to IT utilization.

In this study the generic perceptions of adopting a product or service (as developed in diffusion research) are used to serve as the beliefs used in the Theory of Reasoned Action. Measures for these beliefs and other constructs in the model were created through a rigorous instrument development process. The final stage of the study tested the model in a field survey, which included 540 respondents from seven organizations in a variety of industries. These steps are described in the sections which follow.

2 THEORETICAL BASIS OF THE RESEARCH

2.1 Theory of Reasoned Action

Theory of Reasoned Action (TRA) specifies the relationships between beliefs, attitudes, and behaviors. TRA is based on the proposition that an individual's overt behavior (B) is determined by the individual's **intention** to perform that behavior (BI). BI in turn is a function of two factors, one's **Attitude** towards performing the behavior itself (A_B) and one's **Subjective Norm** (SN):

$$B \cong BI = w_1(A_B) + w_2(SN). \qquad (1)$$

where w_1 and w_2 are the relative weights given to each component by the individual.

Subjective Norm is a function of two components: i) the individual's **normative beliefs** (NB), which are beliefs one has about what each of one's "important others", or salient referents, expects one to do with respect to a particular behavior, and ii) the individual's "**motivation to comply**" (MC) with each of the perceived expectations of the salient referents:

$$SN = \Sigma(NB_jMC_j). \quad (2)$$

NB_j = perceived expectation of the jth referent
MC_j = motivation to comply with the jth referent

One's **attitude** towards a behavior, $\mathbf{A_B}$, is a function of one's **belief** (b_i) that performing the behavior will lead to certain outcomes, and a weighted **evaluation** (e_i) of those outcomes:

$$A_B = \Sigma(b_ie_i). \quad (3)$$

b_i = the expectation of the ith outcome
e_i = the evaluation of the ith outcome

To identify those beliefs which are the basis of attitude in each situation, Ajzen and Fishbein (1980) suggest simply asking respondents to list their beliefs about the behavior in question. It is assumed that beliefs will be listed in the order of relative salience and that only salient beliefs have an effect. Furthermore, because Ajzen and Fishbein (1980) argue that beliefs are unique to each specific situation, a new set of beliefs must be elicited for each new situation.

2.2 Theory of Reasoned Action and IT studies

Researchers studying the use of IT have recently taken different approaches to defining the beliefs which contribute to one's *attitude towards using IT*. Christensen (1987) and Pavri (1988) followed the method suggested by Ajzen and Fishbein (1980) to identify relevant beliefs. More recently, researchers attempted to identify more *generic ways* to define beliefs. For example, Davis (1989) introduced a variant of TRA, which he called a Technology Acceptance Model (TAM). Based on a review of the IS literature, he identified two general constructs, *perceived ease of use* and *perceived usefulness* of the system, as the beliefs hypothesized to determine attitude. In a subsequent study, Davis et al. (1989) compared TAM to a model based explicitly on TRA. The beliefs for the TRA model were first elicited from an initial set of respondents, with the seven most frequently mentioned being chosen for the full study. TAM and TRA models were then compared. The results showed that a "parsimonious" causal structure for predicting behavior could be identified based only on usefulness and ease of use, i.e., the two general beliefs used in TAM had more power than the beliefs identified in the elicitation procedure. This lends support to developing models based on more general perceptions.

In a further study, Mathieson (1991) compared the "Theory of Planned Behavior" (Ajzen, 1991), which is an extension of TRA, to TAM. Mathieson also used an elicitation procedure to identify salient beliefs. He found that both models predicted Behavioral Intention well, but that TAM was "easier to use" because of the use of a standard set of instruments, which eliminates the need to elicit beliefs for every new study or context.

These studies are marked steps forward in the study of attitude within the IT usage literature. However, there still exists considerable inconsistency in the various studies in how attitude is formulated, and especially in how the particular beliefs that contribute to its formulation are identified and explicated. We believe that a fairly consistent approach to defining attitude and perceptions should be undertaken, rather than being dependent on the contingencies of a particular study. Thus, IT researchers should focus on identifying and investigating a generic set of beliefs about using IT to make a more general and cumulative approach to the study of IT implementation possible. The next sections outline such an approach.

2.3 Diffusion of Innovations Theory at the individual level of analysis

IT implementation can be viewed as basically a process of change. For example, Ginzberg (1981) proposed the use of a diffusion of innovations model to study the implementation of IS. Lucas et al. (1990), as the foundations for their model of implementation, refer to attitude models, including TRA and diffusion models. Kwon and Zmud (1987) have also argued for marrying the two streams of research represented by implementation studies and diffusion studies. It is only in recent years that IS researchers have relied on diffusion theories for studying adoption and use at the **individual level** (e.g., Moore, 1987; Brancheau and Wetherbe, 1990).

This research undertakes such a study by using diffusion research to provide a basis for identifying a set of generic perceptions or beliefs which could affect one's attitude towards using IT. It then integrates these perceptions with several constructs from TRA to develop and test a model which helps explain individual use of end-user IT. According to diffusion research, there are a variety of factors that can be identified as affecting the formation of one's attitude and subjective norms, such as the communication network of an individual. However, these issues are outside the scope of this paper.

3 THE CONCEPTUAL FRAMEWORK

The components of the research model shown in Figure 1 are described below.

3.1 Usage

In terms of TRA, personal work station (PWS) usage is the behavior of interest and hence is the dependent variable in this study. A PWS is defined as a set of computerized hardware and software tools designed for personal use by an individual. The key aspect of a PWS is that it is interactive information technology operated directly by a user. For this study, we focus on two dimensions of usage. The first dimension, *diversity* of use (Thompson et al., 1991), is the degree to which one uses a previously adopted product or process in a different use domain. The second is *intensity*, which is the degree to which the product or process is actually put to use (Thompson et al., 1991).

3.2 Attitude towards adopting

According to TRA, one's actual usage of IT will be a function of one's attitude towards its use. In this study we focus on the cognitive aspects, or perceptions, that a person has towards performing a behavior. In diffusion theory, the perceptions which are hypothesized to have an effect on attitude have been cast as the *perceived characteristics of innovations*, and have been shown in a number of studies to be linked to adoption/rejection decisions. Tornatzky and Klein (1982) found that *compatibility*, *relative advantage*, and *complexity* were consistently associated with innovative behaviors. Rogers and Shoemaker (1971) had earlier

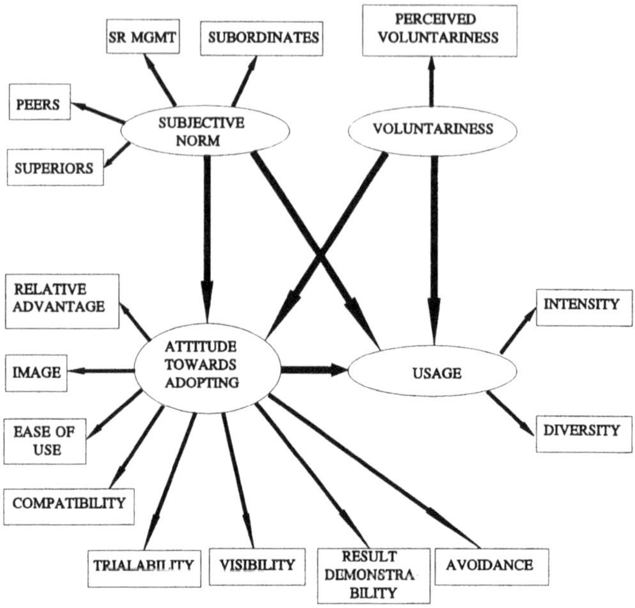

Figure 1 Research model.

identified these three characteristics, as well as *trialability* and *observability*. Because of the popularity of Rogers' work, which has become one of the most cited works in the social sciences, we decided to include these five in the current study. Finally, a sixth characteristic, *image*, was also included since Rogers had indicated that although image might be subsumed under relative advantage, in some instances it was a motivating factor on its own.

The next stage was to develop an instrument to measure these various characteristics (see Moore and Benbasat, 1991 for full details). In the instrument development process, *observability* was found to tap two different constructs, *result demonstrability* and *visibility*, and thus was split. As a result, seven perceived characteristics of using PWS were eventually included in the study, defined as follows:

- **Relative Advantage**: the degree to which using a PWS is perceived as being better than using its precursor.

- **Compatibility**: the degree to which using a PWS is perceived as being consistent with the existing values, and past experiences of the potential adopter.

- **Ease of Use**: the degree to which a PWS is perceived as being easy to use (Note: this term rather than "complexity" was used here to be congruent with the terminology in the IS literature).

- **Trialability**: the degree to which a PWS may be experimented with before adoption.

- **Image**: the degree to which using a PWS is perceived to enhance one's image or status in one's social system.

- **Result Demonstrability**: the degree to which the results of using a PWS are observable and communicable to others.

- **Visibility**: the degree to which a PWS is apparent to the sense of sight.

In addition to the above, an eighth perception, *Computer Avoidance*, was investigated to specifically capture respondents' potential aversion or avoidance reactions to IT. Igbaria (1993) observed that "computer avoidance" influenced behavioral intent negatively. This perception includes management's potential use of IT to monitor workers' performance, IT's potentially negative impacts on one's health, and its potential "deskilling" aspects. It was concluded that these beliefs could potentially influence attitudes towards using IT.

3.3 Subjective norm

One of the potential determinants of behavior is the **Subjective Norm** (SN), as defined in TRA. SN is formed from one's *motivation to comply* with what one believes others expect one to do (termed the *normative belief*). Several individuals may serve as potential "referents" who might influence one's behavior with respect to PWS usage. These include one's co-workers and senior management. Within IS research, there is considerable evidence that several of these referents actually influence IT use, e.g., a popular nostrum for successful IS implementation has been "senior management support" and the presence of a "champion". The expectations of these various individuals that others should use the IT are all subsumed within the SN.

Although TRA does not postulate any interaction effects between SN and attitude, previous research has shown that these effects can exist (e.g., Ryan, 1982). Within IS, Christensen (1987) found that the components of SN had a direct effect on one's eventual behavior, as well as on one's attitude with respect to DSS adoption. Therefore, a link between subjective norm and attitude is included in the model.

3.4 Perceived voluntariness of PWS usage

Degree of **voluntariness** (V) of use explicitly addresses *formal requirements* in one's job to perform a behavior, whereas SN refers to the perceived *social pressure* to perform a certain behavior (Ajzen, 1991, p.188). SN sets an *informal* requirement; it is up to the individual to conform with the expectations of others or not. Voluntariness, however, refers to how an individual perceives *formal* job requirements. It refers to the power an individual has to perform, or not perform, a certain behavior.

The separate nature of SN and V is supported by the Theory of Planned Behavior (TPB) (Ajzen, 1991), proposed as an extension to TRA. According to Ajzen:

> *Behavioral Intention can find expression in behavior if the behavior in question is under volitional control, i.e., the person can decide at will to perform or not perform the behavior (p.182).*

Accordingly, Ajzen has added a new factor to the TPB named **perceived behavioral control**, in addition to **attitudes** and **SN** which are part of TRA. While Ajzen casts perceived behavioral control in terms of abilities, opportunities, and resources available to individuals to enable performance, we view **Voluntariness** as a factor that influences behavior in a similar fashion to perceived behavioral control. This is because Voluntariness, the perception of what an individual thinks he/she is required or not required to perform, and perceived behavioral control, which is described by Ajzen as "volitional control", appear to be closely related constructs. This similarity provides an *a priori* justification for the inclusion of SN and V as two separate, and distinct, factors in our model in the same way that the TPB includes both SN and perceived behavioral control. Furthermore, Hartwick and Barki (1994) observed major differences between voluntary and mandatory users and suggest that more work is needed on this topic.

3.5 Behavior

Behavioral intention, a component within TRA, is not included in the research design. If no other variables intervened once an attitude and subjective norm were formed, or if the behavior were to be performed immediately, then intention could be dropped from the model without a loss of information. Intentions are used to predict behavior, and therefore to be of value "it is important to measure [them] as close as possible to the behavioral observation" (Ajzen and Fishbein, 1980, p.47). Indeed, in this study we are not attempting to predict future behavior; rather, we are attempting to determine how *current* behavior is related to subjective norm and attitude.

4 EMPIRICAL TEST

4.1 The study sample

Data were gathered from both users and non-users of PWS in seven organizations. These firms, representing diverse industries, covered the range of private to public sector organizations. Firms participating also had made the PWS generally available to their employees. Terminals or personal computers were provided, and applications were accessible either locally on personal computers, or on the mainframe or through a local area network. The reason for choosing organizations which made the technology accessible was to make sure that individuals who wished to use the technology had access to it.

A total of 810 questionnaires were distributed, with 540 usable ones returned, for an average response rate of 67%.

Basic demographic statistics were collected to assess how well the sample represented the population of employees within the firms. 60% of the respondents were males. 44% were in supervisory and management positions, 34% were professional and technical employees, and 18% clerical staff. Over 60% had post-secondary education. While no specific data are available, conversation with the company representatives indicated that the proportion of respondents in each category reflects the overall proportions in the organizations.

4.2 Measurement of constructs

4.2.1 Perceived Characteristics of Using PWS. Prior to this study, an extensive construct and instrument development process was undertaken to create several scales to measure the perceived characteristics (described in Section 3.2), including several procedures to ensure the scales' validity and reliability, as described in Moore and Benbasat (1991). After the development process, a total 50 items were chosen to measure these eight perceived characteristics. They were listed in the survey instrument in a random order, i.e., not grouped by perceived characteristics. The items were based on seven point scales, ranging from strongly disagree to strongly agree. An example of an item (for relative advantage) is "Using a PWS improves my job performance".

The reliability statistics for the various scales, *based on the data from 540 respondents who participated in the study*, indicate all scales were above 0.70, and most above 0.80.

4.2.2 Subjective Norm. Items for subjective norm were developed following the recommendations of Ajzen and Fishbein (1980). They were based on seven point scales with "likely-unlikely" anchors. For the normative beliefs (NB) respondents were presented with statements such as "*[Referent A] thinks I should use a PWS in my job*". The various referents, determined through interviews with a sample of respondents, included subordinates, peers, supervisors, and senior management. For the motivation to comply (MC) the statements were phrased "*generally speaking, I want to do what [Referent A] thinks I should do*". Subjective Norms for each referent group were calculated by multiplying their respective NB's and MC's together.

4.2.3 Usage. **Intensity** was operationalized, similar to Thompson et al. (1991), as the *number of hours* an individual uses the PWS. Respondents were asked to indicate the average number of hours of usage per week for *each* PWS function. The total number of hours of use per week was then computed as the sum of these responses. A second item, physically separate from the first item, asked the general question of total hours of use as follows: "*Overall, how many hours per week do you use a PWS?*". A scale for intensity was then constructed from the two items, with a resulting reliability of 0.88.

Diversity, which reflects the number of new task domains in which IT is used, was operationalized, similar to Thompson et al. (1991), as the number of *different functions* that an individual uses on the PWS. The functions chosen to reflect "breath" included: word processing, computer modelling, spreadsheets, graphics, information retrieval, database management, electronic mail, electronic calendars, report generation, and use of interactive programming languages and statistical analysis packages. In addition to these "generic" functions, some specific application areas such as geoscience, accounting, and human resources were included as options. Data on the number of different functions used were obtained from three sources. The first asked when the respondent first used each function. If a date was provided, this was taken as an indication that the specific function was being used. The second source was the number of hours of use per week of each function. A response greater than zero indicated use of that function. A third item asked whether each function, if used, was used on a mainframe or microcomputer. The reliability of the three-item scale was 0.98.

5 FINDINGS OF THE STUDY

5.1 Adopters vs. non-adopters

Table 1 provides comparative statistics for adopters and non-adopters. As can be seen, while the various perceptions of using PWS are generally positive, there are statistically significant differences between adopters' and non-adopters' perceptions for every characteristic except computer avoidance.

Table 1 Comparison of responses: adopters versus non-adopters

I. Proportion of Users Versus Non-Users In Sample

	Adopters		Non-Adopters		Total	
Organizational Level	#	% of level	#	% of level	#	% of Sample
Executive	9	69%	4	31%	13	3%
Middle Management	73	74%	25	26%	98	19%
Supervisory	101	78%	29	22%	130	25%
Professional	95	77%	29	23%	124	24%
Technical	45	76%	14	24%	59	11%
Clerical	78	80%	20	20%	98	19%
Total	418		122		540	
Percent of Sample		77%		23%		100%

II. Variable Means and Tests For Differences

	Adopters	Non-Adopters	Z-Scores	U-Test Signif
Perceived Characteristics				
Image	4.3	3.9	-3.08	.00
Relative Advantage	5.9	4.8	-9.39	.00
Compatibility	5.7	4.4	-9.68	.00
Ease of Use	5.1	4.5	-5.54	.00
Result Demonstrability	5.8	4.9	-7.81	.00
Trialability	4.6	4.3	-2.23	.03
Visibility	5.9	5.3	-5.13	.00
Computer Avoidance	2.1	2.1	-0.04	.97
Voluntariness	3.3	5.0	-10.01	.00
Subjective Norms				
Peers	6.10	.11	-8.07	.00
Supervisors	9.39	.08	-9.06	.00
Senior Management	8.75	-.16	-9.06	.00
Subordinates	5.26	-.53	-7.78	.00

Significant differences between adopters and non-adopters also exist in the subjective norm for all referent groups. Non-adopters report neutral to slightly negative subjective norms, whereas adopters report significantly more positive norms. A negative subjective norm would indicate that the respondent thought that the relevant referent did not expect the respondent to use the PWS. For adopters, the strongest "pressure" to use the PWS comes from their immediate supervisors and senior management, with slightly less pressure from peers and subordinates.

5.2 Results of model test

The model in Figure 1 was tested using structural equation modelling as implemented in LISREL VI (Joreskog and Sorbom, 1984). In order to analyze the results with respect to the research model, the sample was first randomly split into two groups: Sample 1 and Sample 2. Sample 1 was used to initially assess and calibrate the model as necessary, and then Sample 2 was used to validate the results.

5.2.1 Model Fit. The fit of the model to the data was assessed by generally following the guidelines suggested by Bagozzi and Yi (1988). (For full details see Moore and Benbasat, 1993).

The squared multiple correlations and factor loadings for several indicators of attitude were problematic, including the following: image, result demonstrability, trialability, visibility, and computer avoidance. The loading of computer avoidance was not significant. The adjusted goodness of fit index (AGFI), which ranges from 0 to 1, for the overall model was also rather low at .71.

As a result of the analysis of the internal fit of the model, we decided to drop the problematic indicators for attitude. While some indicators were dropped, none of the causal paths in the initial model were altered, and hence *the model's basic structure was not changed.* The model was then run again, still using Sample 1, and the internal fit of the model was re-assessed. In this instance, all the criteria for goodness of internal fit were met.

Once these statistics were evaluated, the next step was to assess the overall fit of the model to the data. Wheaton et al. (1977) suggest that a chi-square five times greater than the degrees of freedom is acceptable, but the smaller the ratio the better. For the full model, however, chi-square/d.f. is approximately 5.3. Furthermore, AGFI, at .71, indicates a somewhat poor fit of the model to the data. Although there is no standard against which to judge these values, they can be used to *compare the initial model against that which eliminated the problematic indicators for attitude.* For this revised model, the χ^2/df ratio improved to 3.5, and the AGFI to .86. This indicated that the revised model fit the data much better than the full model.

The next step was to cross-validate the model. This was necessary to ensure that the final model was not a case of simply fitting the model to the data. Up to this stage, the analysis had been conducted using only one half of the sample, i.e., Sample 1. Cross-validation is conducted by fitting the parameters estimated in the initial (calibration) sample (Sample 1) on a **withheld (validation) sample** (Sample 2) and assessing the goodness of fit indices. The validation exercise showed that all of the assessment indices are relatively good for the model indicating that the model has a fairly good fit to the data. It should be noted that although changes were made to the indicators for some constructs (primarily *attitude*), the fundamental nature of the model was not changed. Since no paths were added or deleted among the constructs in the original model, the test of the model was more one of confirmation than exploration.

5.2.2 Assessment of Model. Figure 2 provides the parameter estimates for the model using the validation sample. All paths are statistically significant.

The standardized procedure provided by LISREL rescales only the *latent variables* (i.e., attitude, subjective norm, voluntariness, and usage) to have a variance of 1.0, while leaving the *observed measures*, or indicators (e.g., relative advantage and ease of use), in their original scales. Each loading of an observed measure, therefore, should be interpreted as the amount of change in the original observed measure given a one standard deviation change in the corresponding latent variable it reflects. In practical terms, the loadings shown in Figure 2 indicate that compatibility has the highest influence on attitude, followed by relative advantage and ease of use. For subjective norm, the most influential indicators are superiors and senior management, while peers and subordinates have lesser influence. For usage, number of functions (diversity), as compared to number of hours (intensity), is the more influential indicator.

In terms of the relationships among the latent variables, attitude has a significant positive effect on usage (.52). Furthermore, attitude has the greatest direct effect of the three constructs affecting usage. Subjective norm has a significant effect on both usage (.18) and attitude (.55). Finally, voluntariness is also inversely related to both usage (-.40) and attitude (-.16).

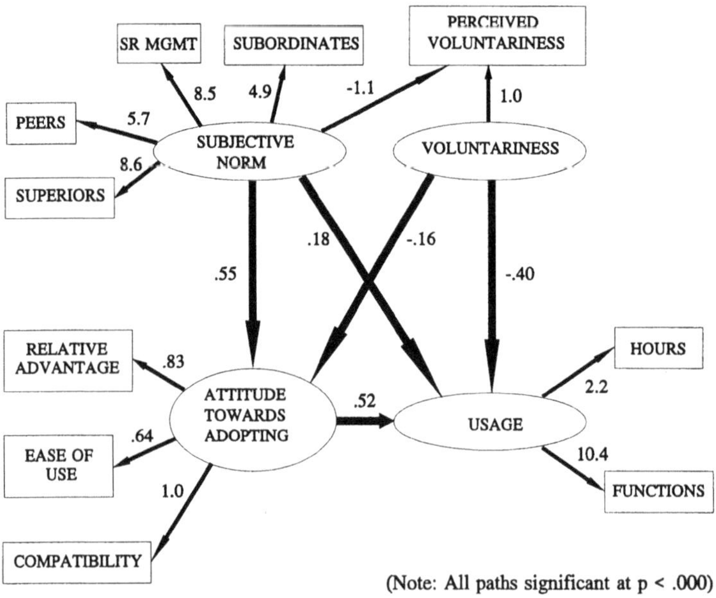

(Note: All paths significant at p < .000)

Figure 2 LISREL standardized solution.

In addition to their direct effects on usage, both subjective norm and voluntariness have indirect effects through attitude. Their total effect can be calculated as the sum of their direct effect (the path coefficient to usage), and their indirect effect (the product of their path coefficient to attitude and that from attitude to usage). For subjective norm, that is:

Total Effect of Subjective Norm on Usage = .18 + (.52 x .55) = .47

The total effects (.47) of subjective norm on usage are close to the effect of attitude (.52). A result not predicted by theory, however, is the fact that its direct effect on usage (.18) is approximately only a third of its direct effect on attitude (.55). Nevertheless, this does parallel the findings of Christensen (1987) who found that the direct effect of subjective norm on one's intention to use a DSS was approximately 54% of its effect on attitude.

As with subjective norm, the total effects of voluntariness can be calculated as follows:

Total Effect of Voluntariness on Usage = -.40 + (-.16 x .52) = -.48

The above result shows that the total effects of voluntariness on usage (-.48) is approximately equal to that of subjective norm, and slightly less than attitude. Nevertheless, its direct effect on usage (-.40) dominates, being approximately 2½ times greater than its effect on attitude (-.16).

In summary, these results provide support for the model. In addition, the squared multiple correlations (which are analogous to R^2) for the structural equations indicate that a fair amount (65%) of the variance in usage is accounted for by attitude, subjective norm, and voluntariness, i.e., a good model fit.

6 LIMITATIONS

This study is cross-sectional. Thus, although much of the analysis is described in causal terms, causality cannot be demonstrated because the study was not longitudinal. The model tested investigated the *concurrent* relationships between subjective norm, attitude and extent of IT use. **Nevertheless**, this research tested a model based on elements of theories proposed in TRA and diffusion of innovation literatures and supported by other empirical research. We believe that our approach is a logical extension of these work and that the variables and relationships tested were appropriate. For example, a recent study by Hartwick and Barki (1994) found support for the use of TRA in a similar context. Even though they operationalized attitudes differently by using a semantic differential scale (e.g., good/bad) to measure feelings concerning system use, i.e., unlike utilizing a set of beliefs generated from the diffusion of innovations literature as was done in this paper, their results and those in this paper are quite similar. Hartwick and Barki (1994) state that:

> *strong support was obtained for TRA, both longitudinally (using predevelopment attitude, subjective norm, and intention to predict post implementation system use) and cross-sectionally (using post implementation attitude, subjective norm and intention to predict contemporaneous system use). (p.458)*

Furthermore, the direct contributions (effects) of subjective norm and attitudes to explaining *usage* in our study (see Figure 2) and to *intentions to use* in the Hartwick and

Barki (1994) study are along the same direction, with attitude having a stronger *direct* effect on behavior than subjective norm in both studies. Similarly, Taylor and Todd (1995) report that the factors affecting behavioral intent, in order of the strength of their influence, were attitude, perceived behavioral control, and subjective norm. Our study also found the same level of impact on behavior, from highest to lowest, for the *direct* effects of attitude, voluntariness (corresponding to perceived behavioral control), and subjective norm. The close correspondence between this study and others provides additional assurance that the results of our study have validity in spite of its focus on concurrent behavior. In summary, the results of this study support the research model, or more conservatively, do not reject it. Nevertheless, longitudinal studies must certainly be undertaken to fully investigate the causal effects of the various factors and their relationships *over time*. An extension to TRA could indeed include the "feedback" loop to subjective norms and attitudes.

7 CONTRIBUTIONS TO RESEARCH

There is a lack of IS research which propose generic theories to deal with a variety of new IT. The primary goal of this research, therefore, was to develop a model for understanding the utilization of end-user IT in particular, and of systems implementation in general. To do this, the study borrowed and integrated concepts from TRA and diffusion of innovations research, and extended them explicitly into the study of IT implementation. It is believed that the results of this study support the model that was developed. This has several implications.

First, this study helps to establish a foundation for further research. By extending the proposed model beyond the study of the utilization of the PWS, it could help researchers understand and investigate other IT implementations, such as executive information systems and expert systems. Second, this study provides support for IS researchers to adopt and use constructs from TRA and diffusion of innovations research. It shows that, as postulated by TRA, both the subjective norm and attitude have significant effects on a potential adopter's behavior and provides support to previous findings that an interaction between these two factors can occur. With respect to diffusion research, this study has shown the link between the perceived characteristics of using PWS and behavior. In particular, the three perceptions which loaded on attitude in the final model, namely relative advantage, compatibility, and ease of use, were also found to be the ones most consistently associated with adoption (Tornatzky and Klein, 1982). This might suggest that such factors as trialability and result demonstrability become less important after one has adopted the technology. This issue certainly deserves further research.

In conclusion, this study has developed and tested a model to explain the degree of use of an IT after its initial adoption. We recommend that its power and applicability to other IT applications be investigated in order to assess the degree to which it could be generalized to all IT domains and the extent to which it could be used to provide prescriptions.

8 ACKNOWLEDGEMENTS

We would like to thank Dr. Wynne Chin, University of Calgary, for his valuable advice on LISREL modelling. This work was partially supported by funds provided by the Natural Sciences and Engineering Research Council of Canada.

9 REFERENCES

Ajzen, I. (1991) The Theory of Planned Behavior. *Organizational Performance and Human Decision Processes*, **50**, 79-211.

______ and Fishbein, M. (1980) *Understanding Attitudes and Predicting Behavior*. Prentice-Hall Inc., Englewood Cliffs, NJ.

Bagozzi, R.P. and Yi, Y. (1988) On the Evaluation of Structural Equation Models. *Journal of the Academy of Marketing Science*, **16**, 74-94.

Brancheau, J.C. and Wetherbe, J.C. (1990) The Adoption of Spreadsheet Software: Testing Innovation Diffusion Theory in the Context of End-User Computing. *Information Systems Research*, **1**, 115-143.

Christensen, G.E. (1987) *Successful Implementation of Decision Support Systems: An Empirical Investigation of Usage Intentions and Behavior*. Unpublished Doctoral Dissertation, University of California at Los Angeles.

Davis, F.D. (1989) Perceived Usefulness, Perceived Ease of Use, and User Acceptance of Information Technology. *MIS Quarterly*, **13**, 318-339.

______, Bagozzi, R.P., Richard P. and Warshaw, P.R. (1989) User Acceptance of Computer Technology. *Management Science*, **35**, 982-1003.

Fishbein, M. and Ajzen, I. (1975) *Belief, Attitude, Intention, and Behavior: An Introduction to Theory and Research*. Addison-Wesley, Reading.

Ginzberg, M. (1981) Key Recurrent Issues in the MIS Implementation Process. *MIS Quarterly*, **5**, 47-59.

Hartwick, J. and Barki, H. (1994) Explaining the Role of User Participation in Information Systems Use. *Management Science*, **40**, 440-465.

Igbaria, M. (1993) User Acceptance of Microcomputer Technology: An Empirical Test. *OMEGA*, **21**, 73-90.

Joreskog, K.G., and Sorbom, D. (1984) *LISREL VI: Analysis of the Structural Relationships by Maximum Likelihood Instrumental Variables and Least Squares Methods*. Scientific Software Inc., Moresville, Indiana.

Kwon, T.H. and Zmud, R.W. (1987) Unifying the Fragmented Models of Information Systems Implementation, in *Critical Issues in Information Systems Research* (eds. R.J. Boland and R.A. Hirscheim), Wiley and Sons, New York, 227-251.

Lucas, H., Ginzberg M.J. and Randall L.S. (1990) *Information Systems Implementation: Testing a Structural Model*. Ablex Publishing Co., Norwood, NJ.

Mathieson, K. (1991) Predicting User Intentions: Comparing the Technology Acceptance Model with the Theory of Planned Behavior. *Information Systems Research*, **2**, 173-191.

Moore, G.C. (1987) End User Computing and Office Automation: A Diffusion of Innovations Perspective. *Infor*, **25**, 214-235.

______ and Benbasat, I. (1991) Development of an Instrument to Measure the Perceived Characteristics of Adopting an Information Technology Innovation. *Information Systems Research*, **2**, 192-222.

______ (1993) *Empirical Examination of a Model of the Factors Affecting Utilization of Information Technology by End-Users*. Working Paper, Faculty of Commerce, University of British Columbia.

Pavri, F. (1988) *An Empirical Study of the Factors Contributing to Microcomputer Usage*. Unpublished Doctoral Dissertation, University of Western Ontario.

Rogers, E.M. (1983) *Diffusion of Innovations*. Third Edition, The Free Press, New York.

_____ and Shoemaker, F.F. (1971) *Communication of Innovations*. The Free Press, New York.

Ryan, M.J. (1982) Behavioral Intention Formation: The Interdependency of Attitudinal and Social Influence Variables. *Journal of Consumer Research*, **9**, 268-277.

Taylor, S. and Todd, P. A. (1995) Understanding Information Technology Usage: A Test of Competing Models. *Information Systems Research*, **6**, 144-176.

Thompson, R.L., Higgins, C.A., and Howell, J.M. (1991) Personal Computing: Toward a Conceptual Model of Utilization. *MIS Quarterly*, **15**, 125-143.

Tornatzky, L.G., and Klein, K.J. (1982) Innovation Characteristics and Innovation Adoption Implementation: A Meta-Analysis of Findings. *IEEE Transactions on Engineering Management*, **29**, 28-45.

Wheaton, B., Muthen, B., Alwin, D., and Summers, G. (1977) Assessing Reliability and Stability in Panel Models, in *Sociological Methodology* (ed. D. Heise), Jossey-Bass, San Francisco, 84-136.

7 BIOGRAPHY

Gary C. Moore is with the TRANSALTA Corporation, Calgary, Canada. He received his Ph.D. in Management Information Systems from the University of British Columbia in 1989. Prior to receiving his doctorate he had a number of years of experience as a practitioner and consultant in the information management field. His research interests include I/S strategy, managing end user computing, I/S-user relationships, and the diffusion of innovations, including the introduction of new information technologies.

Izak Benbasat is CANFOR Professor of Management Information Systems at the Faculty of Commerce and Business Administration, the University of British Columbia, Vancouver, Canada. He received his Ph.D. in Management Information Systems from the University of Minnesota in 1974. His research interests are in studying the adoption of new information technologies, evaluating alternative human-computer interfaces, measuring the effectiveness of decision support tools, and investigating the role of explanations in expert systems. He is a Co-Senior Editor of *MIS Quarterly*, and serves on the editorial boards of *Information Systems Research,* and *Accounting, Management and Information Technologies*.

11

Interorganisational networks and the diffusion process: The case of networks not working

M. Robertson, J. Swan, S. Newell
University of Warwick Business School, Coventry, CV4 7AL, UK
Fax: 44 1203 524965. E-Mail: wbsrbmr@wbs.warwick.ac.uk

Abstract

This research considers the diffusion of CAPM (Computer Aided Production Management) technology in the UK automotive sector, during the mid to late 1980's. The focus is on the role of interorganisational networks in the diffusion process. Previous research has recognised that potential adopters of CAPM technology are subjected to a pro-innovation bias when developing an awareness of the technology, such that adoption is considered always to be the best policy. Using three case companies where adoption of a variant of CAPM known as MRPII (Manufacturing Resource Planning) occurred, the decision making process leading to this investment is explored. Attention is given to the perceived influence of a variety of interorganisational networks on the decision making process.

Whilst, it is acknowledged that suppliers of CAPM technology (hardware and software vendors, management consultants) will support the pro-innovation bias, evidence is also presented here to suggest that a number of other interorganisational networks (including professional associations and academic institutions), reinforce this bias. Causal relationships cannot be inferred from this small number of cases. However, two factors are found to contribute to more positive outcomes, across the companies studied. These are substantial boundary spanning activity, particularly through the use of weak ties, coupled with access to a range of different interorganisational networks.

Keywords

Interorganisational networks, MRPII, production management, consultants

1 INTRODUCTION

This paper is based on case study data gathered from three manufacturing companies operating in the automotive sector in the UK. All three firms invested in a form of CAPM technology known as MRPII, during the late 1980's. The aim of the research was to examine the decision making process surrounding this investment. Specifically, examining the role played by a number of different interorganisational networks which provided potential adopters with an awareness of CAPM solutions.

CAPM technology consists of software based systems and operating procedures that plan and control inventory levels, material flows and the manufacturing operation. The technology aims to ensure that specified products are produced by defined methods to agreed dates within a context whereby the firms assets are utilised optimally. In an integrated form, this technology can support many different functions which draw upon information held on a common database to support their activities. During the 1980's there were three major variants of CAPM technology, MRPII (Manufacturing Resource Planning), JIT (Just-in-Time) and OPT (Optimal Production Technology) (Clark et al, 1992). MRPII technology is considered to be a highly centralised 'push' system of planning and control, pushing materials through the manufacturing operation. It requires organisations to adopt more integrated approaches to work organisation and practices. MRPII technology contrasts with JIT technology. JIT 'pulls' components from one work station to the next during the manufacturing operation, only when the downstream workstation requires them. OPT technology operates by identifying bottlenecks within the manufacturing operation. These three variants of CAPM were considered to be competing, rather than complementary technologies during the late 1980's.

The diffusion of MRPII technology is an interesting area to research. Failure rates, in terms of failure to successfully appropriate the technology, have been found to be as high as 70% in the UK and US (Krupp, 1984, Wilson et. al, 1994). The term 'appropriate' rather than adopt is used here. This form of technology is a multi-faceted, complex 'bundle' of technology rather than a single entity or 'technical fix'. It incorporates both technical and organisational features. It requires specific configuration within individual organisations subject to unique organisational context (Clark, 1987). With respect to MRPII technology then, it is not sufficient to only invest in software, education and training. Attention needs also to be given to the psychological and social construction of organisational and technical systems for MRPII to be successfully appropriated (Pinch & Bijker, 1989).

Adoption of MRPII technology represents a significant capital investment. The software alone can cost anything within the region of £30K to £1M. In order for MRPII concepts to be applied, significant investment must also be made in education and training. Many organisations rely on software suppliers to provide some basic education and training. However, others use specialist consultants throughout the period of implementation (usually 18 months to 2 years). This also represents a further considerable financial investment. Where organisations fail to successfully appropriate the technology, not only do they incur significant capital loss, but the operating environment will have been severely impaired for the duration of the unsuccessful implementation phase.

Organisations were, to a limited degree, aware of the problems and failure rates associated with this technology (Waterlot & Marriot, 1986). However, research found that potential adopters of the technology were subject to a pro-innovation bias. That is, when developing an awareness of the technology, adoption was always considered to be the best policy. Ultimately then, large sections of UK manufacturing industry invested in MRPII technology (NEDO, 1984). Previous research suggested that this pro-innovation bias was largely generated by software vendors and management consultants with a vested interest in promoting MRPII technology (Clark & Staunton, 1989). Further research highlighted professional associations also supporting the pro-innovation bias (Swan J. & Newell, S, 1995). The research found that the developers of the first MRPII software packages, IBM, used The American Production & Inventory Control Society (APICS) as an effective channel through which to diffuse information about their product and the technology generally. The company was able to do this by the active participation of IBM consultants within Chapters of the of the Association across the US and North America. This association has licensee agreements with other associations in many countries throughout the world. Licensees receive much of their information from APICS. Thus the research found that this pro-innovation bias generated by APICS subsequently diffused to practitioners in the UK, through the British Production and

Inventory Control Society (BPICS). It is acknowledged that professional associations are important in the diffusion process as they provide crucial links across networks, so that contact is made between practitioners in industry and individuals in other sectors, such as suppliers, academics, research institutes etc. However, BPICS diffused American ideas about 'best practice' which heavily promoted the use of MRPII technology, to the exclusion of other technologies and therefore provided information that was incomplete, irrelevant or redundant.

This current research extends this analysis. It considers the influence of a range of interorganisational networks on the diffusion of MRPII technology, to try and more fully understand how potential adopters develop an awareness of MRPII.

2 INTERORGANISATIONAL NETWORKS

The concept of inter-organisational networks is problematic in that definitions abound. It is necessary therefore to be clear about how the term 'network' is to be used here. Networks constitute the basic social form that permits interorganisational interactions of exchange (including the exchange of knowledge) between unbounded or bounded groups of organisations (Alter & Hage, 1993). Organisations engage in information exchange and collection in order to reduce uncertainty and networks provide the necessary vector for informational flow. This definition is supported by the industrial network perspective which focuses on the 'space' between organisations (Axelsson & Easton, 1992). Recognising that "there are a number of types of relationship in a network where direct economic exchange is absent though other forms of relationship (primarily informational) may exist, e.g. between competitors" (Axelsson & Easton, 1992:12).

These definitions then are useful in recognising that employees within organisations are involved in a set of exchange relations, which includes the exchange of knowledge and expertise, with other social actors, both within and across industrial sectors. Through the activity of such employees, organisations are more likely to learn about new technologies and consequently make more informed adopt/reject decisions.

Employees involved in this type of activity are defined as 'boundary spanners'(Tushman & Scanlan, 1981). Boundary spanning may be formal or informal. The latter being characterised by the importance and strength of weak ties within and between interorganisational networks (Granovetter, 1973). It is this boundary spanning activity and its influence on the early stages of the diffusion process which forms the basis of this research.

3 INNOVATION DIFFUSION THEORIES

The dominant sociological theorist regarding the diffusion of innovations was Rogers (1962, 1983) - see Clark & Staunton (1989). Rogers second framework consists of five distinct phases described in a sequential manner (knowledge, persuasion, decision, implementation, institutionalising). This framework is useful in that it acknowledged that prior to the decision to adopt (or reject) an innovation, potential adopters are involved in a process of persuasion. The organisation is exposed to a variety of sources of information regarding the innovation, through the activities of boundary spanners - technological gatekeepers, who influence the adopt/reject decision. Importantly, the model highlights the role of suppliers in making potential adopters aware. Thus, the suppliers are shown as active boundary spanners, whilst potential adopters are taken to be relatively passive.

Roger's framework also recognises that there may be a requirement to modify and reconfigure the innovation to make it suitable for a specific organisational context. This is referred to by Rogers as the institutionalising stage. This is particularly relevant to the appropriation of MRPII technology. MRPII technology is classified as a configurational technology. A technology that requires contextual embedding within the adopting organisation, in order to be used optimally (Fleck, 1993).

There are drawbacks however, when attempting to apply Rogers' framework to this research. The diffusion process is described as a simple, linear, sequential process, driven by the needs of potential adopters. It does not adequately address the dynamics of the relationship between suppliers and adopters and the active participation of potential adopters in the diffusion process.

For the purposes of this research then, the Decision Episode Framework (DEF) is more relevant. The DEF was initially proposed by Clark & Staunton (1989), and later developed by (Newell, Swan & Clark (1993). The DEF (shown in Figure 1) does focus on the needs and activities of potential adopters.

Figure 1: The Decision-Episode Framework:The context for user decisions (adapted from Clark et al 1992)

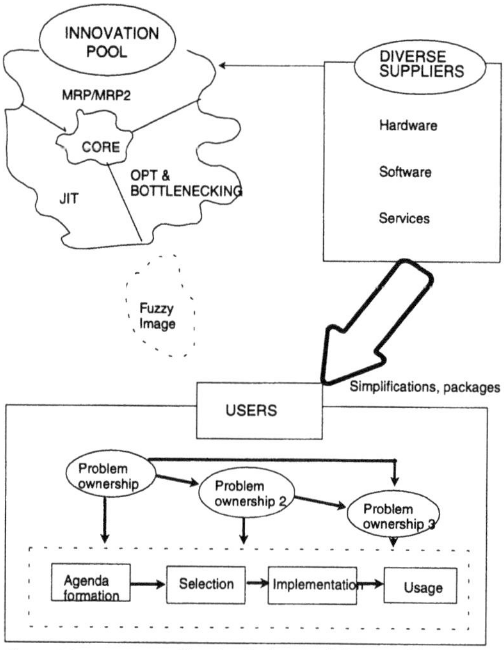

The DEF is an attempt to contextualise both the decision making process and the problems faced by potential adopters when designing CAPM solutions. The framework consists of three interacting elements; the innovation pool; the supply side; and the users. The innovation pool comprises the major variants of CAPM technology with an overlapping core. This illustrates the commonality across the three technologies. The commercial supply side is said to shape availability of the technology to the users and consists of a diverse set of hardware, software and consultancy service vendors, all presenting a favourable and simplified version of the particular technology they provide. The users are presented as decision makers within the firm, transgressing four decision-episodes in an iterative process.

This research focuses on the first two episodes of the DEF; agenda formation and selection. In these, episodes users seek to match their 'fuzzy' image of the innovation with their own requirements. Problems are defined and solutions are generated. However, this does not necessarily occur sequentially. The process is seen as iterative, with many instances of problems chasing solutions (Swan & Clark, 1992). The episodes of agenda formation and selection are crucial because here, there are many opportunities for users to redefine the innovation as presented by the supply side. These design decisions can have important implications for subsequent implementation. However, whilst much research has focused on implementation and usage of CAPM technology, there has been relatively little research on the preceding episodes.

4 METHODOLOGY

The research was carried out during the summer of 1994* . In order to establish comparability, the three companies were selected using the following criteria:

- Manufacturing profile.
- Establishment size.
- Approximate time period within which the decision making process occurred.

There would be inherent problems of comparability if the research did not acknowledge a requirement to compare similar manufacturing profiles. The contextual embedding of CAPM technology imposes a requirement to compare like with like. A company operating batch production techniques is not comparable to a company operating to a make-to order profile. Their CAPM requirements will be qualitatively different. The three companies selected were all characterised by a make-to-order profile.

It was also important to compare companies of similar size. For this research, large companies were selected with employee levels of between 1500 and 3000. Investment decisions in new technology and the management of change will be qualitatively different in a small to medium sized company when compared to a large company.

Interorganisational networks will inevitably change over time, in both composition and relative significance to the diffusion process. Chronologically, all three companies had embarked upon agenda formation and selection of CAPM technology during the late 1980's. They were also geographically proximate. It was assumed then, albeit to a limited degree, that interviewees' perceptions of networks would be relatively similar.

The main methodology used for the research was semi-structured interviews with personnel involved in the decision making process. Each company had set up a project team to consider the introduction of some form of CAPM technology. A total of 12 interviews were carried out with individuals who had formed part of these teams across the three companies. Interviews focused specifically on how the individual had developed an awareness of MRPII and the networks that informed decisions at that time. Whilst adoption was not the focus of the research, inevitably, interviewees also discussed outcomes of their attempts to implement MRPII.

Secondary sources of data, in the form of minutes of meetings and company reports, were also made available during the period of the research. These were used to support interviewees' perception's of the decision making process. Journals from three professional associations dating from 1984 to 1989 were also analysed. This analysis was used to establish what forms, and to what extent, CAPM technologies were being promoted over this time period. The three associations were:-

- BPICS (The British Production & inventory Management Society).
- IMechE (The Institute of Mechanical Engineers)
- IEE (The Institute of Electrical Engineers - Manufacturing Division).

---

* The research was kindly funded by the Economic & Social Research Council

A comparison across three companies cannot be used to infer broader generalisations. It does however, allow the diffusion process to be contextualised. This is a necessary prerequisite, if a fuller understanding of the diffusion of MRPII technology is to be developed.

5 RESULTS

The findings are presented in Table 1.

Table 1

	COMPANY A	**COMPANY B**	**COMPANY C**
Composition of the Project Team	• Special Projects Mgr (Engineering) • Logistics systems Mgr.	• Team Leader ***C** • Mgrl representatives: 1. manf. systems 2. prod control 3. matl's mgmt 4. manf engineering	• Mgrl. representatives: 1. Logistics 2. Sales & Marketing 3. Manf. Systems 4. manf. engineering 5. operations mgmt. • Consultants ***C** (Coopers & Lybrand)
Interorganisational networks accessed			
Professional Associations	BPICS ***C**	IMechE ***C** IEE ***C** BPICS ***C**	BPICS ***C**
Academic Institutions	University of Warwick MBA ***C**		
Other Firms	Reference sites ***C** **Few**	Reference sites ***C** **Few**	Visits arranged through weak ties **Many**
Suppliers	Oliver Wight Consultants	Oliver Wight Consultants	Oliver Wight Consultants
CAPM Solution	MRPII	MRPII	MRPII + JIT
**Outcome (level of appropriation)	Partial implementation 1-2	Failure 1-1	Success 1-4

*** C** Indicates consultant involvement

** Outcome - Levels of CAPM Integration (from Waterlow & Monniot, 1986).

0 No CAPM	No CAPM or presently being installed
1 No integration	Several functions computerised but without regards to integration
2 Partial integration	Several functions linked via common files and coordinated controls
3 Full integration	All CAPM functions using common databases
4 Integration of manf systems	CAPM systems designed in conjunction with material conversion handling, and quality systems against manufacturing strategy objectives.

Table 1 summarises the networks accessed during the decision making process .Antecedent context is not presented other than to state that all three companies had defined a requirement for some form of CAPM technology, in order to replace outdated, disparate systems or to manage increased demand. There was evidence of direct consultant involvement in many of the networks accessed by the project teams in all three companies. Considering the research findings for each company:-

The Logistics Systems manager in Company A first became aware of MRPII when he attended a BPICS seminar in 1985. At the time he was not a member of BPICS. He attended as a guest, and the seminar was free. Free seminars are always given by software vendors and consultants

The Special Projects manager in Company A became aware of MRPII whilst completing a part-time MBA at the University of Warwick. A course option was Manufacturing Planning & Control Systems. An external academic and consultant William Berry, from the University of North Carolina lectured on this option. He is co-author of a book 'Manufacturing Planning & Control systems' (Vollman & Berry, 1985), which focuses solely on the use of MRPII technology. The book is dedicated to the memory of Oliver Wight; 'a pioneer in manufacturing planning and control'. The company founded by this individual - The Oliver Wight Organisation, is a major US consultancy specialising in the provision of education and training in MRPII concepts both in the US and Europe. During the 1980's, the Oliver Wight Organisation was heavily involved in promoting MRPII as best practise with respect to CAPM.

Before Company A Board gave final approval for the introduction of MRPII they asked Oliver Wight consultants to provide two reference site visits. These visits were arranged in order to see MRPII technology applied. Subsequently, the Board gave their approval for investment in MRPII.

In Company B there was consultant involvement in the project team as well as the networks accessed. Failure to introduce various technological initiatives previously, had demonstrated that there was a severe lack of integration and co-operation across functional boundaries. The Manufacturing Director looked to appoint a project team leader who was objective and could remain "above the politics of the company". A consultant known to Company B was appointed as project leader.

All of the team attended mandatory, in-house presentations given by an independent US consultant Hal Mather (Inc.), on the subject of manufacturing control. He was invited to speak in his capacity as a Fellow of the Institute of Mechanical Engineers (IMechE) with which snior members of Company B had links. MRPII as a distinct technology was the focus of the presentations. All of those interviewed in Company B spoke very positively about the knowledge provided by this consultant, reinforcing their comments with reference to his association with the IMechE. Hal Mather is also a Fellow in the Institute of Industrial Engineers (IEE). His book, 'Competitive Manufacturing' (1986), is also an American Production & Inventory Control Society (APICS) publication.

Two members of the team in Company B were also BPICS members. Hence, most of the team attended BPICS seminars where the concept of MRPII was discussed. These seminars were given by vendors and focused solely on the application of this technology. Those interviewed believed that these events were an opportunity to meet other users/potential users of MRPII which enhanced their understanding of the technology.

The project leader was aware that the Oliver Wight Organisation were a specialist MRPII consultancy from previous consultancy assignments. He recommended contacting the Oliver Wight organisation for further information regarding MRPII.

Reference site visits were also arranged in order to establish which software package would be most appropriate if MRPII were to be adopted. The team invited six vendors to tender. All six vendors provided reference sites both in the UK and the US. Following these visits, Board level approval was given to invest in software and an education and training package provided by the Oliver Wight Organisation.

Company C brought in a major firm of consultants to support the decision making process. The team was led by the Managing Director. The team had already developed a detailed business system specification. They were seeking a CAPM solution to support this. Management consultants were to be used to assess software vendor suitability and provide technical expertise considered lacking in the composition of the team.

The Logistics Director was a very active member of BPICS at the time. Through his active participation in branch meetings, seminars and conferences he had developed an in-depth understanding of the MRPII concept. This knowledge was disseminated to the rest of the team.

The major consultancy involved, having considered Company C's business requirements, advocated the adoption of MRPII technology. They arranged for the Oliver Wight Organisation to make a presentation to the Board. The presentation outlined what the technology consisted of and the organisational changes required to support the technology.

The team was aware that their manufacturing profile did not comfortably 'fit' the MRPII concept. Consequently they also actively sought out other companies with a similar profile and arranged factory visits. The purpose of these visits was to ascertain what technologies were being used to aid manufacturing control in organisations facing similar manufacturing problems. These visits were arranged through informal contacts individual team members had with members of other firms e.g. suppliers, competitors, ex-colleagues. Those interviewed indicated that these reference site visits led them to an awareness of other technologies such as JIT and OPT.

The team was conscious that the company's operations were not going to try and 'fit' MRPII technology. The Board was only prepared to invest in the appropriate CAPM solution for the predefined business requirements. The team recommended to the Board that MRPII be implemented in a limited capacity, in order to forecast, schedule, and communicate with the supplier base. A JIT Kanban system, in combination with in-house designed PC based systems, were advocated for detailed shop floor planning and control. These would interface with the MRPII system. In effect , as one team member stated; "we were going to put a shell around the factory and organise shop floor control ourselves ".

Company C used the Oliver Wight Organisation to initiate education and training. This was not successful. Senior team members who attended the Oliver Wight courses were aware that they were being offered," a single point solution". Company C were sufficiently confident of their 'pragmatic' approach to the development of their CAPM systems, they rejected much of the courses' content. Hence, Company C used the Oliver Wight Organisation sparingly for education and training. In-house training courses were developed which encompassed Company C's unique approach to the development of their CAPM systems.

6 DISCUSSION

In all three companies, those interviewed were both aware and wary of the rhetoric and bias of software vendors and management consultants. The supplier network was acknowledged to have a vested interest in promoting the diffusion of specific CAPM technologies. Hence, each company set up a multi-disciplined project team to actively seek out other knowledge domains, that could provide less biased information. On the basis of this knowledge being made available, a decision based on rational / efficient choice could then be taken. Whilst all three companies followed a similar decision making process, the outcome was different in each case.

Company A had limited success. MRPII was implemented partially with some integration across functions. Company A had used an existing software package, and this was considered to inhibit full implementation. Company B experienced severe problems. There was a lack of support for the introduction of MRPII across certain functions. The high levels of data accuracy, a prerequisite to successful implementation, were not achieved. Ultimately the implementation failed and MRPII was not adopted. Company C was most successful and achieved Class 'A'' status as specified by the Oliver Wight certification system (Wight, 1977). Class 'A' indicates that MRPII has been fully implemented, supporting all functions and is integrated with company business strategy.

The research found that there was significant consultant involvement in the majority of interorganisational networks accessed. It was only the network of weak ties accessed by company C that had not been interpenetrated by consultants. Previous research has shown significant consultant involvement in the associations whose members were most closely involved in operations management in the UK and US (BPICS and APICS respectively). This current research supports these findings and extends the scope of professional associations promoting MRPII, to include the IMechE and the IEE. This was highlighted by the involvement of the consultant, Hal Mather, in all three professional associations. His involvement typifies the use made of professional associations by consultants, as an important channel for the diffusion of knowledge about their products and technologies. This consultant activity can also be identified in the analysis of the professional associations' journals. A detailed analysis of the content of these professional associations' journals over the period between 1984 and 1989 found that all three association journals were promoting MRPII to a far greater extent than JIT in the period up to 1989. For example, in that period , the IEE journal contained 43 articles about MRPII, compared to 13 articles about JIT. The role played by consultants in professional associations is also illustrated by their level of activity within the associations. For example, consultant activity in BPICS during 1994 is shown below in Table 2.

Table 2

Membership Category	% of Total Membership	Conference Presentation	Conference Participation	Journal Article Contribution
Practitioner	70	60	26	37
Consultants/ Vendors	23	31	55	76

Whilst consultants actually represent a minority of the BPICS membership they are more involved in the activities of the association as both participants and more especially as presenters of 'new ideas'.

Perceptions of consultants and the knowledge they provide, appears to be distorted positively in their favour through their active involvement in professional associations. Involvement in the professional association network conferred a degree of legitimacy on the consultancy role. The information provided by consultants through their links within the professional association network is perceived to be 'neutral'. During interviews, comments were made about Hal Mather such as "he speaks a lot of sense" and "he understands the real world". These comments were then supported by reference to his position as a Fellow of the IMechE, implying both status and expertise.

Potential adopters of technology may perceive the academic network to be a 'neutral' source of information and assume that the knowledge provided is relatively untainted by vested interests. However, the research highlighted the involvement of consultants in the academic network too. Presented with subject matter firmly grounded in the 'real world' of manufacturing, there is an opportunity for 'experts', other than academics, to disseminate knowledge and expertise within this network. Consultants are in a position whereby they can commodify this knowledge (Zucker, 1991) and hence, the 'neutrality' of the knowledge is questionable. It would not be in the interests of consultants to impart information / knowledge that does not promote their own economic self interest. This research found that the knowledge acquired through the academic network was selective. MRPII technology was presented as the optimal production planning and control tool. Little reference was made to JIT and no reference was made to OPT.

The reference site network is a more obvious example of vendor/consultant involvement. Only those sites that were able to present a positive, unproblematic perception of the technology were selected for factory visits by both the software vendors and consultants. It would not be in the interests of vendors and consultants to organise reference site visits where the technology had failed!

It is important to recognise that it was only the interorganisational network of weak informal ties (used by Company C), which was able to provide information/knowledge regarding other CAPM technologies. The team at Company C had developed a clear business system specification, prior to considering the technology required to support it. The team recognised that sources of information made available through a range of networks, had only helped them to develop an understanding of MRPII. They were aware that this was not sufficient to satisfy their business requirements. Hence, the team at Company C were forced to consider other information sources. Through the use of weak ties, members accessed less formal networks and developed an understanding of all of CAPM variants.

This network of weak ties operated on an informal basis. Relationships had developed and the exchange of knowledge and expertise occurred, in an environment of trust and co-operation. This is in contrast to the more formal knowledge diffusion process, where the exchange of information and knowledge is selective and governed by the economic self-interest of consultants.

Ultimately, the networking activity that occurred across each of the case companies did not provide the 'neutral' information being sought. Other networks accessed actually served to reinforce the pro-innovation bias of vendors/consultants. Consultants, using the guise of professional status, effectively camouflaged themselves within these other networks and were able to disseminate knowledge and expertise which was both selective and in their own interest to impart. This aspect of the diffusion process is not captured either by Rogers or by the DEF.

This analysis suggests an update to the DEF (Figure 3) to include these other networks and to show the inter-relationships between them. It also highlights the dynamics of the relationship between the different interorganisational networks and potential adopters in terms of boundary spanning activity. These interrelationships would be expected to vary across nations. The linkages established will depend on the societal and institutional context in which organisations are embedded. For example, professional associations may play a more significant role in some countries than others (Child et al, 1983).

Figure 3: Update to the DEF

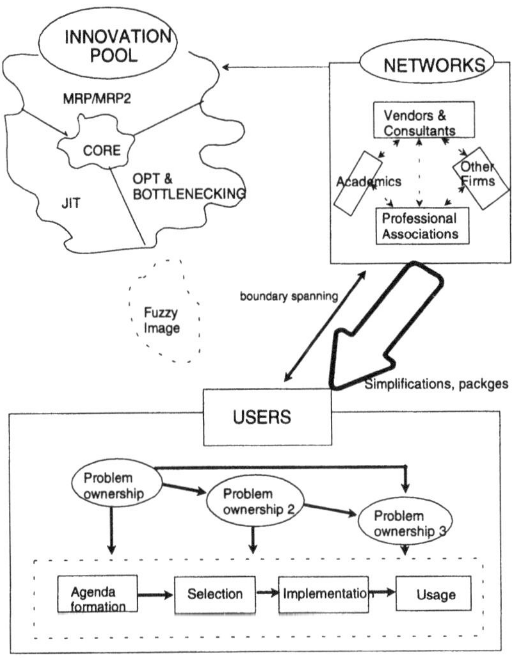

This research has also provided a useful example of institutionalised isomorphic processes operating (DiMaggio & Powell, 1983). DiMaggio & Powell's hypothesis recognises that within certain developed industrial sectors, there is a tendency for firms to develop homogeneously rather than remaining differentiated. This is due largely to the influence of powerful forces such as competition, the state and *professions*. Institutionalised isomorphism is recognised as aiding the diffusion of specific technologies in that as an innovation spreads, a threshold is reached (in terms of adopters) beyond which adoption provides legitimacy rather than improve performance (DiMaggio & Powell, 1983). This research provides insight into the way in which this can occur. Individuals in all three companies visited reference sites and attended professional association seminars, which promoted the concept of MRPII, effectively legitimising the use of MRPII, to the exclusion of other technologies.

This theme is also reflected by Abrahamson (1991) who suggests that within certain organisational groups the adoption of technological innovation is governed more by a fashion perspective, rather than the efficient-choice perspective which dominates the diffusion literature. Efficient choice assumes that organisations act rationally, independently and with certainty, regarding both their own strategic goals and the efficiency of the technology . The fashion perspective suggests that organisations within a group are influenced by fashion setting organisations outside of the group (management consultants, professional associations), which subsequently leads to the diffusion of certain technologies at the expense of others. This may occur even when, (as in these cases), the organisations believe they are acting, following a process of rational decision making. These interrelated concepts suggest that organisations which become active in interorganisational networks may be prone to the effects of institutionalised isomorphism. Fashions, set in many cases by vendors and consultants, subsequently enable the diffusion of certain technologies whilst constraining the diffusion of others. Thus, companies may adopt technologies which are not necessarily appropriate, influenced by the knowledge domains accessed during the decision making process.

CONCLUSION

This research found that during the late 1980's, certain companies within the UK automotive sector were involved in interorganisational networks that promoted the diffusion of certain technologies at the expense of other variants. Using CAPM technology as an example, the research found, in keeping with others, that a variety of networks reinforced and shaped availability of MRPII (Newell & Clark, 1990, Swan & Newell, 1995). Other CAPM technologies existed at this time e.g. JIT and OPT, yet were not actively promoted by these networks. The activity of consultants specialising in MRPII, within these other networks may be an explanatory factor for this. Potential adopters of CAPM technology experienced difficulties in gaining access to networks which *did not* shape availability of CAPM technology at this time. Potential adopters of technology assumed (perhaps wrongly) that outside of the vendor/supplier network, knowledge domains existed that could provide a source of 'neutral' information. However, it is perhaps questionable that this could ever be the case. Consultant activity in these interorganisational networks, whilst legitimate, is going to be driven by an interest in developing new business and in encouraging firms to adopt new technologies.

This research suggests that diffusion rates of CAPM technologies cannot necessarily be predicted by adopting the efficient-choice perspective, which dominates the innovation diffusion literature (Rogers, 1971). MRPII technology was actively promoted by a range of interorganisational networks to the exclusion of other variants of CAPM. Thus, this research has provided an explanation (not necessarily complete), for the successful diffusion of MRPII into organisations, in spite of the high failure rates associated with appropriation of this technology.

REFERENCES

Alter, C. and Hage, J. (1993).. *Organisations Working Together.* Sage, Newbury Park, CA:

Child, J., Fores, M., Glover, I. and Lawrence, P. (1983) A Price to Pay? Professionalism and Work Organisation in Britain and West Germany. *Sociology.* **17**, 63-78.

Clark, P. A. (1987) *Anglo-American Innovation.* DeGruyter, New York

Clark, P., Bennett, D., Burcher, P., Newell, S., Swan, J., and Sharifi, S. (1992). The Decision-Episode Framework and Computer-Aided Production Management (CAPM). *International Studies of Management & Organisation.* **22**, 69-80.

Clark, P. A. and Staunton N. (1989). *Innovation in Technology and Organisation.* Routledge, London

DiMaggio, P. and Powell, W. (1983). The iron Cage Revisited: Institutional Isomorphism and Collective Rationality in Organisational Fields. *American Sociological Review.* **48,** 147-160.

Fleck, J. (1993). Configurations: Crystallizing Contingency. The International Journal of Human Factors in Manufacturing. **3,** 15-36.
Granovetter M. S. (1973). The Strength of Weak Ties. *American Journal of Sociology.* **78,** 1360-1380.
Krupp, J. A. G. (1984). Why MRP Systems Fail: Traps to Avoid. *Production & Inventory Management* **27,** 49-53.
Mather, H. (1986). *Competitive Manufacturing.* Prentice-Hall, New Jersey.
N.E.D.O. (1984). Computers in Production Control.
Newell, S and Clark, P. (1990). The Importance of Extra-organisational networks in the Diffusion and Appropriation of new technologies. *Knowledge: Creation, Diffusion, Utilisation.* **12,** 199-212.
Newell, S., Swan, J. and Clark, P (1993). The Importance of User Design in the Adoption of New Information Technologies: The Example of PICS. *International Journal of Operations & Production Management.* **13,** 4-21.
Pinch, T. P. and Bijker, W.E. (1989) The Social Construction of Facts and Artifacts: Or How the Sociology of Science and the Sociology of Technology Might Benefit Each Other, in *The Social Construction of Technological Systems* (Eds.Bijker, Hughes and Pinch), MIT Press, Cambridge, Massachusettes:
Rogers, E. M. (1962, 1983 3rd Ed.). *Diffusion of Innovations.* Free Press, New York.
Rogers, E. M. (1971). *Communication of Innovation.* Free Press, New York.
Swan J. and Newell, S. (1995). The Role of Professional Associations in Technology Diffusion. *Organisation Studies,* **16** (In press).
Tushman, M. and Scanlan, T. (1981). Boundary Spanning Individuals: Their Role in Information Transfer and their Antecedents. *Academy of Management Journal.***24,** 289-305.
Vollman, A. and Berry, W. (1985). *Manufacturing Control.* Dow Jones-Irwin, Illinios
Waterlow, J. G. and Monniot, J.P. (1986). A study of the state of the art in CAPM in UK Industry, ACME Directorate, Science & Engineering Research Council, 1986.
Wight, O. (1984). *Manufacturing Resource Planning: MRPII.* Oliver Wight Publications, Vermont.
Wilson, F., Desmond, J., & Roberts, H. (1994). 'Success and Failure of MRPII implementation'. *British Journal of Management.* **5**:221-240
Zucker, L. (1991). Markets for bureaucratic authority and control: Information quality in professions and services. *Sociology of Organisations.* **8,**157-190.

BIBLIOGRAPHY

Maxine Robertson is a research fellow currently working with Dr Jacky Swan and Dr Sue Newell on a three year research project funded by the ESRC. The reseach project is a five country comparative study, focusing on the role of professional associations in the diffusion of technological innovation. Jacky Swan and Sue Newell are both psychologists and lecture in Organisational Behaviour at the University of Warwick Business school.

12

Information technology adoption by small business: An empirical study

J.Y.L. Thong and C.S. Yap
National University of Singapore
Department of Information Systems and Computer Science
Lower Kent Ridge Road, Singapore 119260
(email: jthong@iscs.nus.sg; yapcs@iscs.nus.sg)

Abstract

Drawing upon theories from the technological innovation literature, this study examines the relationship between various contextual factors (CEO innovativeness, information intensity, attitude towards IT adoption, IT knowledge, and competition) and IT adoption in small businesses. The results show that small businesses are more likely to adopt IT when they have more innovative CEOs, positive attitude toward adoption of IT, and greater IT knowledge. While CEO innovativeness and attitude toward IT adoption are important determinants of the decision to adopt, they do not affect the extent of IT adoption subsequently. The extent of IT adoption is mainly determined by the level of IT knowledge.

Keywords

Information technology, innovation theories, small businesses, technological innovation

1 INTRODUCTION

An important and fast growing technological innovation during this century is information technology (IT) in the form of computers (Freeman and Perez, 1988). IT provides an opportunity for businesses to improve their efficiency and effectiveness, and even to gain competitive advantage (Ives and Learmonth, 1984; Porter and Millar, 1985). There are many reported cases in the information systems (IS) literature of the positive contribution of IT to large businesses. With the decreasing cost and ever more powerful user-friendly microcomputers and standard software packages, today the benefits are accessible even to the smallest business. Yet, while large businesses have been using computers for some time, small businesses have been slow in adopting these technological innovations.

A review of the published literature shows that to-date there has been little empirical research on the determinants of IT adoption in small businesses. Existing studies (Lind *et al.*, 1989; Yap, 1990) tend to concentrate on large businesses, and findings of these studies are unlikely to be applicable to small businesses because of various fundamental differences between large and small businesses (Cohn and Lindberge, 1972; Welsh and White, 1981). In general, small businesses are characterized by financial constraints, lack of internal IT experts, and a short-range management perspective. Further, the research topic - determinants of IT adoption in small business - is not only of theoretical interest, but also has important practical implications. Consulting firms and IT vendors can target their promotional efforts at small businesses that have not computerized but have characteristics of computerized businesses, since this group of businesses is more likely to adopt IT.

As IT is a technological innovation, it may be fruitful to utilize innovation theories as a reference theory for empirical studies of IT adoption. Rogers (1983), an authority on innovation theory, defined an innovation as an idea, practice, or object that is perceived as new by an individual or other unit of adoption. Thus, an innovation is not only a renewal by means of technology, but it can also refer to renewal in terms of thought and action (Poutsma *et al.*, 1987). The innovation itself need not be new as measured by the time of its discovery or invention. It only has to be perceived as new by the unit of adoption (Zaltman *et al.*, 1973). This suggests that an innovation is any product or process which has been put into practice, and is nontrivial to the business. The innovation presents potential adopters with new means of solving problems and exploiting opportunities.

The characteristics of an innovation can be differentiated along four dimensions (Poutsma *et al.*, 1987). First, there are process innovations and product innovations. Process innovations are innovations that improve the production process through the introduction of new methods, machines, or production systems. Process innovations apply not only to the traditional definition of production but also to data processing, distribution, and services. IT adoption and implementation would fall under this category. Product innovations, on the other hand, refers to the development, production, and dissemination of new consumer and capital goods and services. Second, innovations can be either radical (or shock-like) or incremental (or gradual). Basically, radical innovations are fundamental changes that represent revolutionary changes in technology while incremental innovations are minor improvements or simple changes in current technology (Dewar and Dutton, 1986). IT is an example of a radical innovation. For a small business with little IT knowledge, embarking on IT adoption for the first time is nontrivial as there is a lot of uncertainty and risk involved. The adoption of IT is likely to cause changes in work procedures and increase computer anxiety among the employees. Third, innovations can occur due to technology-push or market-pull. Technology-push implies that an innovation is developed and offered in a matured form on the capital goods market. Under pressure exerted by the competing suppliers and the ascribed superiority of the new innovation, the market is necessitated to absorb the new innovation. In a market-pull, a social need is felt, acknowledged, and translated in terms of technical demand. In response to this demand, a new technology is developed. In the case of IT, both technology-push and market-pull have had an effect on the adoption of IT (King *et al.*, 1994). Four, a distinction can be made between planned and incidental innovation. Planned innovations are innovations that are carried out according to plan where the business aims to control the market through its innovation. Innovations are considered incidental when the innovations occurred as a specific reaction of a business to new market demand. Both approaches are applicable for the adoption of IT.

The technological innovation literature has identified many variables that are possible determinants of organizational adoption of an innovation. This large number of variables suggests that more research is needed to identify the critical ones (Rothwell, 1977). In an agenda for innovation processes research, Eveland *et al.* (1983) contended that a closer consideration of organizational variables with a primary focus on rigorous empirical studies are warranted. However, some researchers have questioned the possibility of developing a unifying theory of innovation adoption and diffusion that can apply to all types of innovations (Downs and Mohr, 1976; Fichman and Kemerer, 1993; Kimberly and Evanisko, 1981). They argued that a unifying theory may be inappropriate due to the fundamental differences between types of innovations. Fichman and Kemerer (1993) claimed that the variations in innovations (e.g. product vs process; administrative vs technical; incremental vs radical) and the adoption contexts in which they may be applied (e.g. individual vs organizational adoption; autonomous vs nonautonomous adoption decisions; competitive vs noncompetitive adoption environments) are simply too great. In a review of eighteen empirical studies of IT diffusion, Fichman (1992) found that IT innovations may have different levels of knowledge burden and locus of adoption (individual vs organization), and classical innovation theory need to be tailored to the adoption context. In response to the lack of a unifying theory of innovation adoption, it is essential to include the distinctive characteristics of context in the development of a strong theory to study innovation adoption (Fichman and Kemerer, 1993; Tornatzky and Fleischer, 1990; Zmud, 1982).

This paper develops and tests a model of IT adoption in small businesses which contains five contextual variables. The five variables are CEO innovativeness, information intensity, attitude toward adoption of IT, IT knowledge, and competition.

2 RESEARCH MODEL

There are two related but distinct research questions: (1) what variables determine the decision of small businesses to adopt IT? and (2) if the decision is to adopt IT, what variables determine the extent of IT adoption? The first research question is concerned with whether a small business is using IT or not while the second research question is concerned with why some small businesses make more use of IT while others less. Based on innovation theories, a model of IT adoption specifically for small businesses was developed (see Figure 1). As this is an early study and the primary purpose is to identify primary relationships, we decided to use a one-stage model relating independent and dependent variables, without any intermediate variables. As more experience is gained, the model can be refined. Each of the variables is discussed below.

2.1 IT adoption

The dependent variable is adoption of IT. In this study, adoption of IT is defined as using computer hardware and software applications to support operations, management, and decision-making in the business (Davis and Olson, 1985). This implies that IT is used productively and is not a 'white elephant'. There are two measures for the dependent variable. The first measure, likelihood of IT adoption, was measured as a binary value: whether the business is computerized or not computerized. This measure is commonly used in diffusion research (Fichman, 1992). A dichotomous measure was used because the first research question of this study is to identify variables that distinguish a computerized small business from a noncomputerized one. Following the example of Alpar and Reeves (1990), a business is defined as computerized if it uses at least one major software application listed in the software application table (see Appendix A). This list excluded word processing packages. The second measure of IT adoption, extent of IT adoption, was measured by the number of microcomputers in use in each business (Lind *et al.*, 1989). This measure indicates the degree to which IT has been adopted. In the case of minicomputer users, the number of terminals was used to derive an equivalent number of microcomputers.

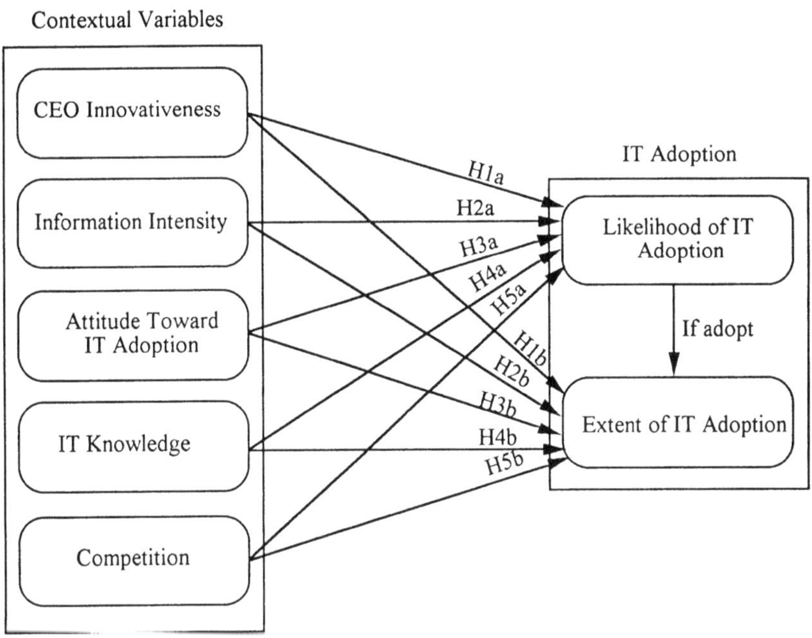

Figure 1 Research model.

2.2 CEO innovativeness

In a small business, the CEO is usually the owner-manager. As the CEO is the main decision-maker, the characteristics of the CEO are crucial in determining the innovative attitude of the small business (Rizzoni, 1991). The CEO's qualities are the determinants of the overall management style of the business (Rothwell, 1977). It is the role adopted by the CEO that determines the innovativeness of the business (Cannon, 1985). In Kirton's (1976) theory of innovativeness, he contended that everyone can be located on a continuum ranging from an ability to do things better to an ability to do things differently. He called the two extreme ends of the continuum adaptors and innovators respectively. In the case of a small business, the adaptor CEO would seek solutions that have already been tried and understood. On the other hand, the innovator CEO would prefer solutions that change the structure in which the problem is embedded - in other words, solutions that have not been tried out and are therefore risky. Unless the CEO has the will to innovate, there is little that others can do to expedite IT adoption or increase the extent of IT adoption.

Hypothesis 1a: The more innovative the CEO, the greater the likelihood of IT adoption.
Hypothesis 1b: The more innovative the CEO, the greater the extent of IT adoption.

2.3 Information intensity

The information processing theory of Galbraith (1973) concentrates on the processes through which the environment influences a business' actions. The degree to which information is present in the product or service of a business reflects the level of information intensity of that product or service. Businesses in different sectors have different information processing needs and those in more information-intensive sectors are more likely to adopt IT than those in less information-intensive sectors (Yap, 1990). For instance, travel agencies are more information-intensive, as their main functions are to process and package tour information. Further, the greater the information intensity, the greater the potential for strategic uses of IT in a business (Porter and Millar, 1985).

Hypothesis 2a: The greater the information intensity of the product/service, the greater the likelihood of IT adoption.
Hypothesis 2b: The greater the information intensity of the product/service, the greater the extent of IT adoption.

2.4 Attitude toward IT adoption

According to Rogers' (1983) innovation theory, formation of a favourable or unfavourable attitude towards an innovation takes place before a decision to adopt is made. In the case of a small business, the CEO is the chief decision-maker. Hence, the CEO's perception toward IT adoption is of prime importance. As IT is a new innovation to the CEO, he or she has no way of knowing whether it will be superior to existing methods of operations. A degree of uncertainty exists as adoption of IT is risky, and each CEO will perceive the degree of risk or uncertainty associated with IT differently. If the CEO perceives the benefits of IT adoption outweigh the risks, then the business is more likely to adopt IT.

Hypothesis 3a: The more positive the attitude toward IT adoption, the greater the likelihood of IT adoption.
Hypothesis 3b: The more positive the attitude toward IT adoption, the greater the extent of IT adoption.

2.5 IT knowledge

Attewell (1992) conceptualized the diffusion of complex technological innovations in terms of decreasing knowledge barriers. Owing to obstacles with developing the necessary skills and technical knowledge, many businesses are tempted to postpone adoption until the barriers to adoption are lowered or circumvented. The implication of this theory is that overcoming the lack of knowledge of the innovation will lead to greater likelihood of adopting the innovation. Typically, small businesses are lacking in IT knowledge and technical skills (DeLone, 1988; Gable, 1991). Many of them rejected the notion that IT could be of any use to their businesses as they had no idea of the benefits that IT could potentially offer. If the IT knowledge barrier of small businesses could be lowered (e.g. more IT knowledgeable employees), they may be more willing to adopt IT.

Hypothesis 4a: *The greater the level of IT knowledge, the greater the likelihood of IT adoption.*
Hypothesis 4b: *The greater the level of IT knowledge, the greater the extent of IT adoption.*

2.6 Competition

By competition, we mean the business environment in which the business operates. Economists generally believe that competition increases the likelihood of innovation adoption (Kimberly and Evanisko, 1981; Link and Bozeman, 1991). It is tough rivalry that pushes businesses to be innovative. Empirically, studies have shown that more intense competition is associated with higher adoption rate (Benvignati, 1982; Globerman, 1975; Levin *et al.*, 1987). Porter and Millar (1985) suggested that by adopting IT, businesses will be able to compete in three ways. IT can change the industry structure and, in so doing, alter the rules of competition. IT can also create competitive advantage by giving businesses new ways to outperform their rivals. Finally, IT spawns new businesses, often from within existing operations of the business. Therefore, a business in an environment that is more competitive would feel a greater need to turn to IT to gain a competitive advantage. On the other hand, a business in a less competitive environment would not be faced with a push to be innovative.

Hypothesis 5a: *The greater the level of competition, the greater the likelihood of IT adoption.*
Hypothesis 5b: *The greater the level of competition, the greater the extent of IT adoption.*

3 RESEARCH METHODOLOGY

3.1 Data collection procedure

In this study, the criteria for defining a small business are adopted from the Association of Small and Medium Enterprises (ASME) in Singapore. A small business is one that satisfies at least two of the following criteria: (1) the number of employees in the business should not exceed 100; (2) the fixed assets of the business should not exceed S$12 million (S$1.00=US$0.60 approximately); and (3) the annual sales of the business should not exceed S$15 million.

The names and addresses of 800 small businesses which fulfil the ASME criteria were obtained from a small business database maintained by the National Computer Board (NCB) in Singapore. The NCB is the main government agency overseeing the promotion of IT to improve productivity and competitiveness in all sectors of the economy. Although the number of businesses supplied by the NCB was large, the proportion of adopters and nonadopters of IT may not be balanced as most of the businesses supplied by the NCB would have adopted IT. Hence, 400 additional businesses were selected at random from the telephone directory.

One questionnaire was designed for data collection. The questionnaire was initially pilot-tested in five small businesses. Based on feedback from these small businesses, minor modifications were made to the questionnaire. The final questionnaire was mailed to the CEOs of the small businesses in the survey sample. A covering letter explained the purpose of the survey and requested the CEO to return the completed questionnaire within three weeks in a pre-paid reply envelope. The respondents were assured of the confidentiality of their responses.

Of the 1200 questionnaires mailed out, 294 questionnaires were returned. However, 122 questionnaires were returned uncompleted as the businesses had changed their addresses or were no longer in operation. The remaining 172 questionnaires gave an effective response rate of 16%. This response rate is considered reasonable notwithstanding that the survey was unsolicited. Responses from 6 businesses were excluded from the final sample as they did not fulfil the criteria of a small business, resulting in 166 usable questionnaires. To ensure that these responses were representative of the larger population, nonresponse bias was assessed by comparing early respondents with late respondents in terms of three key organizational characteristics of the sample. The three characteristics were number of employees, fixed assets, and sales turnover. T-tests showed no significant difference between the two groups of respondents at the 5% significance level, suggesting that nonresponse bias is not a problem. As the CEO is typically the owner-manager in a small business, it is reasonable to assume that the current CEO is the same CEO who decided on IT adoption.

3.2 Measurement of the variables

Standard instruments were utilized as far as possible. Where no standard instruments exist, the research variables were operationalized in close consultation with experienced IS researchers (see Appendix A). CEO innovativeness was measured by the Kirton's (1976) Adaption-Innovation Inventory (KAI) instrument. The KAI is a list of 32 items that is descriptive of the adaption-innovation scale to measure a person's innovativeness. Attitude toward IT adoption was measured by Moore and Benbasat's (1991) instrument. This instrument was adapted to the small business context. The operationalizations of the remaining research variables were developed specially for this study. All perceptual items were measured by 5-point Likert scales representing a range from 'Strongly disagree' to 'Strongly agree'.

3.3 Instrument validation

For each composite research variable, the reliability or internal consistency was assessed by calculating Cronbach's alpha coefficient (see Table 1). All the reliability coefficients were at least 0.70, suggesting that the research variables were reliable (Nunnally, 1978). The construct validity of the specially-developed research variables was examined by factor analysis. A factor analysis indicated that all the factor loadings were greater than the cut-off point of 0.50 as recommended by Nunnally (1978) and the items loaded on their hypothesized variables. Hence, we were confident that construct validity had not been violated. For subsequent statistical analysis, the score for each composite research variable was the sum of a respondent's scores for items defined to measure that variable. Missing data were estimated by using means from the instruments where the items were completed.

Table 1 Descriptive statistics

	Adopter (n=120)		*NonAdopter (n=46)*		*Reliability*
Variable	*Mean*	*Std Dev*	*Mean*	*Std Dev*	*Cronbach alpha*
CEO Innovativeness	96.3	12.2	91.4	13.0	0.81
Information Intensity	11.4	3.0	10.6	3.4	0.89
Attitude Toward Adoption of IT	79.9	9.8	71.3	16.2	0.88
IT Knowledge	5.5	1.9	4.3	2.0	0.75
Competition	10.9	2.8	11.5	2.6	0.70

Table 2 Sample characteristics

	Frequency
Sector	
Manufacturing	49
Commerce	46
Service	71
Hardware	
Microcomputers only	61
Minicomputers only	9
Mini and microcomputers	15
Software Application	
Accounting	88
Sales	70
Inventory control	68
Purchasing	52
Personnel and Payroll	51
CAD/CAM	18
MRP	8
EDI	6
Others	9

4 DATA ANALYSIS

4.1 Characteristics of sample

72% of the responding sample had adopted IT. This figure corresponded closely with the national average of 68% for businesses with less than 100 employees, giving further confidence about the representativeness of the sample (National Computer Board, 1993). The sample characteristics of the 166 small businesses are shown in Table 2. The businesses sampled were in the manufacturing, commerce, and service sectors. The distribution of business sectors is a reflection of the profile of small businesses in Singapore. On hardware, the majority of the businesses had microcomputers only. Finally, most of the businesses had implemented operational and management applications such as accounting systems, sales, inventory control, purchasing, personnel and payroll.

Table 3 Pearson correlation matrix for likelihood of IT adoption

Variable	*(1)*	*(2)*	*(3)*	*(4)*	*(5)*
(1) CEO Innovativeness					
(2) Information Intensity	-0.008				
(3) Attitude toward IT Adoption	-0.017	0.404***			
(4) IT Knowledge	0.130*	0.291***	0.459***		
(5) Competitiveness of Environment	0.038	0.340***	0.203***	0.043	
(6) Likelihood of IT Adoption	0.192***	0.149**	0.302***	0.313***	-0.080

*** $p < 0.01$; ** $p < 0.05$; * $p < 0.10$

Table 4 Pearson correlation matrix for extent of IT adoption (IT adopters only)

Variable	*(1)*	*(2)*	*(3)*	*(4)*	*(5)*
(1) CEO Innovativeness					
(2) Information Intensity	0.111				
(3) Attitude toward IT Adoption	0.104	0.044			
(4) IT Knowledge	0.010	0.184*	0.250**		
(5) Competition	0.043	0.244**	0.050	-0.126	
(6) Extent of IT adoption	0.105	0.230**	0.001	0.356***	-0.119

*** $p < 0.01$; ** $p < 0.05$; * $p < 0.10$

4.2 Correlation matrices

The Pearson correlation matrix for likelihood of IT adoption was examined for the extent of multicollinearity problems (see Table 3). The highest squared correlation among the independent variables was 0.21 between attitude toward IT adoption and IT knowledge. None of the squared correlations was close to 0.80 to suggest a problem with multicollinearity among the research variables (Hair *et al.*, 1992). Similarly, the Pearson correlation matrix for extent of IT adoption was examined (see Table 4). The highest squared correlation among the independent variables was 0.06 between attitude toward IT adoption and IT knowledge. Again, there was no evidence of multicollinearity among the research variables.

4.3 Hypotheses testing

The individual hypotheses with regard to the decision to adopt IT were tested by using logistic regression (see Table 5). It is the appropriate statistical technique when the dependent variable is categorical (e.g. adopters or nonadopters) and the independent variables are interval data (Hosmer and Lemeshow, 1989). Based on the goodness-of-fit statistic (χ^2=124.82, d.f.=134, p=0.703), the model was not significantly different from the perfect model. The results supported hypotheses 1a, 3a, and 4a. The likelihood of IT adoption was significantly associated with CEO innovativeness, attitude toward IT adoption, and IT knowledge. Competition and information intensity were not significantly related to the decision to adopt IT.

Table 5 Logistic regression for likelihood of IT adoption

Dependent	*Independent*	*B*	*Wald*	*p*
Likelihood of IT adoption	CEO innovativeness	1.789	7.273	0.007***
	Information intensity	0.267	1.174	0.279
	Attitude toward IT adoption	1.257	8.161	0.004***
	IT knowledge	0.847	8.731	0.003***
	Competition	-0.413	2.107	0.147

-2 log likelihood: χ^2 = 119.047; p = 0.818; Goodness of fit: χ^2 = 124.820; p = 0.703

*** p < 0.01; ** p < 0.05; * p < 0.10

Table 6 Multiple regression for extent of IT adoption (IT adopters only)

Dependent	*Independent*	*Beta*	*T*	*p*
Extent of IT Adoption	CEO innovativeness	0.157	1.463	0.148
	Information intensity	0.212	1.849	0.069*
	Attitude toward IT adoption	-0.098	-0.848	0.399
	IT knowledge	0.373	3.274	0.002***
	Competition	-0.072	-0.651	0.518

R-squared = 0.268; F = 4.906; p = 0.001

*** p < 0.01; ** p < 0.05; * p < 0.10

The hypotheses relating to the extent of IT adoption were tested by using multiple regression (see Table 6). This technique is appropriate when the dependent variable is of interval scale (Hair *et al.*, 1992). The results supported hypotheses 2b and 4b. The extent of IT adoption was significantly associated with IT knowledge at the 0.05 level. There was also a weak relationship between extent of IT adoption and information intensity (p=0.069). CEO innovativeness, attitude toward IT adoption, and competition were not significantly related to the extent of IT adoption.

5 DISCUSSION

5.1 Likelihood of IT adoption

For small businesses, IT adoption is dependent on the level of CEO innovativeness, attitude toward IT adoption, and IT knowledge. IT represents a radical innovation that is complex and requires a large outlay of financial resources. If the adoption is not successful, the small business could suffer irreparable damages that it may not be able to recover from. Hence, IT adoption is a risky venture. Only CEOs who are more innovative would be willing to take the risk of adopting IT in their businesses.

Small businesses with more positive attitude toward IT adoption are more likely to adopt IT. This result provides support for Rogers' (1983) innovation theory in a small business context. Some of the essential attributes of the innovation which affect the formation of attitude include relative advantage, compatibility, complexity, trialability, and observability. If the innovation is viewed as better than the existing system, is consistent with the needs of the adopting business, is easy to use and understand, allows for experimentation, and the results are easily demonstrable, then there is a higher chance that a favourable attitude toward the innovation is formed. In the context of IT adoption by small businesses, those CEOs who perceive IT adoption to be beneficial to their businesses would be more likely to adopt IT.

In addition, small businesses that are more knowledgeable about IT are more likely to adopt IT. This is consistent with Attewell's (1992) theory of lowering knowledge barriers. To the extent that the small business can lower its knowledge inadequacies, it will facilitate the path to IT adoption. Dewar and Dutton (1986) have found that extensive knowledge is important for the adoption of technical process innovation. Lack of knowledge of the IT adoption process and insufficient awareness of the potential benefits may inhibit small businesses from adopting IT (Senn and Gibson, 1981). To address this, small businesses may supplement their inadequate IT knowledge by engaging external IT experts such as consulting firms and IT vendors (Thong *et al.*, 1994). The external IT experts can act as Attewell's (1992) 'supply-side organizations' that help to lower the innovation risk of the small businesses.

Finally, information intensity and competition do not have any significant direct effects on the decision of small businesses to adopt IT. However, there is evidence that they may have indirect effects on adoption of IT through attitude toward IT adoption. Attitude toward IT adoption is positively correlated with both of these variables. Thus, we speculate that information intensity and competition may influence the business perception toward IT adoption, resulting in the decision to adopt IT. More research needs to be conducted before we can draw more concrete conclusions.

5.2 Extent of IT adoption

There is a possibility that our results may be confounded as some small businesses may have adopted more IT products due to their size. To determine the extent of this problem, we examined the Pearson correlations between organization size, using number of employees as a surrogate measure, and the independent variables. No significant correlation was found, suggesting that organization size was not a confounding variable.

The most significant variable that determines the extent of IT adoption is IT knowledge. Small businesses with greater IT knowledge are likely to use IT more extensively. This finding is again consistent with Attewell's (1992) conceptualization of innovation diffusion as a process of lowering knowledge barriers. As most small businesses do not have a formal internal IT department, they usually computerize with the aid of external IT experts such as consultants or IT vendors. Attewell (1992) suggested that the relationship between the innovation suppliers and the adopting businesses will go beyond selling, and will become structured around the task of reducing knowledge hurdles. When the small business accumulate more IT knowledge through learning by using, it will lower its IT knowledge barriers and be more confident in adopting other IT products. Widespread, routinized, and effective use of the innovation is needed before additional adoption (Fichman and Kemerer, 1993).

The second variable that affects the extent of IT adoption is information intensity. The greater the information intensity of the product or service which the small business is involved in, the greater the extent of IT adoption. This provides some support for the information processing theory. Galbraith (1973) found that when businesses take on uncertain tasks, such as scanning and processing complex information about new innovations, they have to manage the increase in information load with various design strategies. Similarly, a small business dealing with a product or service with high information intensity can make more extensive use of IT to meet its information processing needs.

Contrary to our hypotheses, CEO innovativeness, attitude toward IT adoption, and competition do not have any direct significant effects on the extent of IT adoption in small businesses. While CEO innovativeness and attitude toward IT adoption may influence the initial decision to adopt IT, they do not have any effect on the extent of IT adoption subsequently. This suggests that Attewell's (1992) theory of lowering knowledge barriers takes precedence over individual innovativeness and attitude after the initial IT adoption. In the case of competition, it appears to have no direct 'push' for businesses to increase the extent of IT adoption. However, competition may have an indirect effect on the extent of IT adoption through information intensity. Competition is positively correlated with information intensity ($r = 0.244$, $p < 0.05$). Further research is needed to study this relationship.

6 CONCLUSION

Based on theories from the innovation literature, this paper has developed and tested a model of IT adoption in small businesses. The results show partial support for the model. Small businesses that have innovative CEOs, possess more positive attitude toward IT adoption, and are more knowledgeable about IT, are more likely to adopt IT. There are also some evidence that information intensity and competition may have indirect effects on the decision to adopt

IT. However, only IT knowledge and information intensity are determinants of the extent of IT adoption. This paper has also provided evidence of the efficacy of applying technological innovation literature to the study of IT adoption.

Finally, the limitations of this study are discussed. First, due to the cross-sectional nature of the study, direction of causality can only be inferred. It is not possible to measure directly the perception of the CEO at the time of IT adoption. This is ameliorated to some extent by requesting the respondent to ascertain his or her perceptions before IT adoption. However, we cannot be completely certain that the respondent can back-track his or her mind uninfluenced by the experience of IT adoption to what the state was before adoption of IT. Longitudinal studies need to be conducted to determine the causal links more explicitly. Second, this study has investigated a subset of the variables found to be important in other technological innovations. There are other contextual variables such as performance gap, organization culture and government regulation (Ettlie, 1983; Kautz, 1995; Yap *et al.*, 1994) that may be potential determinants of IT adoption in small businesses. Future research should examine these possibilities.

7 REFERENCES

Alpar P. and Reeves S. (1990) Predictors of MS/OR application in small businesses. *Interfaces,* **20(2)**, 2-11.

Attewell P. (1992) Technology diffusion and organizational learning: the case of business computing. *Organization Science,* **3(1)**, 1-19.

Benvignati A.M. (1982) Interfirm adoption of capital-goods innovations. *The Review of Economics and Statistics,* **64**, 330-335.

Cannon T. (1985) Innovation, creativity and small firm organization. *International Small Business Journal,* **4(1)**, 33-41.

Cohn T. and Lindberge R.A. (1972) *How management is different in small companies.* American Management Association, New York.

Davis G.B. and Olson M.H. (1985) *Management information systems: conceptual foundations, structure, and development.* McGraw-Hall, Singapore.

DeLone W.H. (1988) Determinants of success for computer usage in small business. *MIS Quarterly,* **12(1)**, 51-61.

Dewar R.D. and Dutton J.E. (1986) The adoption of radical and incremental innovations: an empirical analysis. *Management Science,* **32(11)**, 1422-1433.

Downs G.W.Jr. and Mohr L.B. (1976) Conceptual issues in the study of innovation. *Administrative Science Quarterly,* **21**, 700-714.

Ettlie J.E. (1983) Performance gap theories of innovation. *IEEE Transactions on Engineering Management,* **30(2)**, 39-52.

Eveland J.D., Hetzner W.A. and Tornatzky L.G. (1983) Conceptual issues in the study of innovation. *IEEE Transactions on Engineering Management,* **30(2)**, 37-38.

Freeman C. and Perez C. (1988) Structural Crisis of Adjustment: Business Cycles and Investment Behaviour, in *Technical Change and Economic Theory* (eds. G. Dosi et al.), Pinter Publications, New York, 38-66.

Fichman R.G. (1992) Information technology diffusion: a review of empirical research, in *Proceedings of the Thirteenth International Conference on Information Systems*, Dallas, Texas, 195-206.

Fichman R.G. and Kemerer C.F. (1993) Toward a theory of the adoption and diffusion of software process innovations, in *Proceedings of IFIP Conference on Diffusion, Transfer, & Implementation of Information Technology* (ed. L. Levine) Pittsburg, 23-30.

Gable G.G. (1991) Consultant engagement for first time computerization: a pro-active client role in small businesses. *Information & Management*, **20**, 83-93.

Galbraith J.R. (1973) *Designing complex organizations*. Addison-Wesley, Reading, M.A.

Globerman S. (1975) Technological diffusion in the Canadian tool and die industry. *The Review of Economics and Statistics*, **57(4)**, 428-434.

Hair J.F.Jr., Anderson R.E., Tatham R.L. and Black W.C. (1992) *Multivariate data analysis*. 3rd edition, Macmillian, New York.

Hosmer D.W. and Lemeshow S. (1989) *Applied logistic regression*. Wiley, New York.

Ives B. and Learmonth G.P. (1984) The information system as a competitive weapon. *Communications of the ACM*, **27(12)**, 1193-1201.

Kimberly J.R. and Evanisko M.J. (1981) Organizational innovation: the influence of individual, organizational, and contextual factors on hospital adoption of technological and administrative innovations. *Academy of Management Journal*, **24(4)**, 689-713.

Kautz K. (1995) Information technology transfer and implementation: the introduction of an electronic mail system in a public service organization, in *Proceedings of First IFIP 8.6 Working Conference on Diffusion and Adoption of Information Technology* (ed. K. Kautz and J. Pries-Heje) Oslo, 153-165.

King J.L., Gurbaxani V., Kraemer, K.L., McFarlan F.W., Raman K.S. and Yap C.S. (1994) The institutional factors in information technology innovation. *Information Systems Research*, **5(2)**, 139-169.

Kirton M.J. (1976) Adaptors and innovators: a description and measure. *Journal of Applied Psychology*, **61(5)**, 622-629.

Levin S.G., Levin S.L. and Meisel J.B. (1987) A dynamic analysis of the adoption of a new technology: The case of optical scanners. *The Review of Economics and Statistics*, **51**, 12-17.

Lind M.R., Zmud R.W. and Fischer W.A. (1989) Microcomputer adoption- the impact of organizational size and structure. *Information & Management*, **16**, 157-162.

Link A.N. and Bozeman B. (1991) Innovative behaviour in small-sized firms. *Small Business Economics*, **3**, 179-184.

Moore G.C. and Benbasat I. (1991) Development of an instrument to measure the perceptions of adopting an information technology innovation. *Information Systems Research*, **2(3)**, 192-221.

National Computer Board (1993) *Singapore IT usage survey 1993*. National Computer Board, Singapore.

Nunnally J (1978) *Psychometric Theory*. McGraw-Hill, New York.

Porter M. and Millar V.E. (1985) How information gives you competitive advantage. *Harvard Business Review*, **63(4)**, 149-160.

Poutsma E.F., Van Uxem F.W. and Walravens A.H.C.M. (1987) *Process innovation and automation in small and medium sized business*. Delft University Press, The Netherlands.

Rizzoni A (1991) Technological innovation and small firms: a taxonomy. *International Small Business Journal*, **9(3)**, 31-42.

Rogers E.M. (1983) *Diffusion of innovations*. Third Edition, The Free Press, New York.

Rothwell R. (1977) The characteristics of successful innovators and technically progressive firms. *R & D Management*, **7(3)**, 191-206.

Senn J.A. and Gibson V.R. (1981) Risks of investment in microcomputers for small business management. *Journal of Small Business Management*, **19**(3), 24-32.

Thong J.Y.L., Yap C.S. and Raman K.S. (1994) Engagement of external expertise in information systems implementation. *Journal of Management Information Systems*, **11(2)**, 209-231.

Tornatzky L.G. and Fleischer M. (1990) *The processes of technological innovation*. Lexington Books, MA.

Welsh J.A. and White J.F. (1981) A small business is not a little big business. *Harvard Business Review*, **59(4)**, 18-32.

Yap C.S. (1990) Distinguishing characteristics of organizations using computers. *Information & Management*, **18**, 97-107.

Yap C.S., Thong J.Y.L. and Raman K.S. (1994) Effect of government incentives on computerisation in small business. *European Journal of Information Systems*, **3(3)**, 191-206.

Zaltman G., Duncan R. and Holbek J. (1973) *Innovations and organizations*. Wiley, New York.

Zmud R.W. (1982) Diffusion of modern software practices: influence of centralization and formalization. *Management Science*, **28(12)**, 1421-1431.

8 APPENDIX

Appendix A Examples of questionnaire items

	Strongly disagree				Strongly agree
CEO Innovativeness					
I have original ideas	1	2	3	4	5
I would sooner create something new than improve something existing	1	2	3	4	5
I often risk doing things differently	1	2	3	4	5
Information Intensity					
My company is dependent on up-to-date information	1	2	3	4	5
It is very important for my company to have access to reliable, relevant and accurate information	1	2	3	4	5
It is very important for my company to access information fast whenever we need the information	1	2	3	4	5
Attitude Toward Adoption of IT					
Computers increase the productivity of my employees	1	2	3	4	5
My employees find computers easy to use	1	2	3	4	5
I have seen what other small companies have achieved with computers	1	2	3	4	5

IT Knowledge

My employees are all computer-literate	1	2	3	4	5
There is at least one employee who is a computer expert	1	2	3	4	5
I would rate my employees' understanding of computers as very good compared to other small companies in the same industry.	1	2	3	4	5

Competition

It is easy for our customers to switch to another company for similar services/products without much difficulty	1	2	3	4	5
The rivalry among companies in the industry my company is operating in is very intense	1	2	3	4	5
There are many products/ services in the market which are different from ours but perform the same functions	1	2	3	4	5

IT Adoption

For each computer applications in use in your company, please put a tick against the application.

APPLICATION	In-use
Accounting	
Inventory Control	
Sales	
Purchasing	
Personnel and Payroll	
CAD/CAM	
EDI	
MRP	
Others (Please specify)	

9 BIOGRAPHY

James Y.L. Thong is a doctoral candidate in the Department of Information Systems and Computer Science, National University of Singapore. He received his M.Sc. in MIS and B.Sc. (Hons) in computer science from the National University of Singapore. His research is on computerization issues that affect small business with emphasis on information technology transfer, diffusion, and implementation. He has published in the *Journal of Management Information Systems*, *OMEGA*, and *European Journal of Information Systems*.

Chee Sing Yap is Head of the Information Systems Division, Department of Information Systems and Computer Science, National University of Singapore. He holds a B.Sc. (Eng.) from Imperial College, London, and a Ph.D. in information systems from Cambridge University. His research interests include the use of information technology (IT) in small business, government policy and IT in Asia-Pacific countries, and telecommuting. His publications have appeared in *Information Systems Research*, *Journal of Management Information Systems*, *Information & Management*, *OMEGA*, *Informatization and the Public Sector*, *The Information Society*, *Journal of the Operational Research Society* and *European Journal of Information Systems*.

13

Learning at work

K. Thoresen
Norwegian Computing Center
Box 114, Blindern, 0314 Oslo, Norway
Phone: 47-22 85 25 00 Fax: 47-22 69 76 60
Email: Kari.Thoresen@nr.no

Abstract

Organizational implementation of IT systems requires distribution, sharing and pooling of knowledge of how the system can be used in daily practice. This paper analyzes processes of 'learning at work' as they emerge in groups of workers using IT for management and monitoring of the long lines and trunk networks in a telecommunications company. It is shown how resources for learning are socially structured, and how most of the learning takes place as an integrated aspect of the primary work. Thus, learning at work is also learning through work. The concept of 'organizational learning' is discussed relative to the study, and it is argued that the cognitive perspective on organizational learning tends to obliterate some of the important aspects of learning at work.

Keywords

Communities-of-practice, organizational learning, implementation.

1 POINT OF DEPARTURE

How do organizations learn to use their IT systems as a means to carry out their primary work ? It may seem odd to talk about organizations using IT systems, since it is always individuals who use systems. However, there are aspects of adoption of IT that cannot be ascribed to individuals alone. One condition for successful adoption is distributed and shared knowledge regarding use among the networkers. Monopolized knowledge, residing in a computer department or in local gurus mainly, is likely to increase vulnerability and reduce the sustainability of the learning process. A previous study (Bermann and

Thoresen, 1992) showed how the same IT system used in two different hotels contributed to markedly different effects due to the different emphasis on distributed learning.

If we look at adoption and appropriation of IT systems as a variety of organizational change, broad integration is one of the building blocks that facilitates change, as illustrated by Kanter (1988):

> 'If innovations are isolated, in segmentalist fashion, and not allowed to touch other parts of the organization's structure and culture, then it is likely that the innovation will never take hold, fade into disuse, or produce a lower level of benefits than it potentially could (p.299)'

'Learning at work' refers to these processes of distributing and sharing knowledge in the organization as a part of daily practice. These are long-term processes, constituted by a combination of planned and accidental circumstances. It is necessary to distinguish between 'learning' and 'training'. Planned efforts like e.g. training programs or courses, are elements in learning at work, but their impact is variable.

The questions underlying the present study are as follows:

- How does the distribution and sharing of knowledge* regarding use of IT systems take place in organizations ?
- What are the resources used in the above processes ?
- What are the elements - technical and organizational - that facilitate and hinder learning at work ?

To study the questions outlined above, two IT systems in the Norwegian company Telenor have been selected. This paper reports on one of them - NetSys - a system for the management of the long lines and trunk networks in Telenor. NetSys is used by workers from different job categories, whose primary work is related to the management, monitoring and maintenance of the network.

Focus and time-span

The learning perspective underlying this paper differs in some respects from more familiar perspectives, such as diffusion or decision. Scenarios from a decision perspective often adopt a top-down approach, as seen in much of the management literature. As noted by Wardell (1992):

> This scenario, ... , can be broadly characterized as a top-down approach. Overall, the approach explicitly portrays shop-floor activity and the organization of the workplace as being shaped almost entirely by the efforts of managers who respond to a problematic environment. (p.144)

In this paper, the focus is on the daily practice of *the technical and clerical staff and their supervisors.*

---

* The author is aware of the problems inherent in using 'knowledge' in singular. It may give the impression of a unified body of knowledge. See section on 'Expert users' for a more detailed explanation.

Following Herbig and Kramer (1993), *diffusion* is the process of adoption by potential users of a technology or innovation. Adoption may be conceived as a two-stage process where the *initiation* consists of all of the information-gathering, conceptualizing, and planning for the adoption of an innovation, leading up to the decision to adopt, and the *implementation,* all of the events, actions and decisions involved in putting an innovation to use (Van de Ven and Rogers, 1988). The implementation stage can further be said to consist of all events and actions pertaining to modification in both an innovation and an organization, initial utilization and continued use of the innovation when it becomes a routine feature of the organization (Damanpour, 1991).

In the present study, decision to adopt is not a topic, the networkers must cope with what they have. However, coping means both adapting to the existing technical and organizational frameworks, and at the same time, actively shaping the frameworks according to the networkers' needs. The emphasis is therefore on the *interplay between the top-down and bottom-up processes* of integrating NetSys in the organization. This is an aspect of the implementation stage outlined above.

The time-span concerns the period *from initial installation of the system in 1985 until now* with an emphasis on the period of 1993-1995, i.e. fairly late in the implementation process.

Why these topics are interesting

From a practitioner's view, learning at work is necessary to obtain substantial results from investments in IT. Marketing 'hype' implicitly or explicitly claims that results come with the equipment; unfortunately this is contradicted by the experiences of many organizations (see e.g. Keen, Bronsema and Zuboff, 1982, Rowe, 1985, Franke, 1987, Zuboff, 1988, Duimering et al., 1993). Today it is common knowledge that learning and organizational changes are needed in order to reap benefits.

The trend towards integrating systems across organizational boundaries, adds a new dimension of *heterogeneity*. There is widespread recognition of the challenges inherent in this trend, for instance regarding networking (Clement et al., 1994, Wagner, 1994). Another example is the "work-flow thinking" of business process reengineering (see e.g. Hammer, 1990, Jones, 1994, Iden 1995). How does the increased heterogeneity of user groups influence the learning processes ? Will a wider spectrum of training programs be required ? Furthermore, how can heterogeneous groups learn from each other ?

2 ORGANIZATIONAL LEARNING - SOME CONSIDERATIONS

From a theoretical perspective, issues of learning in organizations are often categorized as 'organizational learning'. Organizational learning is one of the fashionable terms in current literature, in particular management literature (see e.g. special editions of Organization Science, 1991, Organization Studies, 1993, and Organizational Dynamics, 1993). It is also a slippery term in the sense that it takes on different, and sometimes unclear meanings depending on the author, the discipline and the area of study.

Dodgson (1993) remarks that 'conceptions of organizational learning are ubiquitous.' He claims that one of the reasons for the popularity of the concept is its broad analytical value. This may be seen in the diversity of use in different disciplines - economic history, industrial economy, management, organization theory, psychology etc. He also views 'organizational learning' as an integrative concept. It can be used to unify various levels of analysis: individual, group, corporate. However, Huber (1991) notes the lack of cumulative work and lack of integration of work from different research groups, which indicates that the broad analytical value may be more of a potential than a reality.

2.1 Grounding organizational learning

The literature on organizational learning is rich and varied (see e.g. Huber, 1991, Orr, 1992, Dodgson, 1993, Cook and Yanow, 1993,). There are, however, complementary strands in the literature that differ markedly in their view of what organizational learning is. These strands see organizations as *cognitive entities*, and as *communities-of-practice*, respectively[1].

Organizations as cognitive entities

This perspective sees organizational learning as modelled after individual learning, in two different ways:

- Individuals learn in organizational contexts. Change comes about because key individuals have the power and influence to change organizational behaviour (see e.g. March and Olsen, 1979, Simon, 1991).
- Organizations are seen, metaphorically, as humans -- with perceptive organs, brains, memories etc. (see e.g. Hedberg, 1981, and Weick, 1991).

Several aspects that were central to the present study were difficult to locate in the literature. While the study of networkers emphasized the centrality of work practice relative to organizational learning, work practice was hardly visible in the literature. Likewise, the everyday dynamics that characterizes organizations, is mostly invisible in the literature. The literature gives an impression of distance to the learners' daily work -- the remote view (see e.g. Dorroh et al., 1994, Levitt and March, 1988). Some problems related to the remote view are outlined below. It is suggested that 'learning at work' is a more appropriate concept for the kind of organizational learning illustrated in this study.

The remote view

Sachs (1994) distinguishes between 'activity'- (or 'work'-) oriented thinking, and 'organization'-oriented thinking for the purpose of representing work for systems design.

> From an organizational perspective, work is conceptualized as a set of clearly defined tasks and operations, described in methods and procedures which fulfill a set of business functions. This view of work differs from an activity-oriented approach which suggests that the range of activities, communication practices, relationships and coordination it takes to

* The line of argument in this section is based on Cook and Yanow, 1993.

> accomplish business functions, is complex and continually mediated by workers and managers alike. (Sachs, 1994, p. 36)

This is in accordance with a number of studies of work practice (Wynn, 1979, Strauss et al, 1985, Suchman, 1983, 1987, Lave and Wenger, 1991, Gerson and Star, 1986, Orr, 1991, 1992) that show how efficient work is characterized by the workers' ability to discover, define and solve problems when they arise, rather than by their skill in following procedures. Task descriptions and procedures may at best function as resources for action (Suchman, 1987). At worst they may be so remote from the practical problems the procedures were intended to solve that they are dismissed by the potential users (Orr, 1991). Most of us know this from our own experience, for instance, when trying to follow instructions for which actions to take when the copier breaks down. From the remote view, contingencies, shortcuts and local adaptation become less visible. The remote view (see e.g. Dorroh et al., 1994, Levitt and March, 1988) obliterates the concrete actions taking place, making it difficult to understand how the reported results came about.

Blomberg (1993) points out:

> Learning about work from a distance tends to result in descriptions of the work that are overly idealized and that fail to reveal unremarkable, yet consequential, aspects of the work (p.11).

One such unremarkable, yet consequential aspect of the work, is the learning that takes place -- learning interwoven with daily practice. Orr (1992) notes the peculiar fact that in the literature on organizational learning, learning is seen as problematic, while ethnographic studies all seem to find that people learn easily, continuously and virtually automatically.

Although it would be an exaggeration to say that this holds for the networkers as well, there are aspects of their learning processes that resonate with the above view (see also section on Resources for learning).

Everyday dynamics

Organizations are fluid entities, in the sense that they are continually changing. They are engaged in long-term change processes as well as short-term changes pervading daily life at work. These everyday dynamics are also visible in the present study and are further discussed in chapter 9 on embedded groups. However, this fluidity make the concept of 'organization' problematic.

Orr (1992) discusses the elusiveness of 'organization' as an entity. Based on studies of service technicians in a large corporation which manufactures photocopiers, he claims that the term 'organization' does not capture the multiple realities of 'organization' as experienced by its members. For one thing, membership is fluid. For the service technicians:

> ....even field service as an organization is not a coherent entity either. There is 'this district' as opposed to 'that district', and then there is 'this team' as opposed to other teams or the district itself. Within teams there are workgroups, and within workgroups there are 'Customer Service Teams.' These are composed of two or three individual technicians. Thus there is an array of organizations at play in the service organization, with substantial-

> ly or wholly overlapping memberships, and yet there is a clear choosing of which membership is appropriate at a given time. (Orr, 1992, p.3-4)

The basic question raised here concerns the problems inherent in delimiting the unit of analysis when it is dynamic. It is often difficult to glean from the literature what kind of entity is referred to as an 'organization'. A company ? A team ? A group of managers ? A department ? Although there is a high degree of consensus that the fundamental learning entity is an individual (Fiol and Lyles, 1985), the leap from the individual to the organization, at whatever level, remains vague.

Organizations as communities-of-practice

The focus on organizations as communities-of-practice represents a cultural perspective, rather than an organizational or managerial. Examples are found in e.g. Lave and Wenger (1991), Brown and Duguid (1991), Orr (1992) and Cook and Yanow (1993).

A characteristic of organizations as communities-of-practice is their *ability to carry out collective activities.* The ability to act is attributed to the group, not only the individual or the sum of individuals. A symphony can only be played by the orchestra, not by any individual musician, not even by the sum of individual musicians. Rehearsals and performances are dependent on mutual interactions in real-time between the conductor and the orchestra members, and among the orchestra members: listening, correcting, enhancing, changing the elements of the musical performance as it unfolds. Thus it makes sense to say that a group acts, and that the individual musicians can act on their abilities only in the context of an orchestra. Focus shifts from individuals in organizational contexts, to groups of individuals in a web of commitments regarding a production process.

In Lake City, the whole group of networkers are involved in order to keep the network in optimal shape. The group's actions encompass both things the individual alone can do, but also actions involving cooperation and interdependence. The various subgroups depend on each other to carry out the orders, and each subgroup in turn can only do this by cooperating among themselves and with other work groups.

Another characteristic of organizations as communities-of-practice is that the ability to act is *based on knowledge that resides in the organization as a whole.* An individual networker may know how to carry out her own activities, but she depends on other networkers' knowledge. The person resonsible for signing off completed orders knows about the technical details of sign-offs. However, that is insufficient in order to provide the collective product. She depends on networkers all over the region to do their part and sign-off locally, and she can't just sit and wait for it to happen. She actively checks where there are missing sign-offs, she calls the relevant persons to find out why they are late, and breathes down their neck if necessary. It is not her knowledge only, neither is it the accumulated knowledge of a number of individuals -- it is *collective knowledge* that comes into being through interactions regarding work.

The third characteristic points to a phenomenon which is almost absent in the cognitive perspective: *Organizational learning is preservative as well as innovative.* The preservative variety of learning concerns not losing professional identity, to continue to be able to do what they are good at. Cook and Yanow (1993) point out how a group of flutemakers of high reputation strives to maintain their professional identity as makers of 'the finest flutes in the world' while accommodating an innovation in the form of a new scale. The same concern runs like a red thread through my material: the obligation expressed by the networkers to provide high quality network services despite the turbulence of organizational and technological changes. In some cases, what is called 'resistance to change' in the literature, may in fact be preservation.

Organizational learning is seen as *the acquiring of knowledge that enables the group to carry out their collective activities.* By taking into account the actual work that is carried out, the relationship between knowledge and work becomes visible. Chapter 9 and 10 discusses some of the resources and strategies employed by the networkers for this purpose.

3 THE CONCEPT OF LEARNING

The concept of learning underlying this paper emphasizes the relationship between knowledge and action. I have gradually come to see learning as *a potential change in the repertoire of actions, based on knowledge.* Some points in this specification need clarifying.

First, the change may be potential, not necessarily manifest. The networkers may know how to carry out specific tasks, e.g. from courses or manuals, but do not try it out in their daily work, for instance due to division of work. This correspond to the concept of 'role-constrained' learning (March and Olsen, 1976).

Second, learning is not limited to improvement -- change may imply an increase or a reduction of the repertoire of actions. Work skills once learned may diminish if not practiced regularly. A variety of help-seeking approaches may, for instance, be replaced with one standardized approach. Hedberg (1981) used the concept of 'unlearning' to denote a process through which learners discard knowledge.

Third, there is not necessarily a fixed sequence between knowledge and action. Knowledge may precede action, but action may also precede knowledge. The networkers may find their way through the system by trial-and-error approaches, and use such approaches to develop a more coherent understanding of the system. It is the 'maybe-it-will-work-if-I-push-that-button' syndrome that most of us are familiar with.

Hanks (1991) expresses a similar view on learning:

> The individual learner is not gaining a discrete body of abstract knowledge which (s)he will then transport and reapply in later contexts. Instead, (s)he acquires the skill to perform by actually engaging in the process, under the attenuated conditions of *legitimate peripheral participation* (author's italics) (p.14).

Thus, a condition for learning at work is the access to close cooperation and communication with coworkers regarding work. The paper focus on the processes through which this occur.

4 TELENOR AND ITS BUSINESS CONTEXT*

Telenor is the former 'Televerket', which until recently was the only national tele-operator in Norway. For more than a century it has been one of Norway's largest public institutions, occupying a monopoly position in the telecommunications field until a deregulation opened up the Norwegian market in the late 1980's. The European Union has launched January 1, 1998 as the D-Day for free telecommunication markets in Europe, and international alliances are continually being forged.

One of the target groups for new operators in Norway is that of large companies, which are also a major source of income for Telenor. This makes Telenor vulnerable to competition regarding the large customers. In most of the private customers market, and parts of the company market, Telenor may keep its dominating position, due to its history and its size. It is still by far the largest operator in the Norwegian market. Pressure is expected from larger operators with higher productivity and lower costs, and from specialists of customized value-added services.

Two of the Telenor's organizational changes -- changes originating as responses to the environment, are essential to this study: from public monopoly to a (semi)-private company; and from a functional bureaucracy to a divisionalized structure. A cultural transformation -- from a corporate culture based on administration of public services to customer-orientation -- is part of the parcel. The transition from a public monopoly to a company, although wholly owned by the state, took place formally January 1, 1995. Preceding the formal event, a series of reorganizations have taken place, accompanied by downsizing. The number of employees in the period 1965-1992 reached a peak of more than 22.000 in 1987 before declining to slightly more than 18.000 in 1991. Top management claims that further reduction is needed, in order to meet the competition.

In 1992-93 the divisionalization took place, including a geographical change where 27 tele-areas were allocated to 7 regions (Figure1). At the end of 1994 the divisions were reorganized into separate units. During the later years, a number of subsidiary business units have been established, owned directly or indirectly by Telenor.

At the time of the field work, the main divisions in the mother company were the private market division, the company market division and the network division. Of a total turnover of roughly 2 billion NOK in 1994, the private market division counted for 34 %, the company market division for 26 % and the network division for 3 %. However, this figure represents only the external turnover for the network division. In 1995, more than 90% of expected turnover for the network division will come from internal invoicing.

As seen from Figure 1, all regions encompass these divisions, giving a matrix-based structure. TRP (Telenor Resource Pool) is intended to develop new business areas and offer further education for surplus personnel. There are central and regional staff functions for IT, research, education, material administration, property management etc.

---

* The section is based upon information from 'Åpen linje' -- the Telenor internal newspaper, in particular the articles by S.Karlsen.

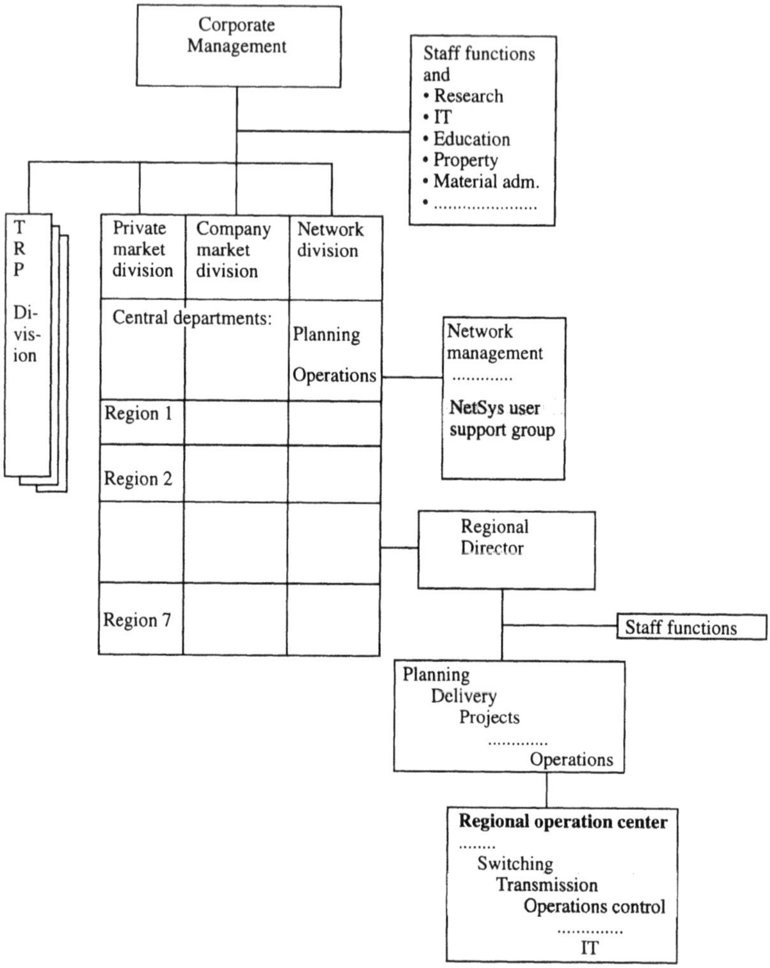

Figure 1. Simplified organizational chart of Telenor showing the relevant organizational units (shaded) and their location in the overall organizational framework. On the *regional level*: transmission and operations control (which includes both network allocators and operations control personnel), and on the *central level:* network administration, which encompass the user-support group. NOTE: This reflects the organization at the time of the field work.

The study takes place in the network division during the turbulent times from 1993-1995. It is important to understand the impact of the turbulence in shaping the intervening conditions for the results reported here. Regarding the practical work, new routines, power distribution, reporting channels, etc. were re-established. Some positions were filled with substitutes who sometimes did not know for how long they were to stay, or only reluctantly took on the jobs. The atmosphere of upheaval and unpredictability felt by the employees during this period, regarding for instance employment security, work load, job changes and rights to participate in decision processes at all levels, was marked. The change was felt all the more strongly due to Telenor's long history of stability, also regarding industrial relations.

5 METHODOLOGY

The material for this study was collected during field work in Telenor during the fall of 1993 and January-March 1995. The empirical material includes interviews with and observations of 11 persons - four women and seven men- working with different types of network management ('the networkers') in one of the regions. The networkers included operation control personnel, network allocators and transmission technicians. Nine of these work in the regional operation center in Lake City and two in a decentralized unit of the operation center. There are other groups that use NetSys in Lake City, for instance planners, but these are not included in the study so far. The empirical material further includes four persons - two women and two men - from the centrally located user-support group for NetSys, the IT system in question. Both the networkers and the user-support group belongs to the network division.

The interview framework was inspired by socio-technical analysis. Experience from previous projects (Pape and Thoresen, 1987, 1990) convinced us that socio-technical analysis was well suited for analyzing formal and informal work-related interdependencies, which are essential for learning purposes. The limitations of the method are partly due to the lack of operationalization of the social analysis, in particular regarding reproduction and development of knowledge. Therefore the interview framework emphasized the informal social networks involved in defining and solving work-related problems, including NetSys.

Other information sources are interviews and discussions with one of NetSys' chief designers, participation in a one-week regular NetSys training course, participation in a Users' Forum meeting and document studies.

Grounded theory (see e.g. Glaser and Strauss, 1967, Glaser, 1978) has been used for data analysis. The emphasis is on developing concepts and integrating these concepts for the purpose of theory building. The study does not support conclusions regarding the relative importance of the phenomena observed, due to the small number of networkers and the fact that the field site is limited to one region. Comparisons between several regions are required in order to answer such questions.

The study intends to contribute to substantive theory. In grounded theory, substantive theory is developed for a specific empirical area, in contrast to formal theory which is developed for a conceptual area. However, the material is still in the early stages of analysis, and grounded theory will be used for reframing topics for further field work and data analysis.

6 NETSYS - A BRIEF OVERVIEW

NetSys is a system for administration and management of the long lines and trunk networks in Norway. The first version in general use was introduced in 1985, and NetSys is now used in all Telenor areas, with approximately 1200 active users. Despite resistance from some groups, NetSys has displayed a remarkable stamina. It has been able to incorporate new telecommunication technologies unheard of at the time of its conception. The centralized database has grown steadily and now represents an unquestionable asset to Telenor. Additional applications built on the same design rationale have contributed to the organizational integration of NetSys.

The description below concentrates on some of the features that are most relevant for use. A more detailed description is given in Thoresen (1995).

Configuration

The configuration contains three large mainframes with a centralized database. The users have terminals, PC's and printers connected to the central mainframes. The terminals may either be old, dedicated IBM terminals, or newer X-terminals, which run an emulated 3270 version presented on the X-terminal. Most terminals are located in the respective offices of the different groups. This means that few transmission technicians have access to terminals while they are in the field, the terminals are used when the technicians return from field work.

At the time of the fieldwork, the PC's were mainly used for graphical presentations, together with a graphical plotter, but Lake City had not started to use the graphical module. At present, the 3270-terminals are replaced with PC's.

Modules

The main module in NetSys is the database, with information about the resources and connections in the long lines and trunk network. The database is used by all networkers. Before NetSys was implemented, Telenor had central and local archives which were updated when new circuits and nodes were installed, disconnected, allocated or expanded. With NetSys, the archives were converted into a centralized database covering the country as a whole.

There are a number of additional modules, and one is important in this paper: *OrdSys* - an electronic mail system used for distributing orders concerning work to be carried out on the network by the transmission technicians. Before OrdSys, orders were printed out locally in a variety of text-based formats. After OrdSys, the orders can only be issued through the system, thus forcing the transmission technicians to use NetSys more. This implied a major step towards integration of NetSys in the organization.

Design rationale

The NetSys database is designed as a model of the physical network*. Conceptual data modelling was used as inspiration for the designers. These foundations later turned out to be inadequate. Today, the designers do not view the data definitions as models in a strict sense, but as syntactical definitions.

The design idea behind the physical network model is that the model should be common for various network technologies and independent of organization. Technological independence would facilitate the incorporation of new network technologies without costly redesign and programming. Unlike systems based on work functions, NetSys would be easily adaptable to various work tasks and contexts. Although the designers realized that in reality this is not fully achievable, their ambition has nevertheless been to develop something close to a context-free model of the physical network. Not only are there no attempts to capture work procedures, they are deliberately deleted as far as possible in the design process. Users are free to move around in the network model according to their own needs, in a modeless dialogue.

Content and functionality

At the time of data collection, NetSys featured 87 different screens, a number of batch system reports and graphic modules. The NetSys database contained close to 8000 nodes, 23.000 distances between nodes and 300.000 circuits.

The contents and layout of screens 'mirrors' the network model. The relevant attributes of a node, or a circuit, or a group etc. are displayed in a table-like format (for more detailed illustrations, see Thoresen, 1995). Commands and screens are text-based, and the system provides simultaneous dialogues in a Windows-like format. NetSys can be used with a flexible and complicated set of access permissions defining graded 'read' and 'write' access, assigned to work groups or persons with different work responsibilities.

7 NETSYS AND THE USER GROUPS

The newly established regional operation center in Lake City is one of 7 regional operation centers. The center is responsible for the optimal functioning of the network in their own region. They use several computer systems for this task, one of them is NetSys.

The operation control (OC) personnel monitor the network. In Lake City they are 6-8 persons, spending most of their work day in the operation control room (the OC room). The heart of the room is the OC desk with several alarm systems up and running. The OC personnel take turns at the desk, where alarms appear on the screen. Information about malfunctions also come in by fax, by phone or by other personnel shouting across the room. Operating the OC desk can be a stressful task, and the turn-taking was initiated as a response to the stress. The OC room also holds personnel from other work groups, among them fault recording personnel. Both private and company customers call to re-

---

* Information on design rationale is due to A.Meisingset . For papers discussing similar ideas, see Meisingset (1993).

port malfunctions of all kinds. With the new divisions, fault recording personnel belongs to the private market or the company market division, not the network division.

When action is needed, the OC personnel forward alarm messages by phone or fax to other persons in the areas of the region where the malfunction is supposed to be. Later they follow up how things are going. They are responsible for warning the customers that will be affected when parts of the network go down. Since Lake City is the regional center, they must approve or reject requests from other Telenor areas in the region to disconnect parts of the network. Such decisions may be part of a planned operation, like digitalization, or part of emergency situations - to get the network up and running after failures.

The OC personnel use NetSys with read access only: to look up routings when customers complain, and to find out what parts of the network will be affected if circuits are cut in a particular area. They print out lists of which customers must be warned, who should be offered replacement phones etc. They use the system once or twice a day, between 15-30 minutes in all. When there is no network trouble, they may not use it for weeks.

The network allocators are the expert NetSys users. In Lake City, two persons have this job. Their job is to provide optimal use of the resources of the transmission network in their region: routing, technologies, reserves etc. The network allocators are located in a separate room in the OC room, in close contact with the OC personnel.

Through OrdSys the network allocators get input from regional and central planning departments regarding what installations are to be carried out in their region. However, the orders they get from planning may be seen as rough 'skeletons'. They are not always complete, and they may not always be correct. Since the network is continually under development, it is difficult for planners to be updated as to the status of the physical network. The planners may for instance indicate which exchange should be used, but don't always know whether that exchange is prepared or not. A part of the network allocators' job is to forward the orders, in revised versions, through OrdSys to the transmission technicians. The revised orders describe how and where the physical work on the network is to be carried out. They plan in detail what the planners have done in the large.

The other part of the network allocators' job concerns the NetSys database. They are responsible for updating the database and for data quality in their region. The network allocators use NetSys more or less the whole day, 4-6 hours at a minimum. Since they are expert users they are frequently interrupted, by local OC personnel who need their help, or by other NetSys users from across the region.

The transmission technicians make up the third group that use NetSys. They are the people who carry out the practical work on the long lines and trunk networks. A group of 10 persons in Lake City install, test and repair transmission equipment.

They get their orders through OrdSys printed out in the morning, travel to places where they carry out their work, return and do paper work and sign-offs on orders, and prepare for the new orders. They have a technical assistant, a woman who more or less runs the place when the technicians are out in the field. She is also the main NetSys user for the technicians. As a group, the transmission technicians use NetSys with both read and write access, though they are only allowed to perform one 'write' function: entering data for sign-offs. Most of them use NetSys at least 2-3 times a week, but for short periods of 5-15 minutes only.

Some transmission technicians dislike NetSys and have invented ways of working around the system. The sign-offs are delegated to the technical assistant, and the technicians may ask her for instance to look up a preview of the distance they will work on the next day. Sometimes they call her when they are out in the field. Some make it a policy to use NetSys as little as possible.

8 RELATIONSHIP BETWEEN WORK AND LEARNING

What are the elements that facilitate or hinder learning at work ? To answer the question, it must be kept in mind that learning NetSys is *an aspect of learning and doing the primary work**. It is not a separate process, except on special occasions like e.g. formal courses or demonstrations of new functions. Thus, learning at work is situated, in the sense that it is:

> tied in essential ways not to individual predispositions or conventional rules but to local interactions contingent on the actor's particular circumstances. A consequence of action's situated nature is that communication must incorporate both a sensitivity to local circumstances and resources for the remedy of troubles in understanding that inevitably arise (Suchman, 1987, p.28)

At first, it was puzzling that NetSys was seldom a topic when the networkers were talking among themselves at lunch, in meetings or in the coffee room. It emerged as a topic, however, embedded in their work tasks. The 'curriculum' is shaped by the demands of the primary work. The fact that Telenor has an obligation to inform certain customers when they are affected by network malfunctions is an opportunity for the networkers to learn to use NetSys to retrieve lists of these customers. A request to cut an optic fibre cable from a networker in a nearby valley may prompt the networkers in Lake City to learn to retrieve the relevant NetSys data to assess the feasibility of the request.

The close relationship to primary work is also reflected in the degree of familiarity with the system. For the Lake City networkers, use of NetSys is just one activity in a larger set of activities aimed at keeping the region's network in optimal shape. For the central user-support group, use of NetSys is a means by which to provide the networkers with advanced knowledge of NetSys use, which occupies most of user-support's day. These differences in primary work manifest themselves in the frequency of use of different screens. While the networkers have a high usage score for 9 of 87 screens, the user-support group scores high for 21 screens. Their primary work requires them to answer all sorts of questions about all screens. Most of the networkers do not need to know about that many screens, since their daily practice concentrates upon the use of some screens only. On the other hand, the networkers know a lot more about the network in

---

* 'Primary work' are the tasks in which computer use is embedded (see Gasser, 1986). The networkers' primary work is to keep the network in optimal shape and utilize its resources optimally.

their region than the user-support personnel; who do not issue orders nor change the regional databases.

The concept of *legitimate peripheral participation* (Lave and Wenger, 1991) illustrates a similar view on learning as a situated activity:

> Learning viewed as situated activity has as its central defining characteristic a process that we call *legitimate peripheral participation* (authors italics). By this we mean to draw attention to the point that learners inevitably participate in communities of practitioners and that the mastery of knowledge and skill requires newcomers to move toward full participation in the sociocultural practices of a community (p.29).

Legitimate peripheral participation is thus a precondition for learning, a precondition that emphasizes identity and membership of communities-of-practice.

The following sections will discuss some of the elements that contribute to participation in the networkers' communities-of-practice. Focus is on what might be called 'textural' aspects of the work organization. Textural aspects, as different from the structural aspects, refer to the fine-grained, interlocking and dynamic relationships among the networkers during daily practice*. These relationships cannot be seen from an organizational chart, texture emerges from studies of practice as it unfolds during daily work. Analyzing texture is one approach for obtaining the close view discussed previously.

9 NETWORKS IN FLUX

Since NetSys is appropriated as an integrated part of primary work, it becomes vital to understand those aspects of the primary work central to learning at work. Two phenomena emerge from the empirical data as particularly relevant, both related to the informal organization necessary to coordinate and carry out the work. Below, concepts for those two phenomena, *links* and *embedded groups,* are outlined. The intention is to provide tools for understanding the character of the informal organizational networks, and how parts of the social texture are shaped.

9.1 Links

A link refers to the relation between two persons carrying out different types of work. Links are important because they form the basis for cooperation. They pave the way for embedded groups, and facilitate the emergence of informal networks for many kinds of problem-solving. It is also characteristic that links have a kind of after-life: they often persist although the work-oriented relationship that brought them into being no longer exists. Thus links are a part of the socially structured resources used by the networkers in their daily practice.

Links may be due to *direct* relations, when the types of work are temporally next to one another in a sequence of work activities. The transmission technician may for

* The texture metaphor is also found in weaving, where texture denotes the surface created by the multiple combinations of warp and weft, and in geology, where texture denotes the geometric aspects of, and the mutual relations among the component particles or crystals of a rock, as seen in the microscope.

instance not install the equipment themselves, but instead put it into operation when others have installed it. There may also be *indirect* links, where the types of work are further apart in a time sequence. When someone orders equipment, a person retrieves that equipment from the store, though not necessarily the person who initially received the order.

Links may exist or not. When they exist, they may have different states. They may be *active*, in the sense that some link is well established and can be trusted. They may be *dormant*, e.g. a link which was previously active may become active again. Links may be *dead*, for instance when someone quits. A link may have a *location* within or across one's unit and take on different *forms*, like delegation or assistance. Links are seldom bounded by formal authority structures and boundaries.

Active links are necessary prerequisites for learning. Links provide insight into larger parts of network management, by contacts with people with different knowledge and work tasks than one's own.

9.2 Embedded groups

The physical network is fluid in the sense that it is continually changing: malfunctions are repaired, areas are digitalized, new equipment and circuits are installed etc. This fluidity is to some extent reflected in the informal organizational networks, which continually reshape themselves to suit the requirements of the physical network. The reshaping occurs according to type of work to be performed, the urgency with which the work must be performed, and the scope of the work.

This dynamic reshaping gives rise to *embedded groups,* established for the purpose, but not visible in any chart nor visible from organizational positions far from the embedded groups themselves. They are groups in the sense that they cohere for some work-related purpose, although *stability* and *membership* may vary. They usually know each other and communicate freely.

Embedded groups are in many ways similar to communities-of-practice (Lave and Wenger, 1991, Brown and Duguid, 1991):

> In using the term community, we do not imply some primordial culture-sharing entity. We assume that members have different interests, make diverse contributions to activity and hold varied viewpoints. In our view, participation at multiple levels is entailed in membership in a *community of practice* (authors' italics). Nor does the term community imply necessarily co-presence, a well-defined, identifiable group, or socially visible boundaries. It does imply participation in an activity system about which participants share understandings concerning what they are doing and what that means in their lives and in their communities (Lave and Wenger, 1991, p.98).

Embedded groups are integrative forces, pulling together a wide variety of resources across existing boundaries. The groups may be in the same or different *locations*, they may exist for long or short periods, and they may be more or less *visible*.

However, the lack of visibility also creates dangers. Invisible work is often less valued. The informality strengthens the flexibility of the embedded groups, but the flexibility may be undermined by attempts to formalize with rules and procedures. The ability to react adequately and quickly to a variety of more or less predictable situations requires some freedom of action.

Compared with most of the communities-of-practice described by Lave and Wenger (ibid), the embedded groups in this study differ in some respects. They are more heterogeneous regarding the types of work they perform, they may be more short-lived, and they include a larger variation of organizational positions and geographical locations.

The formal organization structure in Lake City features three groups - the transmission technicians, the operation control personnel and the network allocators. Overlaid on this formal structure, and stretching out into other parts of Telenor, are multiple overlapping embedded groups, more or less stable, which emerge and disappear with different activities, time and space.

One example is that of the *ad hoc groups,* for instance the informal task forces established on the fly to deal with malfunctions in the network. Such task forces are usually geographically distributed, cross formal organizational boundaries and are composed of persons from different job categories.

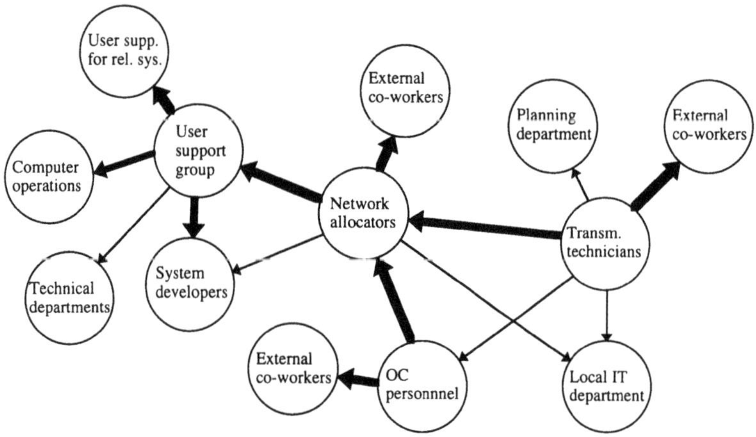

Figure 2 Network of informal NetSys related communication in Lake City and the user-support group. Arrows indicate who asks whom, arrow widths indicate frequency. Each circle denotes an organizational unit, 'external co-workers' is a collective term for persons in units not otherwise specified.

There are also more stable groups, although membership may vary. One example is the network of NetSys users (see Figure 2). The group is not visible on any organizational chart, but everyone knows who its members are, who the experts are within the network, and which experts can be asked. The group is distributed geographically, as well as over a number of organizational units and types of work. Each circle denotes a separate organizational unit, and the widespread distribution of the network illustrates one of the problems outlined in section 2.1 on 'Grounding organizational learning'. What kind of organizational entity is actually the learning unit in this case ?

The graph illustrates the answers to the question "who do you ask when you have problems with NetSys ?", which explains the directedness of the graph. A more complete graph should also encompass the answers to the question "who asks you about NetSys problems ?".

It is worth noting that this is not a 'flat' network in the sense that the nodes are person independent. There are personal relations involved, depending on who one knows, trust and like. There are types and degrees of expertness (see section below on 'Expert users'). Figure 2 should therefore be interpreted as two embedded groups: one constituted by the community of all NetSys users, and the other, not visible in the graph, the core of more expert NetSys users. The boundary between these two groups is not stable, however. It undulates according to accessibility (the experts may not be available), growing experience and job changes.

Another example of a relatively stable embedded group is the arrangement found in the transmission department. The technical assistant is formally employed in the Operation Control group, but works for the transmission technicians. She is 'borrowed' by the transmissions technicians, and even does some work for the regional operation center's top management.

Texture and organizational learning

The above discussion on links and embedded groups is a first attempt to clarify some of the textural aspects of an organization. The fluidity and elusiveness that 'organization' brings with it is due to the fact that the organization performing the work is both different from the formal organization as well as dynamic. The embedded groups are resources for information exchange and learning. The links described in the previous section are preconditions for these groups.

A textural approach to analyze organizational learning requires a change in focus from the formal structures to the actual structures that unfold when work is carried out. In the case of the regional operation center in Lake City, *the organization in question is fluid, and constituted at any given time by the dynamic interaction pattern between persons with respect to their work.* Analyses of acting or learning must take this into account, by specifying actors/learners and the particulars of the fluidity, like who interacts with whom, for what purpose, at what time and in what way.

10 RESOURCES AND STRATEGIES FOR LEARNING

Networkers have access to different types of learning resources. Some of these are pedagogical efforts concentrating on NetSys. These are central or local training courses held by the user-support group or by local experts. Others are learning resources integrated in the daily work in Lake City. These may be personal resources, such as individual systems of yellow stickers, notebooks, kardexes etc. They may also be socially structured resources, accessible for larger groups. Below some of these resources are outlined

10.1 Overlapping competence

A well known approach to developing a broadly competent workforce is to encourage overlapping competence. Semi-autonomous groups, as advocated in socio-technical theory and practice, is one way of dealing with this challenge. The rationale for developing overlapping competence may differ depending on the context. Bermann and Thoresen (1992) in a study of hotel work, found that overlapping competence were encouraged because of the central value associated with the welfare of the guests. They should not encounter the 'sorry,-but-you-must-ask-somebody-else'-attitude.

Different approaches to develop overlapping competence may be part of a conscious learning strategy, or it may be a result of accidental circumstances. Below some ways of developing overlapping competence amongst the networkers are described, together with the rationales behind each.

Approaches to overlapping

The OC staff views overlapping competences as an explicit ambition. To operate the OC desk one must deal with events in all telecommunications field. The weekend shifts in the OC room require OC personnel to work alone, necessitating a broad background to deal with all sorts of events.

To fulfill these requirements, it was an explicit policy to recruit specialist personnel, each with her own specialty like transmission, switching, installation etc. This would cover the range of qualifications necessary to run the operation control center as a whole. The turntaking at the OC desk is one way of developing overlapping competence.

The transmission technicians were in a somewhat different situation. Previously they were all-rounders, mastering different types of technologies. During the last 5-10 years the degree of specialization had increased, due to technological and organizational changes. Equipment changes faster than previously: new varieties appear several times a year while some old equipment could last several decades. The equipment is also more complicated, and more time is required to understand and operate it.

The technicians have a system of *semi-overlap:* each is responsible for knowing a technological field neigbouring upon their own specialty. 'The boundaries between jobs are jelly-like', one of the technicians remarked. In this way they can substitute for each other and to some extent reduce the vulnerability inherent in specialization. 'But the dream is to go all-round again' was also stated. The semi-overlap approach gives rise to another variety of embedded groups: those with similar technological knowledge and skills.

10.2 Contexts that hamper learning

The conditions for learning were not favourable at the time of my field work. The operation control group had recently been established and the new arrangements, within the regional operation center and between the center and the subordinate areas, were not always in place. This required a considerable amount of articulation work (Strauss, 1993, Gasser, 1986), and the management of real-time contingencies (Star, 1991) in particular.

Most of the OC workers were new in their jobs and worked hard to manage the new situation. Not all positions had yet been filled, so there was some undermanning. Furthermore, the Olympic Games were two months away, which brought an extraordinary work load. The OC workers' strategy for coping with the situation was to lower the priority of activities not absolutely necessary for getting the job done. Learning more of NetSys was one of the activities that could be set aside for the time being. This worked because some expert users were physically close by and could be relied upon for trouble-shooting.

For the transmission technicians, the most obvious obstacle for learning NetSys was the fact that transmission technicians spend little time in their offices where the NetSys terminals are located. NetSys is a highly complex system to learn, which adds to the problems encountered by the technicians. Their strategy was to some extent *hedging*, i.e. avoiding use whenever possible, leading to a specialization wherein the technical assistant does most of the NetSys work. The relationship between the design of NetSys and its characteristics of use is further analyzed in Thoresen (1995).

However, the degree of hedging varies between regions and between areas within regions, and over time. Not all transmission technicians have a technical assistant, so they are forced to learn NetSys themselves. Furthermore, the position of assistant is gradually being eliminated as part of the reorganizing and down-sizing, and more transmission technicians will have to make do on their own.

In general, there are many ways in which establishing links may be restrained or discouraged. Work overload often leads to voluntary specialization. To get the job done, everyone does what s/he is best at and can do most effectively. This tends to reduce the number of links. Management may enforce formal structures, e.g. by insisting on following the 'proper' information channels instead of shortcutting them. Thus the learning environment may be impoverished, and the flexibility of the work organization decreases. This is well known from working-by-the-rules strategies.

Pressure for efficiency further increases the workload and reduces the opportunities for maintaining and developing broad competence within the workforce.

10.3 Job trajectories

The concept of *job trajectory* is useful to understand how overlapping competence is developed through a mixture of planned and accidental circumstances. Strauss (1993) specifies 'trajectory' as follows:

> (1) the course of any experienced phenomenon as it evolves over time ....
> and
> (2) the actions and interactions contributing to its evolution (p.53-54).

The networkers job trajectories are constituted by the succession of jobs and organizational positions they have occupied during their career, and the corresponding skills and knowledge they have acquired. 'Positions' also include participating in e.g. projects, and union work, which is fairly common in Telenor.

Telenor has until recently been considered a company where one could spend one's entire work-life. Its size, variety of job categories, job security, in-house educational opportunities and country-wide location made it a desirable workplace. The average employment time in my sample was more than twenty years, varying between 6 and 40 years. During this period, all the networkers had changed jobs and work places several times, sometimes voluntarily and sometimes enforced, due to reorganizations, downsizing and technological changes.

A characteristic of the networkers' job trajectories was that most job changes were related to the network in some way or another. The women started out with an education as telephone operators. Three of them (the fourth shifted to a technical education) then moved or were moved in many steps, and interrupted by in-house administrative courses, into their present jobs. Some of the men also started as telephone operators, but later entered the in-house courses for technical personnel: as installation workers, engineers, transmission technicians and sometimes lower-level management in the network field. These job categories in turn cover a variety of types of work. It is reasonable to believe that their competence extends well beyond their present job.

10.4 Expert users

The expert users are not a homogenous group. There are local and central expert users, and they vary according to type and scope of knowledge, accessibility, primary work and how they view their expertise. Different types of knowledge may be related to the physical network, or the database and its navigation. The scope of their expertise with NetSys may range from only a few specialties to NetSys in its entirety. Instead of expert users, it would be more appropriate to speak about *types and degrees of 'expertness'*.

A striking phenomenon with respect to one type of expertness is the need for knowing the whereabouts of Telenor employees, particularly those in the region. This means both the organizational location and the precise physical location at the time they are needed.

One example of this phenomenon concerns the need for rapid establishment of embedded groups for dealing with network failures. Establishment is carried out in relay chains - perhaps originating in the operation center, yet soon taken over by networkers in other parts of the region who report back and forth. Due to a number of recent reorganizations where people have been shuffled around, keeping track of who is where becomes a major concern. One type of expertise is to be able to quickly locate the right person. This task is facilitated by the information resources embedded in the varied job trajectories; the 'old hands' usually know someone in many Telenor workplaces. The 'old girls network' is particularly useful, since many are employed in Information Service, where locating people is their primary work.

The *main local experts* are the network allocators. They form the core of an embedded group in Lake City, with associated circles of more or less stable membership. They are in daily contact with the decentralized network allocators in other areas of the region, redistributing orders among themselves to adjust their work load, substituting for one another handling telephone calls etc.

Their expert position is based on the existing division of work, where network allocation and use of NetSys is specialized. They have also appropriated other resources for learning by dominating Users' Forum, the official participatory body for further development of NetSys. Their participation in Users' Forum provides close informational and influential contacts with the user-support group, and a country-wide social network among themselves which is influential due to their expert position.

The *central experts* are located in the user-support group. They have two main responsibilities: providing information and guidance, including courses, to all NetSys users, and heading further development of NetSys, in cooperation with the Users' Forum and two groups of in-house system developers. They are accessible to all NetSys users, and know a large number of them from teaching the internal courses. In Lake City, it is mostly the network allocators who contact them. The user-support group manager is a woman with background from the old manual network archives. She has participated from the very beginning of NetSys - in design and development of the system, the user-support arrangements and the courses.

10.5 Meeting-places

The existence of meeting-places to exchange information and pick up useful news is essential to learning at work. Meeting-places may be related to *activities*, like regular meetings or shift changes, and they may be related to *physical environments* promoting communication and learning, like coffee rooms. They may be planned as meeting-places or not, - the point is that they function as opportunities for learning, and that they are cultivated as such.

Co-location is generally an important prerequisite for learning at work. The location of the network allocators in close proximity to the OC room makes communication easy. Figure 1 shows that the OC personnel primarily used the closest experts, who were the network allocators - 'Transmission is 20 meters away' as one OC worker remarked.

The physical environment of both the OC room and the transmission technicians' room are *open landscapes*. A landscape constitutes an informal meetingplace, with some advantages seen from a learning point of view (although they may be disadvantageous from a work environment point of view). It is easy to find somebody to ask, and the surrounding talk is a source of information. The technical assistant and the transmission technicians exploit this in their office landscape. The morning session in particular, when the print-outs of orders are distributed, functions as a meetingplace to inform the technical assistant and her co-workers about who will work where, who should not be disturbed, etc.

A particular form of communication in landscapes is *out-in-the-air-questions*. These are questions that are thrown out in no particular direction, and rely on somebody being able to answer. This form of communication is viewed as a sign of good working relations: 'Nobody says that you're asking too much, you always get an answer.' Similar communication practices are reported by Jordan (1992) and Heath and Luff (1991), although with a stronger emphasis on mutual updating. Jordan (ibid.) suggests that 'out-louds' work in workplaces where information resources are non-hierarchically distributed, a characteristic often associated with a good work environment.

More formal meeting-places are, for instance, group meetings, Users' Forum meetings and training courses. The training courses play an important role for a variety of reasons. They contribute to the establishment of *personal relations* between the user-support personnel and the NetSys users, as well as among the NetSys users. Personal relations facilitate links and are conditions for the various informal networks to thrive. The courses also serve the purpose of *confirmation* - people realize that their experiences are similar, or dissimilar, to others'. The courses function as an arena for exchange of ideas of new or better ways of doing things. One aspect of the instructors' contribution is particularly interesting, since they frequently are links in *learning chains* - when information is transferred from one workplace to another through intermediaries. The user-support personnel's broad contact with the networkers provides them with information about problems and solutions all over the country, which they forward to those attending the courses.

It should be noted that training courses are valued among the networkers*. This is different from Orr's (1992) service technicians who found the courses too limited for their purpose. Part of the reason seems to be the differences in grounding the courses in practice. The NetSys instructors take care to anchor the teaching, excercises, and examples in practice. Development of new courses takes place in cooperation with the target groups. The user-support group manager's background from archiving, not from IT, is important to ensure this grounding. There is also a general awareness among the user-support personnel of the situatedness and contingencies of daily practice, in contrast to canonical practice.

11 SUMMARY

Learning at work for the networkers in Lake City is *facilitated by* legitimate peripheral participation in practice, implying physical nearness to each other, use of telephone to easily reach remote coworkers, access to expert users, meeting-places, workplaces that allow peripheral awareness and out-in-the-air questions.

It is *hindered by* restraints on legitimate peripheral participation brought about by work pressure, division of work, enforced organizational boundaries, physical characteristics of the workplace, complexity of NetSys and varying degrees of usefulness of NetSys for different groups.

The networkers' learning of NetSys is smoothly embedded in their practical work: actions and interactions within communities-of-practice aimed at keeping the network in good shape. This is not to say that there are no hindrances. The point is that when *opportunities for learning arise within the context of daily practice,* they are also exploited by the networkers. Thus, learning at work is also learning *through* work.

The cognitive view of organizational learning tends to delete or abstract the work carried out. One of the dangers of this non-visibility is that the concrete actions and the concrete resources needed to successfully appropriate IT disappear in general formulations.

---

* This is true mostly for those attending the more recent courses. The early courses were not well received.

12 ACKNOWLEDGEMENTS

Thanks to Arve Meisingset and Birgit Andvin for their critique, comments and helpfulness in elucidating NetSys' trajectory and commenting on the paper. Thanks also to Susan Leigh Star, Lucy Suchman, Ina Wagner, Mike Hales, Julian Orr, Frieder Nake and Peter Holmes for encouragement, for help in clarifying topics and presentation, and for literature guidance. The anonymous reviewers provided many helpful comments. Thanks also to the networkers in Lake City and the user-support group for their patience and willingness to share their working knowledge with me.

The work was supported by Grant No. 100684/410 from the Norwegian Research Foundation and the Norwegian Computing Center.

13 REFERENCES

Bermann, T. and Thoresen, K. (1992). Konferansesenteret. In Thoresen, K. and Keul, V. (Eds.), *Omstilling med IT,* NKS-Forlaget, Oslo, 99-116 (Norwegian only)

Clement, A., Kolm, P. and Wagner, I. (1994). *NetWORKing: Connecting Workers In and Between Organizations.* IFIP Trans.A-38, North-Holland, Amsterdam, 1-250.

Cook, S.D.N. and Yanow, D. (1993). Culture and Organizational Learning. *Management Inquiry,* Vol.2, No.3.

Damanpour, F. (1991). Organizational Innovation: A Meta-Analysis of Effects of Determinants and Moderators. *Acad. of Management Journal,* Vol.34, No.3, 555-90.

Dodgson, M. (1993). Organizational Learning: A Review of Some Literatures. *Organization Studies,* 14/3, 375-94.

Dorroh, J.R., Gulledge, T.R. and Womer, N.K. (1994). Investment in Knowledge: A Generalization of Learning By Experience. *Management Science,* Vol.40, No.8, 947-58.

Duimering, P.R., Safayeni, F. and Purdy, L. (1993). Integrated Manufacturing: Redesign the Organization Before Implementing Flexible Technology. *Sloan Management Review,* Vol.34, No.4, 47-56.

Fiol, C.M. and Lyles, M.A. (1985). Organizational Learning. *Acad. of Management Review,* Vol.10, No.4, 803-13.

Franke, R.H. (1987). Technological Revolution and Productivity Decline: Computer Introduction in the Financial Industry. *Technological Forecasting and Social Change,* 1, 143-54.

Gasser, L. (1986). The Integration of Computing and Routine Work. *ACM Trans. on Office Information Systems,* Vol.4, No.3, 205-25

Gerson, E.M. and Star, S.L. (1986). Analyzing Due Process in the Workplace. *ACM Trans. on Office Information Systems,* Vol.4, No.3, 257-70.

Hammer, M. (1990). Reengineering Work: Don't Automate, Obliterate. *Harvard Business Review,* July-August 1990, 104-12.

Heath, C. and Luff, P. (1992). Collaboration and Control. Crisis Management and Multimedia Technology in London Underground Line Control Rooms. *Computer Supported Cooperative Work,* Vol.1, No.1-2, 69-94.

Hedberg, B. (1981). How Organizations Learn and Unlearn. In Nystrom, P.C. and Starbuck, W.H. (Eds.), *Handbook of Organizational Design,* Vol.1,Oxford University Press, 3-27.

Herbig, P.A. and Kramer, H. (1993). Low Tech Innovation: Resurveying the Basic Meaning of Innovation. *Management Decision,* 31/3, 4-7.

Huber, G.P. (1991). Organizational Learning: The Contributing Processes and the Literatures. *Organization Science,* Vol.2, No.1, 88-115.

Iden, J. (1995). Workflow Management: What Does the Literature Say ? *Report No.36, ISSN 0803-6489.* Univ. of Bergen, Norway, Dept. of Information Science, 1-18.

Jones, M. (1994). Don't Emancipate, Exaggerate: Rhetoric, Reality and Reengineering. In Baskerville, R., Smithson, S., Ngwenyama, O. and De Gross, J.I(Eds.), *Proceedings of IFIP Conference,* 357-77.

Jordan, B. (1992). Technology and Social Interaction: Notes on the Achievement of Authoritative Knowledge in Complex Settings. *IRL Report NO. IRL92-0027,* 1-58.

Kanter, R.M. (1988). *The Change Masters* Unwin Paperbacks, London, UK, 1-432.

Keen, P.G.W., Bronsema, G. and Zuboff, S. (1982). Implementing Common Systems: One Organization's Experience. *Systems, Objectives, Solutions,* 2, 125-42.

Levitt, B. and March, J.G. (1988). Organizational Learning. *Annual Review of Sociology,* Vol.14, No.3, 319-40.

March, J.G. and Olsen, J.P. (1979). *Ambiguity and Choice in Organizations.* Universitetsforlaget, Oslo, Norway, 2.edition, 1-408.

March, J.G. (1991). Exploration and Exploitation in Organizational Learning. *Organization Science,* Vol.2, No.1, 71-87.

Meisingset, A. (1993). Human-machine interface design for large systems. *Telektronikk,* Vol.89, No.2/3, 11-20.

Orr, J. (1991). Contested Knowledge. *Anthropology of Work Review,* 12(3), 12-7.

Orr, J.E. (1992). Ethnography and Organizational Learning: In Pursuit of Learning at Work. *NATO Advanced Research Workshop, 'Organizational Learning and Technological Change.* Siena, Italy, September 22-26.

Pape, T. and Thoresen, K. (1987). Development of Common Systems by Prototyping. In Bjerknes, G., Ehn, P. and Kyng, M. (Eds.), *Computers and Democracy,* Avebury, UK, 297-311.

Pape, T. and Thoresen, K. (1990). Evolutionary prototyping in a change perspective. A tale of three municipalities. *Information Technology & People,* 6:2-3, 145-70.

Rowe, C.J. (1985). Identifying causes of failure: a case study in computerized stock control. *Behaviour and Information Technology,* Vol.4, No.1, 63-72.

Sachs, P. (1994). Transforming Work: The Role of Learning in Organizational Change. HICSS-27 Monograph on *Representations of Work,* Ed. L.Suchman. Hawaii International Conference on System Sciences, 36-43

Simon, H.A. (1991). Bounded Rationality and Organizational Learning. *Organization Science,* Vol.2, No.1, 125-134.

Star, S.L. (1991). The Sociology of the Invisible: The Primacy of Work in the Writings of Anselm Strauss. In Maines, D. (Ed.), *Social organization and Social Processes: Essays in Honour of Anselm Strauss.* Hawthorne, NY, Aldine de Gruyter.

Strauss, A., Fagerhaugh, S., Suczek, B. and Wiener, C. (1985) *Social Organization of Medical Work.* The University of Chicago Press, U.S., 1-310.
Strauss, A.L. (1993). *Continual Permutations of Action.* Aldine de Gruyter, NY, 1-280.
Suchman, L. (1983). Office Procedures as Practical Action: Models of Work and System Design. *ACM Transactions on Office Information Systems,* Vol.1, No.4, 320-8.
Suchman, L. (1987). *Plans and Situated Actions.* Cambridge University Press, U.S., 1-203.
Thoresen, K. (1995). Design for Heterogeneity. Proceedings of *Computers in Context: Joining Forces in Design,* Aarhus, Denmark, August 14-18, 1995, 60-72.
Van de Ven, A.H. and Rogers, E.M. (1988). Innovations and Organizations. Critical Perspectives. *Communication Research,* Vol.15, No.5, 632-51.
Wagner, I. (1994). Networking Actors and Organizations. *Computer Supported Cooperative Work (CSCW),* 2, 5-20.
Wardell, M. (1992). Changing Organizational Forms: From the Bottom Up. In Reed, M. and Hughes, M. (Eds.), *Rethinking Organization. New Directions in Organization Theory and Analysis.* Sage Publ., 144-64.
Weick, K.E. (1991). The Nontraditional Quality of Organizational Learning. *Organization Science,* Vol.2, No.1, 116-139.
Wynn, E. (1979). *Office Conversation as an Information Medium.* Ph.D. Thesis, Berkeley, Dept.of Anthropology.

14 BIOGRAPHY

Majored in geology in 1966 at the University of Oslo, assistant professor at the Mineralogical-Geological Museum in Oslo. Research scientist at the Norwegian Computing Center since 1972. Professional interests: change processes, participatory design, and work environment issues related to information technology in organizations. Research approaches include both action oriented and analytic studies in post offices, town and country planning departments, hospitals, hotels, and telecommunication companies.

14

Information Technology and Organizational Change: The Role of Context in Moderating Change Enabled by Technology

Mahmoud Watad
Monmouth University
West Long Branch, NJ 07764 U.S.A.
Tel (908) 571-3663
Fax (908) 571-3656
Email: mwatad@mondec.monmouth.edu

Sonia Ospina
New York University
40 W. 4th St., Room 600
New York, NY 10003 U.S.A.
Tel (212) 998-7478
Email: sospina@is2.nyu.edu.

Abstract

This study uses data from 140 Information Systems projects implemented in public organizations to analyze the role of organizational context in moderating change enabled by the introduction of computer-based technologies. The analysis supports the notion that neither technology nor managerial action alone can be considered deterministic forces in shaping organizational change and consequently in determining the outcomes of the introduction of IT. The findings provide some evidence to suggest that as managers mature with the use of technology, they will be in a better position to coordinate the human and the technological aspects of organizational change. Additionally, the findings indicate that while managers seek alignment between the organizational mission and the use of computer-based information systems, there is a narrow and limited application of information technology to solve organizational problems.

Keywords

Technology, organization, learning, change, public, context, computers

1 INTRODUCTION

Organizational change does not take place in a vacuum. It occurs in particular settings which respond to change dynamics sensitive to factors such as the nature of the job, and the social and technical conditions framing both intentions and perceptions. This article explores the role organizational context plays in moderating the changes associated with the introduction of Information Technology (IT) in public service organizations. We argue that technology in general, and IT in particular, can not be considered a deterministic force in shaping organizational change; instead, change is moderated by many contextual factors emerging in particular organizational settings.

While organizational context itself is a difficult construct to operationalize, it is possible to study particular circumstances under which interactions take place and decisions are made in organizations. The combination of these defines the specific background that, in conjunction with managerial action, affects planned change. In this article we use "organizational mission" and "stage of automation" (i.e. the level of maturity of the organization in using computer-based technology) as operational indicators of context.

The analytical strategy to explore the role of context in mediating the relationship between IT and organizational change consists in assessing the impact of these two contextual variables in 140 Information Systems projects implemented in 14 municipal organizations. These projects have in common the introduction of the same type of technology (all projects introduced technology based on communication and information storage devices) and the same type of managerial judgment (all interventions were premised on a managerial decision to introduce such devices). Assuming then, that managerial action and technological availability were relatively constant, we analyze the role of mission and stage of automation in affecting the reported changes.

If the same type of technology is introduced in the same public-sector decision-making environment, and it produces different organizational impacts, then the organizational context may in fact be critical to understand change associated with the introduction of information technology. Indeed, for the cases studied, the contextual variables analyzed did influence the impacts resulting from the introduction of IT, as reported by the managers responsible for the introduction of the projects.[1] This provides evidence to support the emerging perspective of organizational change (see Section 2), by highlighting the interconnected effect of managerial action, technological availability and organizational context.

The practical value of our conclusions lies in supporting the notion that technology does not automatically determine the desired consequences in a change process. Instead, it enables the outcomes to emerge according to conditions which are context specific. Thus to assume an automatic relationship between introducing a specific technology and achieving a specific outcome may be shortsighted. Therefore, when introducing a new technology, managers must monitor its use, as well as provide the necessary adjustments for getting the most out of its introduction. Ultimately, a successful introduction of information technologies requires a careful

---

[1] The perceptions of public managers regarding the impacts associated with IT tap **perceived** rather than **actual** impact. Literature on Information Systems support and accept this approach (Danziger and Kraemer, 1986; Kraemer et al, 1993).

consideration of the contextual factors which may affect the way the new technology is understood, used and adapted to achieve the desired benefits. This is particularly important in the case of public organizations, where the permeability to the political environment may influence the context specific circumstances to be considered in the managerial decision-making process (Rainey, 1991).

2 INFORMATION TECHNOLOGY AND ORGANIZATIONAL CHANGE

Markus and Robey (1988) identify three organizational paradigms that help explain how change enabled through information technology affects organizations.[2] They are: technological determinism, the organizational imperative, and the emergent perspective of organizational change. Technological determinism views information technology as an exogenous variable that determines the behavior of organizations and their members in a generic way. In this view, the consequences of manipulating a given technology will always be the same, independent of actors and contexts. Hence the notion that for any given technological intervention there will be a predictable outcome.

The organizational imperative approach to change reflects the strategic choice paradigm of management theory. It assumes that managers can control the process of change directly, based on their search for rational solutions to organizational problems. In this view organizational actors have unlimited technological choices to produce a desired impact. While technological determinism downplays managerial choice, the organizational imperative approach assumes that the latter is the critical factor in understanding the link between information technology and organizational change.

Finally, the emergent perspective attributes change to the "unpredictable interaction of technological features and actors' intentions" (Markus and Robey, 1988). In this view, the aggregate effect of participant action, technological artifacts and organizational context determines the actual consequences of the intervention. If neither the technology itself, nor the rational manager, him or herself, totally control the process of change, other contingencies which affect possible outcomes must be considered in the analysis and in the management of change. This highlights the role of context, broadly defined as the set of circumstances or facts that surround a particular event or situation.

All three perspectives of change reviewed above share the assumption that IT is an organizational intervention or form of planned change. Yet the emergent perspective has the advantage of assuming that there are differences between "planned" change and the "actual" change which may emerge (Goodman and Burke, 1982). While both the organizational imperative approach and technological determinism provide some insights, their frames are insufficient to understand change enabled by information technology in organizations.

The organizational imperative approach assigns too much weight to rationality and managerial control over the change. It downplays the fact that information technology by itself is a resource

[2] The roots of this linkage go back to Leavitt and Whisler (1958). In their landmark article "Management in the 1980's," they speculated about the impact of IT on organizations, suggesting a "radical reorganization of middle management levels" and an increase in productivity as "fewer people...do more work."

brought to organizations from the external environment. Since managers are not the creators of the technology they are bringing in, and they do not have control over the evolution of the technology as artifact, they can only control its application. Furthermore, to fully control its use, managers must have perfect understanding of it, and the users must modify their skills continuously to adapt instantly to the evolving technology. These preconditions to automatic adjustment are not possible in the real world. At least the available literature does not support their existence neither in the private nor in the public sector. Managerial action is a necessary but not a sufficient factor to explain organizational changes produced by the introduction of IT.

Technological determinism also falls short in its explanations of the dynamics of change, in particular when the task is complex and the environmental demands are numerous. This paradigm overemphasizes the independent role of technology and underemphasizes its social nature. This perspective is premised on a view of technology as an object that has measurable features independent of who is manipulating it (Woodward, 1965; early Perrow, 1967; and Thompson, 1967). In contrast, revisionist contingency theorists[3] have emphasized the subjective nature of technology, defined by the way participants interpret it in specific social contexts (Dornbush and Scott 1975; Weick, 1969). The latter view claims that technology itself is less a force determining organizational outcomes (Noble, 1984), and more a mediating factor affected in turn by other social and political processes which represent material and social determinants of change (Davis and Taylor, 1976; Perrow 1983). Indeed, if technology is a social object, its applications may be sensitive to the context of the technological intervention itself. In fact, the organizational setting will play a major role in providing the "meanings" assigned to technology.

For both those who espouse the revisionist approach of contingency theory and the emerging paradigm of change, a given technology could have a different definition and could be treated differently by specific organizational participants. Moreover, if technology may be defined by the context of its use, then its consequences will be affected or moderated by the context in which it is introduced. For example, Barley (1986), studied how identical CT scanners (a computer-driven technology) introduced into two different radiology departments (in two different hospitals) affected the structure of these departments. His conclusion was that "identical technologies can occasion similar dynamics and yet lead to different structural outcomes" (Ibid, P 105). To explain his results, he argued that technology is a social object that may produce consequences shaped by the context of the technological intervention.

Olson and Turner's work (1986) has also supported the emergent view of change. These authors argue that the impact of information technology on organizations is the result of a complex set of interrelated choices driven by technological availability and managerial assumptions regarding technology. In their view, the effect of IT on organizational components does not follow one single and predictable direction, nor is there a single dimension of change which can be directly linked to IT interventions.

While there is clear cause-effect relationship in the technological and the strategic choice views of change, the emergent perspective highlights the importance of interrelated factors, thus

---

[3] Contingency theory (Lawrence & Lorch, 1967; Pugh et al., 1969; Blau & Schoenmherr, 1971; Jenkins, 1978) postulates that organizational structure is contingent on the type of work performed and on the environmental demands placed upon the organization. The revisionist group updates this theory by relaxing the direct cause-effect relationship proposed earlier.

proposing a matrix type rather than a linear relationship between information technology and organizational change. It is the interaction of organizational context, participant actions, and technological artifacts that determines the actual consequences of the IT intervention. A thorough analysis of the organizational impacts associated with an information technology intervention requires thus direct attention to the context in which technology is introduced. This goal underlies the analytical strategy of this article.

3 THE RESEARCH SETTING: IT INTERVENTIONS AND REPORTED IMPACTS

To provide a brief overview of the projects studied, in this section we describe the interventions, their impacts, the stage of automation, and the type of mission performed by the organization in which they were implemented. We will use this information to analyze the impact of "mission" and "stage of automation" on the changes managers reported.

The intervention

Data about the information system projects were obtained from reports submitted by city managers to the Mini-Micro Computer Coordinating Council. This is a voluntary committee formed by computer managers and staff of all city agencies. The reported projects were implemented in municipal agencies delivering services which ranged from human and enforcement services to community development, environmental and capital services, and city-wide support services. For example, a pilot project implemented by the Housing Inspector Office introduced the use of radio-based handheld computers in an effort to reduce the inspectors' time spent in the office and traveling from the office to inspection sites, thus increasing the time spent performing inspections and changing the direction of the information flow.

The impact of change

The classification used in this article to describe the organizational impacts of the studied interventions is based on an elaborate framework which is fully developed and explained elsewhere (Watad, 1993). In this framework the introduction of IT into an organizational setting can produce two types of impacts: it may affect other organizational elements, such as the organization's structure, or it may affect organizational outcomes associated with effectiveness, such as the level of productivity. These two sets of dimensions are depicted in Figures 1 and 2.

Figure 1 presents the critical elements of an organization which may be affected by change: structure, technology, people, tasks and goals, and environment (Scott, 1987; Leavitt, 1965). Technology is the body of knowledge, methods, and tools employed in carrying out specific tasks. Tasks are units of work performed for the organization to realize its goals. Organizational structure refers to authority and responsibility lines, patterns of communication, as well as the norms, values, and symbols emerging from the organization's activities. People refers to the capabilities, motivations, intentions and commitment of individuals available to the organization. And finally, environment includes external social, economic, and cultural factors that influence

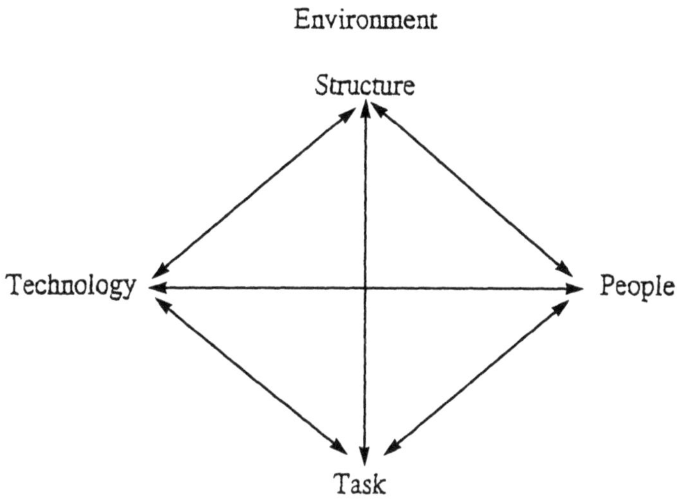

Figure 1 Organizational Elements Model

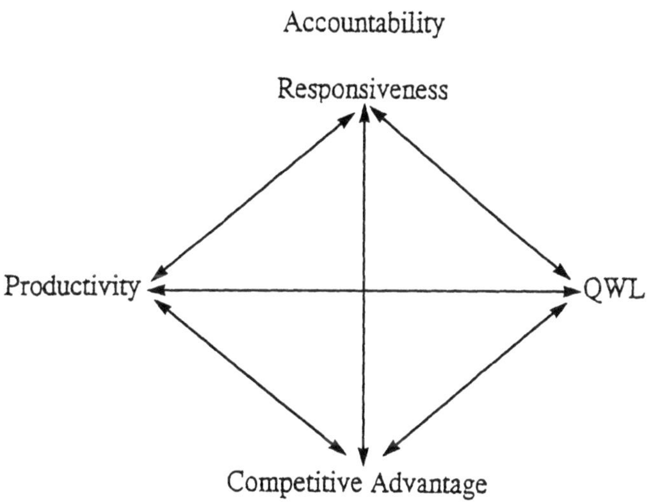

Figure 2 Organizational Outcomes Model

an organization's activity.

In contrast to the elements, organizational outcomes refer to effectiveness criteria.[4] A review of the literature on the organizational impacts of Information Technologies suggests that the wide array of criteria associated with organizational performance can be classified in one of four major outcome themes, as depicted in Figure 2.[5] These are: quality of work-life (QWL), responsiveness, competitive advantage, and productivity. A fifth external outcome of concern to public organizations is accountability toward its environment. Quality of work- life deals with employees' well-being. Responsiveness relates to the speed of delivery and the provision of information to satisfy customers. Competitive advantage includes efforts to improve the quality of the product or the service. Productivity is the ratio of inputs to outputs with respect to processing time and operating costs. Accountability refers to the organization's capability to explain its actions to its constituencies (Bozeman and Straussman, 1990).

An impact in one element may trigger a chain effect which has consequences on one or all of the others. For example, a manager may bring IT into a unit to change the method to perform a task. Benefits such as 'making the task easier to complete' or 'obtaining greater control over the task, may require modifications in other elements, such as the people performing the task. Employees may need training to learn the new method. Job duties and job titles may change, thus affecting the organization's structure. Organizational outcomes are equally interdependent. For example, changes that seek higher productivity may cause unintended transformations in the quality of work life; or an organization which seeks higher responsiveness may achieve this at the expense of harming its competitive advantage.

Our analysis focused on the benefits reported by managers after the introduction of IT in the studied projects. These were classified according to whether they represented impacts related to organizational outcomes or to organizational elements (Watad, 1993). Table 1 summarizes the impacts associated with IT as reported by managers who participated in the study. It shows, for example, that in 70% of the 140 projects, managers reported 'reduction of processing time' as a benefit of the intervention. This represents a change in the organizational outcome of Productivity. In contrast, only in 2% of the projects did managers report that the IT introduction 'improved morale' or 'reduced stress' of the organizational participants. This represents a relative absence of change in the organizational component of People. These frequencies provide the background for the analysis of the role of context, which is the primary focus of this article.

The context of change

While there are many possible contextual factors to consider in the introduction of IT, this article focuses on two, stage of automation and mission.[6] The first variable, stage of automation,

---

[4] Organizational theorists agree on the centrality of effectiveness but they disagree on its definition (Heffron, 1989). Campbell (1977) has identified thirty measures of organizational effectiveness. Heffron (1989) has added five outcome measures for public organizations.

[5] For a description of this framework and a review of the literature sustaining its validity, see Watad, 1993.

[6] We considered other variables such as business function and locus of decision-making. However, in order to develop the argument presented in this article, analysis was kept as simple as possible.

Table 1 Frequency Distribution for Impact Variables (maximum frequency is 140)

Impact Variable	*Frequency*	*%*
T4 Streamlining Operations	136	97%
S1 Division of Work	135	96%
K2 Method Alteration	133	95%
K6 Access to Information	110	79%
P2 Processing Time	98	70%
K1 Ease of Task Execution	97	69%
K7 Control over Work	87	62%
K4 Accuracy in Task Execution	60	43%
T1 Acquiring Knowledge	58	41%
A1 Accountability	55	39%
T2 Process Alteration	54	39%
P3 Reducing Cost	52	37%
R1 Delivering Service	34	24%
P1 Increasing Output	30	21%
T3 Decision Making	27	19%
R3 Providing Information	26	19%
C2 Quality of Service	23	16%
S3 Communication Patterns	19	14%
E3 Inter-Org'l Relationship	18	13%
W1 People's Skills	12	9%
R2 Knowledge\ Customers	12	9%
K5 Task Consolidation	11	8%
E2 New Relationships	9	6%
E1 Contact\ Environment	7	5%
K3 Scheduling Flexibility	7	5%
S2 Work Flow Alteration	7	5%
Q1 Stress	3	2%
S4 Centralization	3	2%
Q3 Morale	3	2%
S6 Impersonal Control	2	1%
S5 Decentralization	2	1%
C1 Linking services	2	1%
Q2 Job Satisfaction	2	1%
C3 New Product\ Service	1	1%
S7 Shifting Power	1	1%
W3 Initiation	1	1%
W2 Abstract Thinking	0	0%

T=Technology, S=Structure, K=Task, W=People, E=Environment, P=Productivity, C=Competitive Advantage, R=Responsiveness, Q=QWL, A=Accountability refers to the experience of organizational actors with information technology at the time of the intervention. Projects were either implemented to automate a manual business function or to upgrade an existing automated information system.[7] These stages represent two different levels of maturity with respect to the use of information systems. The two categories embody qualitatively different experience bases with which to manage the intervention. Extensive experience and familiarity with computer-based technology, developed over time, can provide a more focused approach to implement new information technology to transform existing processes and functions. The use of this indicator as a contextual variable presumes the notion of technology as a social object which is highly sensitive to the actors' subjective perceptions of its meaning. However, there is no need to assume that managers involved in the upgrade stage are the same as those involved during first time automation. The higher level of maturity comes from the organizational learning which takes place after an organization introduces a new technology. Thus maturity refers to the organization more than to the individual managers involved in the change process.

Table 2 shows the distribution of the projects according to the "stage of automation". From a population of 140 projects, 32 projects were classified as "upgrade," while 108 were classified as "1st time automation". This distribution suggests that the use of information technologies in the organizations studied for the most part was introductory and not advanced. The fact that most projects (77%) were introduced for the first time may be an indication of public organizations' lack of maturity with the use of IT, or it may be an indication of the lack of computing skills in these organizations.

Table 2 Two Stages of Automation

Stage of Automation	*Frequency*	*Percent*
First Time Automation	108	77%
Upgrade/ Transition	32	23%

All projects were classified
Maximum frequency is 140

The second contextual variable is the type of mission accomplished by the organization where the intervention took place. We use a service operations definition of the mission of an organization to classify the public organizations studied. Service missions ensure that collective action in organizations is geared toward providing value added through the consumption of the

[7] The upgrade category also included projects that were transitional in their nature but which included a previous IT base, for example, the shift from mainframe based to PC/LAN based projects.

service. Thus, from the consumers' perspective, organizations may be classified into two main categories according to their mission: those facilitating services for consumers and those delivering services to consumers (Fitzsimmons and Sullivan, 1982).

The first type of organization provides services which assist consumers in achieving other ends, as in the case of transportation (getting somewhere), sanitation (maintaining public health), etc. The second type of organization provides services which, in one way or another, transform the consumer voluntarily or involuntarily, as in the case of education or health services, criminal justice agencies, etc. The basic difference between the two categories, for the purpose of this discussion, is that the first type of organization focuses on the community as whole as its prime consumer, while the second focuses on the individual as its prime consumer.

Table 3 presents the frequency distribution of the projects according to their mission. From a population of 140 projects only 37 projects resided in organizations dealing directly with the individual ("to consumer"). Ninety-two took place in "for consumer" organizations, which dealt with the community as whole. The remaining 11 were classified as citywide service projects and were therefore excluded from the analysis.[8]

Table 3 Mission Classification by the Target of Service

Type of Service	*Frequency*	*Percent*
Service to the Individual*	37	26%
Service to the Community**	92	66%

* To consumer
** For consumer
8% were classified as Citywide internal services
Maximum frequency is 140

4 RELATING CONTEXT TO ORGANIZATIONAL IMPACTS

To explore the relationships between the contextual variables and the organizational impacts associated with IT, we conducted a subgroup analysis in two stages[9]. The first stage applied the

[8] These projects deal with functions internal to the city's operations such as the inter-agency electronic mail system.

[9] Two stages are necessary when projects are classified into groups, largely because some of the impacts with low variation (which were excluded) become very significant in relation to one group. For example, the task consolidation variable was excluded because its frequency in the population was only 8%, but it appeared in the 2nd order group with 30% frequency. In addition, two stages are necessary because the first produces "significance"

Chi-square procedure between each contextual variable and the impact variables to find significant associations. The second stage of the analysis measured the difference in the relative frequency of the occurrence of the impact variables between the subgroups[10].

As an example, considering stage of automation, the first step explored if there was a significant relationship between this dimension and each of the impact variables, such as "increasing output" or "reducing processing time". For those cases where the relationship was significant, the second step then explored the number of times an impact variable was reported by managers for each of the two stages of automation. Higher frequencies would indicate the managerial focus or intentions to produce a specific type of organizational benefit as managers introduced the technology. The same logic was applied to explore the relationship of organizational mission to the organizational benefits. The results are presented below.

Stage of Automation

Table 4 summarizes the results of the analysis to answer the question of significant differences in the reported organizational impacts, between those organizations which implemented projects to upgrade an existing technology, and those which implemented projects to automate functions for the first time. In addition to those associations that were significant, the table also includes those cases where the difference in the relative frequencies between the two levels was above 10%.

One may hypothesize that projects introduced for the first time may produce results which are less bold in terms of their consequences (for example, "enhancing control over work"). In contrast, those benefits produced by projects aimed at upgrading an existing automated system would have broader consequences for transforming the business functions of the organization (for example, emphasizing "increasing output"). This was in fact the case in the projects studied.

Table 4 suggests that when managers introduced IT for the first time into their units, their primary concern was reducing processing time of the operations, delivering services faster and enhancing control over work. The first two benefits represent factors directly linked to the organizational outcomes of productivity and responsiveness (see Figure 1). The underlying thread of these two benefits is a managerial desire to improve the speed with which services are produced and delivered. The third benefit, control, represents an impact on either the "structure" or the "task". This is linked to the managerial desire to enhance task execution as well as improve the monitoring of work.

Table 4 also demonstrates that when managers upgraded existing information systems their primary concern was to achieve better communication patterns, to increase output, to increase the ease of task execution, to alter the work flow, and to achieve better access to information. "Communication patterns" and "altering work flow" represent indicators of organizational structure. "Access to information" and "ease of task execution" represent indicators of the task element. The focus on these indicators represents a managerial interest

---

while the second reveals "magnitude".

[10] In this context a group of projects refers to those projects that fit a value of the contextual variable. For example, the "stage of automation" variable has two values, one for each group. Therefore, projects are divided in two groups, one is "first time automation" and the second "upgrade".

to improve the structural patterns and task related factors in their organization. "Increasing output" is an indicator of the organizational outcome of productivity. The focus on this component represents management's concern on increasing the capacity of their production system in order to satisfy more customers.

Table 4 Impact Variables Frequencies by Stage of Automation: Comparing Impacts' Frequencies in the "Upgrade" Group Versus "First-Time Automation" Group.

Impact Variable	*Upgrade*	*Automation*	*Difference*
S3 Communication patterns	34%	7%	27%
P1 Increasing Output	34%	18%	17%*
K1 Ease of task execution	84%	69%	15%
S2 Altering work flow	16%	2%	14%
K6 Access to information	88%	76%	12%
R1 Delivering service	6%	30%	-23%**
K7 Control over work	44%	68%	-24%*
P2 Processing time	44%	78%	-34%**

Number of projects in the upgrade group was 32 and in the first time automation group was 108. The percentages in the middle columns were calculated by dividing the number of times an impact variable was perceived occurring in each group by the total number of projects in the corresponding group.

The significance level was determined by using Chi-square procedure
** significance level less than 5%
* significance level less than 1%

Putting these findings in theoretical perspective, it is possible to suggest that the context provided by the level of maturity, as a proxy of the stage of automation in the organization, has a direct influence on the impacts associated with the introduction of IT. This supports the emerging perspective of change. Since the same type of technology did not produce the same type of impacts in both the upgrade and the automation group, it is possible to rule out the notion that technology by itself is the driving force of the change process. Indeed, findings from the stage of automation analysis suggest that there is a difference in managers' perceptions when they upgrade existing automated projects than when they introduce technology for the first time. One may conclude, that when managers upgrade existing systems their focus shifts from short sighted objectives such as reducing processing time, improving delivery of services, and enhancing control over work, to more long-term objectives such as increasing the ease of task execution, improving communications patterns, and increasing output. In short, their shift from speed and control over work to ease of performing task and increasing capacity may indicate a broadening of their approach. Maturity may pave the road to a long term qualitative change in the organization, when the technology will become completely subsumed into the business operation.

Organizational Mission

Table 5 presents the findings from examining the effect of the organizational mission on the impacts associated with the introduction of IT. It reveals that in organizations which deliver services to consumers and therefore deal with the individual directly (for example a health organization), managers are more interested in affecting organizational outcomes than they are in affecting internal elements of the organization. In contrast, managers in organizations that deal with the community as a whole (for example a sanitation department), emphasize elements more than outcomes. Indeed, the first four indicators of this table represent the organizational outcomes of productivity ("increasing output"), responsiveness ("delivering service" and "knowledge of customers"), and accountability ("accountability"). In contrast, the last four indicators represent the organizational components of technology ("knowledge analysis" and "decision-making"), environment ("inter-organizational communications), and task related factors ("access to information").

For example, the frequency of occurrence of the benefit "increasing output" in organizations targeting the individuals was 38%, while the frequency for community-oriented organizations was 15%. There is a 23% point difference between the frequencies managers reported this impact according to the organizational mission. Furthermore, this impact seemed to be more common in organizations that provide services to individual consumers. On the other hand, managers in organizations with missions aimed at the community reported changes in organizational elements more frequently.

Some strategic thinking seems to occur in public service organizations as public managers align the IT introduction with the mission of their organizations. It is interesting to note from these findings, for example, that while organizations providing services for the community introduce technology to enhance knowledge and analysis, organizations that provide services to the individual introduce technology to be more accountable toward their environment. One possible explanation for this pattern is that the organizational context which emerges in the process of addressing the two types of mission affect managers' search for solutions. In the organization with the mission geared toward individuals, managers focus on the immediate concern of consumer needs. This forces them to find timely responses, thus focusing attention on short term solutions to the problems. In the organizations with a community-based mission, managers do not have direct consumer pressure. Long term capital projects can afford lengthier time frames for decision making. Indeed, managers in these types of organizations usually deal with large scale projects which require complex analysis and elaborate decision making to produce unstructured solutions. The pressure for effectiveness stems from internal considerations more than from factors in the external environment.

This interpretation is consistent with our notion that the different missions create different organizational contexts, which in turn affect the direction of change produced by the introduction of information technology. Given the same managerial decision to introduce the same type of technology in particular organizational contexts, the mission of the organization moderates the types of impacts produced during the implementation process. This represents further evidence for the emergent view of organizational change.

Table 5 Impact Variables Frequencies by Organizational Mission Type: Comparing Impacts' Frequencies in the "Individual Customer" Group Versus the "Community" Group.

Impact Variable	*Individual*	*Community*	*Difference*
P1 Increasing output	38%	15%	23%**
R1 Delivering service	35%	18%	17%**
A1 Accountability	46%	34%	12%
R2 Knowledge of customers	14%	3%	10%
E3 Inter-Org'l Communications	3%	12%	-9%
T1 Knowledge-analysis	35%	46%	-11%
T3 Decision-making	5%	25%	-20%*
K6 Access to information	62%	85%	-23%*

Number of projects in the "individual" group (to consumer) was 37 and in the "community" group (for consumer) was 92. The percentages in the middle columns were calculated by dividing the number of times an impact variable was perceived occurring in each group by the total number of projects in the corresponding group.

The significance level was calculated from Chi-square analysis
** significance level less than 5%
* significance level less than 1%

5 CONCLUSION

This article provides evidence for the relevance of context to understand the organizational change associated with the introduction of IT into public-service organizations. Neither IT nor strategic choice alone control the change process. Instead, change is moderated by factors linked to the organizational setting. The findings presented here, therefore, support the emergent perspective of organizational change.

Awareness of the emergent perspective of organizational change can provide insights for public managers engaged in efforts to solve organizational problems by introducing new information technology. It suggests that managers must take into consideration in their managerial philosophy and style the following two paradigms of mutual adjustment: the first proposes keeping in mind the relationship between the human and the technical aspects of the production system they manage. The second proposes to focus simultaneously on the external demands posed by the environment and the internal resources required to meet these demands.

With respect to the first paradigm, the findings from the "stage of automation" analysis suggest that managers address problems and search for solutions differently, according to each level of maturity in the use of technology. This has important human resources management implications for succession planning and recruitment. For example, it may be important to consider this characteristic in the process of recruiting and training new managers, because if they lack sufficient experience with IT, this could affect their decisions about how to coordinate technological innovation with the management of human skills.

Organizational effectiveness requires the optimal coordination of people skills and technological innovation. Since public organizations tend to have more stable human resources because of institutional constrains in their staffing, public managers must be skillful both in managing human resources and in understanding information technology. In particular, they must be able to evaluate the pool of skills available and either adjust the technological innovation to such skills or provide enough training to upgrade the skills to the necessary level. In either case, the fragmentation of authority over personnel decisions typical of the public sector requires that the manager be more alert in developing these strategies to accomplish the desired coordination (Brock, 1984).

The findings provide some evidence to suggest that as managers mature with the use of technology, and as its use becomes easier, they will be in a better position to coordinate the human and the technological aspects of organizational change. In the studied projects, that managers widened their concerns for speed and control to include ease of task execution and increased communication flow represents an enhancement of the mentioned coordination efforts. It also indicates a broader concern to include both the technical and the human aspects of information technology in the change effort. This represents a better utilization of human resources and a clear integration of information technology into the managerial task.

With respect to the second paradigm, the findings from the "mission" analysis suggest that for the cases studied, there is an alignment between the organizational mission and the use of computer-based information systems. While managers in organizations with community based missions utilized an inward focus, managers focusing on missions for individual consumers utilized an outward focus. This suggests the existence of strategic thinking. However, that the focus was primarily inward in one case and outward in the other, indicates a narrow and limited application of information technology to solve organizational problems.

Organizational effectiveness requires a comprehensive approach for applying technology and a balanced focus between external and internal concerns. A localized focus will ignore --by default-- important contextual factors which, according to the emergent approach espoused in this paper, represent critical determinants of organizational change enabled by IT interventions. The practical result of ignoring such contextual variables will be an increase of unintended consequences associated with the introduction of IT, which may be negative in nature. This will in turn require a costly adjustment in organizational elements.

Given the recent reinventing government trends inspired by the national political climate, and the limited resources public managers face, the effective use of technology will require by necessity a comprehensive rather than a localized managerial focus. Moreover, recent literature in public management has emphasized the need to pay attention to the consumer and to develop a client orientation, to counteract the effects of an excessive focus on the internal workings of the bureaucracy (Barzelay, 1992). While this trend is welcome to balance the previous emphasis, public managers must remember that both extremes are equally problematic, and that an effective approach to public management requires a much more balanced concern with internal and external forces. An example of balance suggests investing in front line employees (internal element) so that the customers will be served better (external element).

6 REFERENCES

Barley, S. R. (1986) Technology as an Occasion for Structuring: Evidence from Observations of CT Scanners and the Social Order of Radiology Departments. *Administrative Science Quarterly*, **31**, 78-108.

Barzelay, Michael, (1992) *Breaking through bureaucracy: a new vision for managing in government*, Los Angeles, CA: UC Press.

Blau, P. & R.A. Schoenherr. *The Structure of Organizations*. New York: Basic Book, 1971.

Bozeman, B., & Straussman, J. (1990) *Public Management Strategies*, San Francisco, CA: Jossey-Bass.

Brock, J. (1984) Managing people in public agencies. *Personnel and Labor Relations*, Lanham, MA: UPA.

Campbell, J.P. (1977) On the Nature of Organizations Effectiveness. In P.F. Goodman, J.M. Pennings, and Associates, *New Perspectives on Organizational Effectiveness*. San Francisco: Jossey-Bass.

Danziger, J.N. & Kraemer K. (1986) People and Computers: The *Impact of Computers on End Users in Organizations*. NY: Columbia University Press.

Davis, L.e. and J.C. Taylor. (1976) Technology, Organization, and Job Structure. In R. Dubin, *Handbook of Work, Organization, and Society*. Skokie, IL: Rand-McNally.

Dornbusch, S.M. & W.R. Scott. (1975) *Evaluation and the Exercise of Authority*. San Francisco: Jossey-Bass.

Fitzsimmons and Sullivan. (1982). *Service Operations Management*. New York: McGraw Hill, 1982.

Heffron, F. (1989) *Organization Theory and Public Organizations: The Political Connection*. Englewood Cliffs, NJ: Prentice Hall.

Goodman, P. & Burke, L. (1982) Studies of Change in Organizations: A Status Report. In Goodman and Associates (Eds.), *Change in Organizations: New Perspectives in Theory, Research, and Practice*. San Francisco, CA: Jossey-Bass.

Jenkins, W.I. (1978) *Policy Analysis: A Political and Organizational Perspective*. London: Martin Robinson.

Kraemmer, K., Danziger, J., Dunkle, D., & King J. (1993). The usefulness of computer-based information to public manages. *MIS Quarterly*, 129-148.

Lawrence, P. R. & Lorsch, J. (1967) *Organization and Environment*. Cambridge: Harvard University Press.

Leavitt, H.J. (1965) Applied Organizational Change in Industry: Structural, Technological and Humanistic Approaches, in *Handbook of Organizations*, pp. 1144-70, ed. James G. March. Chicago: Rand McNally.

Leavitt, H.J. and Whisler, T.L. (1958) Management in the 1980's. *Harvard Business Review*, November-December: 41-48.

Markus, M.L. & Robey D. May (1988) Information Technology and Organizational Change: Causal Structure in Theory and Research. *Management Science*, Vol. 34, No. 5.

Noble, D. (1984) *Forces of Production: A Social History of Industrial Automation*. New York: Knopf.

Olson, M.H. and Turner, J.A. (1986) Rethinking Office Automation. *Data Base*, Summer 1986.

Perrow, C. (1967) A Framework for the Comparative Analysis of Organizations. *American Sociological Review*, **32**, 194-208.

Perrow, C. (1983) The Organizational Context of Human Factors Engineering. *Administrative Science Quarterly*, 28, 521-541.

Pugh, D.S., D.J. Hickson, C.R. Hinings, & C. Turner. (1969) The Context of Organizations Structures. *Administrative Science Quarterly*, **14**(1): 91-114.

Rainey, H. (1991) *Understanding and managing public organizations*, San Francisco, CA: Jossey-Bass.

Scott, W.R. (1987) *Organizations: Rational, Natural, and Open Systems*. Englewood Cliffs, NJ: Prentice-Hall.

Thompson, J. D. (1967) *Organizations in Action*. New York: McGraw-Hill.

Watad, M. (1993) Dissertation: *The organizational benefits associated with the introduction of information technologies in public service organizations*. Ann Arbor: UMI

Weick, K.E. (1969) *The Social Psychology of Organizing*. Reading, Mass.: Addison-Wesley.

Woodward, J. (1965) *Industrial Organizations: Theory and Practice*. London: Oxford University Press.

7 BIOGRAPHIES

Mahmoud Watad is Assistant Professor of Management in the School of Business Administration at Monmouth University. His research focuses on information management; information technology diffusion and implementation; organizational effectiveness and change; and the determinants (i.e. culture) and consequences (i.e. economic development) of technological change. After obtaining a B.S. in mechanical engineering and a M.S. in materials engineering, he earned a Masters in public affairs from the University of Texas at Austin, and a Ph.D. in management from New York University. Before joining Monmouth University, he worked as director of computing resources in New York City government for more than five years.

Currently he is studying the strategic use of telecommuting in the state of New Jersey, and its degree of diffusion in the state's economy.

Sonia Ospina is Associate Professor of Public Administration in the Robert Wagner Graduate School of Public Service at New York University. Her main interests are organization and management theory; public management; human resources management; and sociological perspectives on work, employment and social policy. Her work has appeared in Business and Economic Review, Review of Public Personnel Administration, Public Productivity and Management Review, Handbook of Public Administration and *Gestión y Política Pública*. She is the author of Illusions of Opportunity: Employee Expectations and Workplace Inequalities (forthcoming) from Cornell University/Industrial Labor Relations Press. She has an M.S. in policy analysis and public management and a Ph.D. in sociology, both from the State University of New York at Stony Brook.

KEYWORD INDEX

INDEX OF CONTRIBUTORS

GPSR Compliance
The European Union's (EU) General Product Safety Regulation (GPSR) is a set of rules that requires consumer products to be safe and our obligations to ensure this.

If you have any concerns about our products, you can contact us on

ProductSafety@springernature.com

In case Publisher is established outside the EU, the EU authorized representative is:

Springer Nature Customer Service Center GmbH
Europaplatz 3
69115 Heidelberg, Germany

www.ingramcontent.com/pod-product-compliance
Ingram Content Group UK Ltd.
Pitfield, Milton Keynes, MK11 3LW, UK
UKHW020140290926
15471UKWH00003B/608
* 9 7 8 1 4 7 5 7 4 9 7 6 2 *